A USER'S GUIDE
TO THE MILLENNIUM

J. G. BALLARD

A User's Guide to the Millennium

ESSAYS AND REVIEWS

Picador USA ♋ New York

Picador® is a U.S. registered trademark and is used
by St. Martin's Press under license from Pan Books
Limited.

Library of Congress Cataloging-in-Publication Data

Ballard, J. G.
    A user's guide to the millennium : essays and
reviews / by J.G. Ballard.
        p.   cm.
    ISBN 0-312-14440-7 (trade cloth)
    I. Title.
PR6052.A46A16   1996
824'.914—dc20   96-62
                                                 CIP

First published in Great Britain by
HarperCollins*Publishers*

First Picador USA Edition: May 1996

10   9   8   7   6   5   4   3   2   1

Acknowledgement

My thanks go to David Pringle for his invaluable help in collating this selection of my essays and reviews of the past thirty years, and for his many editorial suggestions.

Contents

A USER'S GUIDE
TO THE MILLENNIUM

1 FILM

Casablanca, Brando
and Mae West, *Star Wars*
and *Blue Velvet* . . .

The Sweet Smell of Excess

Writers in Hollywood 1915–1951
Ian Hamilton

In his prime the Hollywood screenwriter was one of the tragic figures of our age, evoking the special anguish that arises from feeling sorry for oneself while making large amounts of money. His plight is summed up in *Sunset Boulevard*, where Joe Gillis ends his unhappy career lying face down in the swimming pool he always wanted, rather than admit his failure and go back to the humble newspaper office in Dayton, Ohio.

Nowadays, of course, his successors lie face up in their Hollywood pools, with not a tragic shudder among them, and the huge fees they receive, often for scripts that are never filmed, could buy most provincial newspapers outright. But the problem of the screenwriter's role still remains, especially when the director is once again taking almost all the credit for any success. What part is played by the film script, how much does the screenwriter contribute to a film, and does he merit the status which literary people generally assign him? The difficulty of answering these questions lies at the heart of the unsatisfactory Hollywood careers of Chandler, Fitzgerald, Faulkner and Nathanael West, which fixed for ever the popular myth of the literary artist exploited and degraded by a philistine industry.

With some reservations, Ian Hamilton seems to accept this point of view, tracing the history of the screenwriter from the silent era, when regiments of ex-newspapermen were hired to rough out storylines and supply static captions, to the birth of sound and the recruitment in the 1930s of a far classier and more self-important literary set – the serious novelists, Broadway playwrights and Algonquin wits, who were patronizing about the crudities of popular film but had noticed that the green slopes of Beverly Hills were covered, not with leaves, but thousand-dollar bills. All of them, to varying degrees, made the mistake of assuming that the primary creative contribution to a film would come from themselves.

Much of Hamilton's book is drawn from the standard defensive biographies of Chandler, Fitzgerald and co., and a stale air hangs over these anecdotes. He never asks why these pre-eminently literary writers so failed to get to grips with Hollywood. Like most outsiders he under-estimates the importance of the producer, in many ways the greatest creative force in film. He knows nothing about screenwriting or, for that matter, the writing of fiction, and misconceives the function of the scriptwriter, which lies closer to the original role of story-outliner and caption-supplier.

As far as the novel is concerned, the importance of the writer is still paramount, though all of us have learned to keep a close eye on the rear-view mirror. In the theatre the playwright is at least the equal partner of the performers, but in film the writer is shouldered aside by director, actor, producer and editor, who together transform the printed word into something far more glamorous and evocative.

Years ago I was offered the chance to do the novelization of a film then being made by a leading British director. The script outlined a hackneyed story about a malevolent stowaway, with dialogue that rarely rose above 'Chow-time. Where's Dallas?' 'Topside.' 'Uh-huh.' What amazed me was not that someone had decided to film this script, but that he had been able to form any idea of the finished movie from these empty lines. Yet the film was *Alien*, one of the most original horror-movies ever made, and the throwaway dialogue perfectly set off the terrifying vacuum that expanded around the characters.

By some unexplained alchemy, a film can effortlessly transform senti-mental clichés into something emotionally compelling, as in *Sunset Boulevard*'s last lines: 'Life, which can be strangely merciful, had taken pity on Norma Desmond. The dream she had clung to so desperately had enfolded her . . .' No serious novelist would dare to end a book with these lines, and no middlebrow writer would have the talent to invent them. But Billy Wilder is the exception. He may have quarrelled with Raymond Chandler (over *Double Indemnity*), but they were really on the same side, both lovers of the word. Wilder's films, dominated by their bitter-sweet dialogue and filled with theatrical characters who always seem aware of their audience, are untypical of anything in today's cinema.

Alfred Hitchcock (whom, puzzlingly, Hamilton scarcely mentions) is a far better guide to the true relationship between screenwriter and film. Reading the script of *Psycho*, the ancestor of so much present-day cinema, one is struck by the off-kilter construction – Janet Leigh's almost unmo-tivated crime, and the grotesque retribution carried out by the 'innocent'

Norman Bates. The real villain, Mother, does not appear until the last moments, when she adroitly turns into her son. Despite all this, *Psycho* is one of the most powerful films ever made, a psychotic *Little Red Riding Hood* in which Granny disguises herself as the wolf. Chandler, Fitzgerald and Faulkner could never have written the script (by Joe Steffano) and would have ruined the film had they tried. The novelistic constraints of motive and characterization would never have allowed Hitchcock to achieve those states of extremity where his imagination thrived, though few screenwriters would accept this.

The most interesting films of today – *Blue Velvet*, *The Hitcher* and the 30-second ads for call-girls on New York's Channel J (some of the most poignant mini-dramas ever made, filmed in a weird and glaucous blue, featuring a woman, a bed and an invitation to lust) – are a rush of pure sensation. *Blue Velvet*, like *Psycho*, follows the trajectory of the drug trip. Paranoia rules, and motiveless crimes and behaviour ring true in a way that leaves a traditionally constructed movie with its well-crafted plot, characters and story looking not merely old-fashioned but untrue.

As Hamilton points out, the disappointments of the 1930s and 1940s screenwriters were compounded by the Hays Office and its ludicrous moral code. However, cinema was then a public medium, watched by audiences made up of complete strangers, and the restrictions accorded with the conventions of ordinary social life – on those occasions when we stray into the bedroom of a strange woman we usually find, alas, a husband with one foot on the floor in the approved Hays manner. Now, though, cinema is becoming a private medium. We watch on video either alone or with one or two intimates, and the imaginative demands for greater sexual freedom are all the more urgent – needless to say, I think there should be more sex and violence on television, not less. Both are powerful catalysts of social change, at a time when change is desperately needed. And both might give the screenwriter a new lease of life in liberating him from the written word.

Independent on Sunday
1990

Magical Days at Rick's

Round Up the Usual Suspects: the Making of Casablanca
Aljean Harmetz

Nostalgia may not be all it used to be, but films really were better in the 1940s and 1950s, and this account of the making of *Casablanca* clearly shows why. Hollywood today seems set on returning to the simple and unsophisticated spectacle of the nickelodeon era, when my grandfather's generation gazed in amazement at express trains speeding over viaducts. Fortunes are now spent on the kind of computerized special effects that appeal to the Super Nintendo mind-set of the present-day twelve-year-old, for whom adult relationships, political beliefs and the bitter-sweet ambiguities of love and loyalty – the magical stuff of *Casablanca* – are as remote and boring as the kabuki theatre.

Most critics consider *Citizen Kane* the best film ever made, but the best-liked must be *Casablanca*. Yet no one involved in making the film ever imagined that it would achieve its legendary status. As Aljean Harmetz records, when shooting ended in August 1942, everyone was glad that the production was over. There was fierce rivalry between Jack Warner, the studio boss, and the film's producer, Hal Wallis. The director, Michael Curtiz, had constantly abused his crew and bit players, and with one or two exceptions, the actors had disliked each other. Paul Henreid was contemptuous of Humphrey Bogart's acting skills, while Ingrid Bergman was baffled by her role and said of Bogart: 'I kissed him but I never knew him', a line worthy of a movie all its own. The film's dramatic climax, when the hero renounces the woman he loves and nobly returns her to the husband, was decided upon only at the last moment, and the famous closing words – 'Louis, I think this is the beginning of a beautiful friendship' – were written and inserted weeks after shooting had ended.

One of the myths about *Casablanca* is that the director and screenwriters made up the story as shooting went along. In fact, almost every key character and scene were present in the original play, *Everybody Comes to Rick's*, by Murray Burnett, who had visited prewar Vienna and been appalled by Nazi behaviour. On his way back to America, he paused in a bar in the South of France and thought: 'What a setting for a play!'

But the transformation of this unsuccessful play into a Hollywood legend required a huge range of talents, from the seven scriptwriters to the producer, director and the leading stars. As important was the strong cast of supporting actors who gave *Casablanca* a dramatic depth that no contemporary Hollywood film can match. Producers today rarely allow the camera to leave the face of the $10-million leading actor. By contrast, *Casablanca* is rich in supporting roles that give the film a telling authenticity – the cast-list is packed with Jewish refugees, some of them playing refugees, and the others playing the Nazis.

Round Up the Usual Suspects is filled with surprises, and a feast for movie buffs and late-night viewers of classic films. It had never occurred to me that the patrician Claude Rains was a born-and-bred cockney, or that he and Bogart, off the screen as on, could have struck up a close and lasting friendship. Some academic film critics have suggested that *Casablanca* is a thinly veiled parable of homosexual passion, to which one can only say: 'Play it again, Sam' – the film's most famous line but one that never actually appears in it. Now that is the true measure of a legend.

Daily Telegraph
1993

Hollywood Sex Idols

Brando: A Life In Our Times
Richard Schickel

Mae West: Empress of Sex
Maurice Leonard

Is Marlon Brando the Mae West of contemporary cinema? At first sight, no two Hollywood stars could seem less alike, but reading these biographies one begins to sense how much they resemble each other, especially in the way that they enjoyed immense fame as the avatars of a new kind of sexual frankness, and then fell victim to the celebrity they had helped to create.

Both Brando and Mae West rose to stardom by projecting a powerful and lazy carnality rarely seen before them, though Brando always had the advantage of the bigger breasts. Both completely overwhelmed the parts they played, and were great on-the-set re-writers of their scripts, adding a depth and bite for which they were rarely given credit. After their first runaway successes, both saw their careers collapse when Hollywood reset its sails in a changing social and commercial climate, and sank into a series of lacklustre films from which they briefly rescued themselves by sheer force of will. And, by the end, both became enduring camp icons, adored for the same mix of failure and combative pride that lovers of camp have always found irresistible, as in the case of Barrymore and Judy Garland, and the butt of the kind of cruel joke that Richard Schickel quotes. What do Elvis Presley and Marlon Brando have in common? Answer: many people believe both of them are still alive.

Schickel, the astute and generous film critic of *Time*, writes as an unabashed fan of Brando, and a member of the generation whose frustrated coming-of-age in the smug years of Eisenhower prosperity was galvanized by the appearance of the young Brando as the unforgettable Stanley Kowalski in *A Streetcar Named Desire*. Sly, illiterate and aggressive, and supremely confident of his sweating and animal body, Brando's Kowalski became the idol of a rebellious generation, if not ready to rape their mothers, represented by the prim and self-deluding Blanche Du Bois, at least ready to rape their mothers' values.

Schickel convincingly traces the bruised outsider of Brando's early films – *The Men, Streetcar, The Wild One* and *On the Waterfront* – to his middle-class Illinois childhood, outwardly respectable but deeply marred by his alcoholic parents. He suggests that the children of alcoholics, trying to deflect attention from their shame, seek out those even more troubled than themselves, and that this explains Brando's choice of the underdog roles in which he excelled. Whatever the accuracy of this, it's certainly true that Brando's characters have sustained more violent beatings over the years than those of any other Hollywood actor.

By the mid-fifties Hollywood was desperate to defend itself against the rising power of television. Led by Darryl Zanuck, the studios began to invest in lavish cinemascope spectacles, and the first and greatest phase of Brando's career was over. He found himself for the next two decades playing in a series of Technicolor schlockbusters such as the ludicrous *Desirée* (in which he appeared as a shy and spaced-out Napoleon, keenly looking forward to St Helena, one feels), *Sayonara* (slow death on Mount Fuji), and *The Fugitive Kind* (in which he became the first actor to be paid a million dollars for a single film).

By now, elevated to superstar status, he could no longer find the demeaning roles that satisfied his need to be humiliated, and as the years passed he seemed to grow ever more depressed, hiding behind a screen of weird accents and mannerisms. Schickel praises his fey and foppish Fletcher Christian in *Mutiny on the Bounty*, and in particular his 'English' accent – every bit as extraterrestrial as any of Meryl Streep's – and it is sobering to reflect that, to Americans, most of us sound like this.

Then, at last, he broke free, first with *The Godfather*, and again in what I feel is his greatest role of all, *Last Tango in Paris*, in no sense a pornographic film but a stunning portrait of male middle-aged despair, in which he wrote a large part of his own dialogue. After this he made a few guest appearances in second-rate films and reserved his best performances for the world outside the film set, culminating in what many observers considered to be his brilliant impersonation of a father convinced of his son's innocence at Christian Brando's trial for murder.

Of Mae West it's safe to say that for her the distinction between film set and reality was never worth more than a sidelong glance and a faint switch of the hips. Determined to make the most of her sexuality, whatever the location, she was only too happy if a crowd came in and stayed to watch. On stage from the age of seven, as a child vaudeville performer, she never left it until her death in 1980 at the probable age of eighty-seven.

Sex, the Broadway play she both wrote and starred in, put her on the map in 1927, and landed her in jail for ten days, guilty of 'corrupting the morals of youth', although I like to think that, far more valuably, it was the morals of the middle-aged that Mae managed so wonderfully to corrupt. A gangster's bag-man named George Rauft, smooth as a gigolo, collected the box-office receipts, and later, as George Raft, starred with Mae in her first film, *Night after Night*. 'She stole everything but the cameras,' Raft observed. In a series of spectacular successes she single-handedly saved Paramount from bankruptcy, perfected her screen persona and polished to a gemlike brightness the string of one-liners that survive to this day, above all the immortal 'Is that a gun in your pocket, or are you just glad to see me?' and, in reply to 'Goodness, what lovely diamonds' – 'Goodness had nothing to do with it.' Most were long-standing vaudeville gags, but no one ever delivered them like Mae West.

Above all, she brought humour into sex, then as now, sadly, a deadly serious business. Sex, for Mae West, as Maurice Leonard comments, was not only fun but went unpunished, a revolutionary notion whose hour had come in those Depression years. Even Benito Mussolini became a devoted fan – Mae West was an example of 'virile, healthy womanhood', the Duce opined. But the puritanical Hays Office, and the code of restrictions that the film industry accepted, spelled the end of her career. Nervous of the moralistic Hearst press, producers were afraid to offer her roles.

Gutsy to the end, she reinvented herself as a camp icon, presiding over a Hollywood apartment decorated like a boudoir-scale Versailles, touring in *Diamond Lil*, and making guest appearances in over-the-top extravaganzas like *Myra Breckinridge*, when her memory had gone and her lines were relayed to her through an earphone. Over the years she drifted into eccentricity, urging enema kits on to her friends, obsessed with spiritualism, and surrounding herself with retinues of muscle-builders. The concept of an octogenarian nymphomaniac which she patented and so brilliantly sustained (amazingly, there had long been rumours that she was a man) showed that she had never lost her touch, and makes her a continuing inspiration to the rest of us.

Guardian
1991

Push-button Death

From Hanoi to Hollywood: The Vietnam War in American Film
edited by Linda Dittmar and Gene Michaud

Was there a Gulf War? Already the question seems less absurd than it would have done a week ago, despite the destruction rained from the air and the huge number of casualties on the Iraqi side. After the arcade video-game of the bombing campaign, the '100 hours' of ground fighting, filtered through the military and TV censors, were scarcely enough to root the reality of the war in our minds. Push-button death is a game with few risks, at least to the television viewer. The devastated Basra escape highway looked like a traffic jam left out to rust, or a discarded Mad Max film set, the ultimate autogeddon. The absence of combatants, let alone the dead and wounded, suppresses any reflexes of pity or outrage, and creates the barely conscious impression that the entire war was a vast demolition derby in which almost no one was hurt and which might even have been fun.

Will Hollywood cope more happily with the Gulf War than it did with Vietnam? Reportedly, several Desert Storm movies are in active preparation, and one can easily imagine Chuck Norris or Stallone rushing the berms and single-handedly strangling the Republican Guard in their own tank tracks.

Soon after the disastrous US intervention in Lebanon, President Reagan was heard to say: 'Boy, I saw *Rambo* last night; now I know what to do next time.' In retrospect, this seems a remarkably shrewd comment, and no doubt his military aides snapped their fingers as they recognized an astute career move. At first sight, the Gulf War and the invincibility of the American killing machine might seem the purest expression of the Rambo ethos. But as many of the contributors to *From Hanoi to Hollywood* point out, the hero of *Rambo: First Blood Part II* was the very opposite of a technological superhero – all he had going for him were his hate-driven will, his Indian hunting skills and, of course, immortality, qualities which General Schwarzkopf had no need to call upon.

The Vietnam War lasted at least ten years, and continued in the American mind long after its routed troops were airlifted from the roof of the Saigon embassy in 1975, perhaps only ending with George Bush's recent press conference pronouncement: 'The Vietnam syndrome is dead.' Yet during the war Hollywood released only one Vietnam film, John Wayne's preposterous *Green Berets*. Such was the war's legacy of 'lies, errors and impotence', in the editors' words, and so deep the crisis in the American imagination provoked by the war, that it was only in the late 1970s that the first large-scale Hollywood films began to appear.

Many of these films, from *The Deer Hunter* and *Apocalypse Now* to *Coming Home* and *Born on the Fourth of July*, openly confront the tragedy of American failure in the war (the vastly greater tragedy that befell the Vietnamese is rarely touched on), and the unhappy position of the returning veterans who, for the first time in American history, found that being a veteran was not something of which to be proud. Despite their huge budgets and the self-conscious literary references to *Heart of Darkness* and Fenimore Cooper, Hollywood's Vietnam films rarely match their lofty ambitions, and only succeed in presenting the war as a bloody Superbowl. They trivialize death not because they accord it no value, but because they treat it with the bogus respect of a poignant camera angle.

Nonetheless, two great lines survive the unending gunfire: from *Apocalypse Now*, Colonel Kilgore's 'I love the smell of napalm in the morning', worthy of some Armalite-toting Robert Lowell, and Rambo's plaintive 'Do we get to win this time?' from *First Blood Part II*, in many ways the most interesting of the American war films, though universally detested by the essayists in this book. *Platoon*, which they grudgingly prefer, seems to me a tiresome buddy film, while *First Blood Part II* does contain an ambiguous and many-layered message – that all governments and military bureaucracies are corrupt, that the ordinary fighting man is an expendable victim, but that he alone loves his country and is prepared to die for it.

The essayists, almost all American academics, condemn virtually the entire output of Hollywood Vietnam films, faulting them for evading any serious consideration of what they see as America's misguided and racist involvement in Vietnam and for failing to offer any insight into the long-term consequences of the war. But Hollywood, especially when it puts on its battle fatigues, is not a branch of the peace or civil rights movement, and it puzzles me that these well-meaning academics could expect the conventions of the entertainment movie to cope with the complexities of the war, and one moreover that America lost.

Though the undisputed genius of popular entertainment, Hollywood has rarely made a successful war film. The realities of war, which Americans have totally mastered while they are awake, run counter to everything they hold dear when they dream. The best war films ever made – Rossellini's *Open City*, the Japanese *Fires on the Plain* and *The Burmese Harp*, and the greatest of them all, Klimov's *Come and See*, about partisans fighting the Germans in Byelorussia, are visions of desolation, meaninglessness and despair, qualities that are true to war but do nothing for the box office.

As well, the conventions of the entertainment movie reduce war to the subjective experience of a single hero, for whom combat is the ultimate catharsis that allows him to find his true self. This rarely happens in war, as Leo Cawley, himself a Vietnam veteran, comments in the best essay in the collection:

> There is almost no human activity that is as intensely social as modern warfare . . . When a military unit loses its internal cohesion and starts to fight as individuals there is such a radical and unfavourable change in the casualty ratio that it is almost always decisive . . . Every general staff in the world since 1914 has known that the bravery of individual soldiers in modern war is about as essential as whether they are handsome.

Guardian
1991

Hobbits in Space?

Can I offer a dissenting opinion? There seems to be a profound need everywhere to admire *Star Wars*, and a resentment of any response other than loving affection. *Star Wars*, written and directed by George Lucas, is engaging, brilliantly designed, acted with real charm, full of verve and visual ingenuity. It's also totally unoriginal, feebly plotted, instantly forgettable, and an acoustic nightmare – the electronic sound-wall wrapped around the audience is so over-amplified that every footfall sounds like Krakatoa.

In that case, why all the fuss? And what does the amazing success of *Star Wars* indicate, for good or ill, about the future of s-f cinema? Although slightly biased, I firmly believe that science fiction is the true literature of the twentieth century, and probably the last literary form to exist before the death of the written word and the domination of the visual image. S-f has been one of the few forms of modern fiction explicitly concerned with change – social, technological and environmental – and certainly the only fiction to invent society's myths, dreams and utopias. Why, then, has it translated so uneasily into the cinema? Unlike the western, which long ago took over the literary form and now exists in its own right, the s-f film has never really been more than an offshoot of its literary precursor, which to date has provided all the ideas, themes and inventiveness. S-f cinema has been notoriously prone to cycles of exploitation and neglect, unsatisfactory mergings with horror films, thrillers, environmental and disaster movies.

The most popular form of s-f – space fiction – has been the least successful of all cinematically, until *2001* and *Star Wars*, for the obvious reason that the special effects available were hopelessly inadequate. Surprisingly, s-f is one of the most literary forms of all fiction, and the best s-f films – *Them!*, *Dr Cyclops*, *The Incredible Shrinking Man*, *Alphaville*, *Last Year in Marienbad* (not a capricious choice, its themes are time, space and identity, s-f's triple pillars), *Dr Strangelove*, *The Invasion of the Body Snatchers*, *Barbarella* and *Solaris* – and the brave failures such as *The Thing*, *Seconds* and *The Man who Fell to Earth* – have all made use of comparatively modest special effects and relied on strongly imaginative ideas, and on ingenuity, wit and fantasy.

With *Star Wars* the pendulum seems to be swinging the other way, towards huge but empty spectacles where the special effects – like the brilliantly designed space vehicles and their interiors in both *Star Wars* and *2001* – preside over derivative ideas and unoriginal plots, as in some massively financed stage musical where the sets and costumes are lavish but there are no tunes. I can't help feeling that in both these films the spectacular sets are the real subject matter, and that original and imaginative ideas – until now science fiction's chief claim to fame – are regarded by their makers as secondary, unimportant and even, possibly, distracting.

Star Wars in particular seems designed to appeal to that huge untapped audience of people who have never read or been particularly interested in s-f but have absorbed its superficial ideas – space ships, ray guns, blue corridors, the future as anything with a fin on it – from comic strips, TV shows like *Star Trek* and *Thunderbirds*, and the iconography of mass merchandising.

The visual ideas in *Star Wars* are ingenious and entertaining. Ironically it's only now that the technology of the cinema is sufficiently advanced to represent an advanced technology in decline. I liked the super-technologies already beginning to rust around the edges, the pirate starship like an old tramp steamer, the dented robots with IQs higher than Einstein's which resembled beat-up De Sotos in Athens or Havana with half a million miles on the clock. I liked the way large sections of the action were seen through computerized head-up displays which provided information about closing speeds and impact velocities that makes everyone in the audience feel like a Phantom pilot on a Hanoi bombing run.

In passing, the reference to Vietnam isn't undeserved – the slaughter in *Star Wars*, quite apart from the destruction of an entire populated planet, is unrelieved for two hours, and at times stacks the corpses halfway up the screen. Losing track of this huge bodycount, I thought at first that the film might be some weird, unintentional parable of the US involvement in Vietnam, with the plucky hero from the backward planet and his scratch force of reject robots and gook-like extraterrestrials fighting bravely against the evil and all-destructive super-technology of the Galactic Empire. Whatever the truth, it's strange that the film gets a U certificate – two hours of *Star Wars* must be one of the most efficient means of weaning your pre-teen child from any fear of, or sensitivity towards, the deaths of others.

All the same, as a technological pantomime *Star Wars* makes a certain amount of sense. There's the good fairy, Alec Guinness, with his laser-wand and a smooth line in morally uplifting chat; the pantomime dame/ wicked witch, the Dark Lord Darth Vader, with black Nazi helmet, leather face-mask and computerized surgical truss; the principal boy, the apparently masculine robot Artoo-Detoo who in fact conceals a coded holographic image of the Princess Leia, which he now and then projects like a Palladium Dick Whittington flashing her thighs.

However, George Lucas has gone badly astray with his supporting cast – what looks like an attempted tour de force, the parade of extrater-restrials in the frontier-planet saloon, comes on hilariously like the Mup-pet Show, with shaggy monsters growling and rolling their eyeballs. I almost expected Kermit and Miss Piggy to swoop in and introduce Bruce Forsyth.

What is missing in all this is any hard imaginative core. *Star Wars* is the first totally unserious s-f film. Even a bad episode of *Star Trek* or *Dr Who* has the grain of an original idea, and the vast interplanetary and technological perspectives of *2001* were at least put to the service of a steadily expanding cosmic vision. The most one can hope, I think, is that the technical expertise now exists to make a really great s-f film. *Star Wars*, in a sense, is a huge test-card, a demonstration film of s-f movie possibilities.

20th Century-Fox's advance publicity describes the modern motion picture as 'the most magnificent toy ever invented for grown men to play with and express their fantasies' – presumably with Lucas's approval, and *Star Wars* may well be more prophetic than I give it credit for. In many ways it is the ultimate home movie, in which Lucas goes back into his toy cupboard and plays with all his boyhood fantasies, fitting together a collection of stuffed toys, video games and plastic spaceships into this ten-year-old's extravaganza, back to the days, as he himself says, when he 'dreamed about running away and having adventures that no one else has ever had'.

Time Out
1977

A User's Guide to
the Millennium

When it turns to science fiction, cinema closes its eyes and moves into a rich and uneasy sleep. The collective dreams and nightmares of the twentieth century have found their most vivid expression in this often disparaged but ever popular genre. A few great directors, from Fritz Lang to Steven Spielberg, have worked in science fiction, but until the sixties most s-f films were little more than B-movies. With limited special effects, minor actors and minuscule budgets, and usually ignored by the critics, the only things that these films had going for them were powerful stories, unrestrained imagination and, first and foremost, a hot line to the unconscious. In these often modest films, as almost nowhere else in the popular arts of our age, classical myth and scientific apocalypse collide and fuse.

Like most of my fellow s-f writers, American and British, I nurse ambivalent feelings towards the science-fiction movies. Despite our heroic efforts, it is not the printed word but the film that has defined the images of science fiction in the public mind and also, incidentally, exerted a huge influence on architecture, fashion and consumer design. Even now, the future is anything with a fin on it.

Far from being a medium of escapist entertainment, the science-fiction film has always been a sensitive barometer of the cultural and political climate of the day. Our deepest fears of an irrational superscience stalked its blue corridors long before latter-day environmentalists became concerned for our planet's future. In the fifties, Cold War paranoia and the terrors of nuclear Armageddon prompted a cluster of remarkable science-fiction movies, among them *Invasion of the Body Snatchers*, *Them!*, *The Day the Earth Stood Still*, and *The Incredible Shrinking Man*, which were handicapped by their meagre – by present-day standards – special effects. Unlike the novelist, the film director cannot leave his locations to the reader's imagination.

In the sixties, however, the special effects at last began to match the inspiration of the filmmakers. Indeed, within a decade the technology of film design became sufficiently advanced (as in *Star Wars*) to show an advanced technology in decline.

At its worst, the science-fiction film offers the sheer exhilaration of the roller coaster. At its best, and to its credit, it tries to deal with the largest issues facing us today, and attempts, however naively, to place some sort of philosophical frame around man's place in the universe.

Forbidden Planet (1956)

This remarkably stylish colour film is a quantum leap forward in visual confidence and in the richness of its theme – an update of Shakespeare's *The Tempest*. Walter Pidgeon plays the Prospero figure, Dr Morbius, a brilliant but flawed scientist living alone with his daughter on an isolated planet. Robby the Robot is the ever obliging Ariel, and the crew members of a visiting spaceship are the stranded mariners.

The film's real originality, however, lies in making the brutish Caliban figure an externalization of Morbius's own libido. This gives an unsettling force to the final confrontation, as Morbius's lustful id, never seen directly, throbs and oozes along in full Oedipal splendour, melting down steel doors on its way towards a quivering Anne Francis. The special effects were unequalled until *2001: A Space Odyssey*.

Dr Strangelove or: How I Learned to Stop Worrying and Love the Bomb (1964)

Nearly twenty-five years after its release, Stanley Kubrick's black satire has lost none of its impact. In this story of an insane US Air Force general who launches an all-out nuclear attack on the Soviet Union, Kubrick cunningly mixes documentary realism with the ultimate in graveyard humour – the death of mankind treated as scarcely more than the last sick joke.

Kubrick's masterstroke is to tilt the dramatic action of the film so that the audience's sympathies slide across the value scale and eventually lie with the targets being satirized. We come to admire the magnificent B-52s with their sleek A-bombs and brave if baffled crews; we despise the wimpish president for trying to do a deal with the Kremlin, and we almost welcome the nuclear Armageddon when it comes. By enlisting us on the side of our darkest fears, Kubrick exposes all the sinister glamour and unconscious logic of technological death.

Alphaville (1965)

This moody and powerful allegory is Jean-Luc Godard's most accessible film, made for that consumerist and politically conscious sixties audience that he dubbed 'the children of Marx and Coca-Cola'. *Alphaville* blends utopian satire, pop art and comic-book imagery to create the alienated landscape of the distant planet Alphaville, whose cowed population is tyrannized by an evil computer. However, Alphaville is in every way indistinguishable from contemporary Paris. The 'spaceship' of secret agent Lemmy Caution is his Ford Galaxy, and similar linguistic plays link the action together in a far more convincing way than might seem possible.

For the first time in the science-fiction film, Godard makes the point that in the media landscape of the present day the fantasies of science fiction are as 'real' as an office block, an airport or a presidential campaign. His original title was *Tarzan versus IBM*, but the film transcends its pop imagery to create a disturbing world that resembles a chromium-plated *1984*. Sadly, after *Alphaville* Godard abandoned the genre.

Barbarella (1968)

Sex, which many enthusiasts thought they had invented in the sixties, here makes its appearance in the science-fiction film. The relationship between sex and science fiction or, more to the point, its virtual absence from the genre, has always been a puzzle – explained, I would guess, by the fact that science-fiction writers constitute an authentic community of naifs, generally nervous of change, politically ultraconservative, eager not to think about what adults do after dark.

At any rate, it is inconceivable that the masters of classic science fiction could have come up with this rich and saucy confection, in which the interplanetary sex adventures of the French comic-strip heroine are elegantly transferred to the screen. Roger Vadim, who in *And God Created Woman* created Brigitte Bardot, here turns his affectionate and ironic eye on another of his wives, Jane Fonda, who achieves immortality as she cavorts naked in a fur-lined spaceship.

Silent Running (1971)

Douglas Trumbull, who supervised the special effects in *2001*, directed this moving ecological fable, and there are strong echoes of Kubrick's epic in the scenes of giant starships sailing along the tideways of space. The premise – that one day in the future all the vegetation on Earth has died, and that the last remaining trees are stored in vast, orbiting space vehicles – may take some swallowing, but the theme is so well handled that the film taps into all our unease about the abuse of this planet and its environment.

Much of *Silent Running*'s success is due to Bruce Dern's superb performance as a watchman and gardener in one of the forgotten greenhouses. His dogged, cantankerous manner exactly suits the character of this last conservationist alive, who refuses orders to dump the vegetation, kills the crew, and sets off into deep space with only the trees for company.

Dark Star (1974)

Dark Star is the *Catch-22* of outer space. The anarchic spirit of Joseph Heller's novel, with its inverted logic and padded-cell humour, presides over John Carpenter's extraordinary low-budget feature. Reportedly made for $60,000, *Dark Star* was originally filmed in 16mm by a group of students at the University of Southern California, and later transferred to 35mm. Watching this brilliant extravaganza, one is forced yet again to accept that talent alone is always enough.

Like many ostensible satires – in this case, of the science-fiction movie itself – *Dark Star* soon transcends its own subject matter. The sealed world of the spaceship, with its exhausted, near psychotic crew, its 'dead' captain in his cryogenic capsule periodically revived to be asked for advice, and its intelligent bombs that have to be argued out of detonating prematurely, soon begins to resemble that other spaceship called Earth.

The Man who Fell to Earth (1976)

A brave failure, Nicolas Roeg's excursion into science fiction reveals the excitements, and hazards, of illustrating a conventional genre theme – the visiting alien destroyed by an uncaring Earth – with images taken largely from outside that genre. Here the alien is played by rock star David Bowie, whose strange, hypersensitive presence instantly convinces us that he has come from another planet. His growing estrangement is seen not as a reaction to the brute incomprehension of others, but in terms of his own seduction by our television and communications landscape, with its unlimited tolerance of deviant behaviour.

Above all, the Bowie figure is seduced by the fragmentation and sheer ironic style of life on Earth, perfectly exemplified by Roeg's film technique – a mix of elegant photography and fashionable dislocations. But with his alien dismantled and demoralized, Roeg has nowhere to go, since he cannot rely on the genre's conventions to rescue his film. And without the genre's conventions the behaviour of his hero becomes merely modishly psychotic.

Close Encounters of the Third Kind (1977)

Spielberg's mastery of the science-fiction medium was already evident in *Duel*, his 1971 classic of highway paranoia. From autogeddon he moved on to two major themes of science fiction, monsters (*Jaws*) and interplanetary travel (*Close Encounters* and *ET the Extra-Terrestrial*). That these have become three of the most successful films in the history of the cinema underlines my long-held belief that science fiction defines the popular imagination of the twentieth century.

Close Encounters combines lavish special effects with the complex and poetic story of a power-company technician whose life is transformed by a series of UFO visitations. He becomes obsessed with a strangely shaped mountain in Wyoming, a model of which he constructs in his family living room. The film proceeds by a series of powerfully allusive images, which climax with the arrival of the alien spaceship, a visionary landing that resonates for years in the spectator's mind.

Alien (1979)

Alien is a tour de force of pure horror, a barrage of brutal eruptions (some literally so) that obscure the existence, behind the blood and terror, of an extremely elegant s-f film. Returning to Earth, the crew of the *Nostromo* is diverted to a remote planet and there unknowingly picks up the alien organism, which then proceeds to metamorphose its way through the cast until defeated by the courage and wiles of Sigourney Weaver, the s-f film's first feminist heroine.

While all this is going on one has barely a pause to notice a host of fine details: the claustrophobic world of the spaceship, with its fraying camaraderie; the entropy of long voyages, time slowing down so that a brief conversation seems to last all day; the stylish interior of the *Nostromo*, a cross between a computer terminal and a nightclub; the final appearance of the alien, an insane mesh of ravenous teeth straight from the paintings of Francis Bacon that materializes just after Weaver strips down to her underwear. Dinner, fortunately, is delayed, at least until the sequel.

Mad Max 2 (1981)

This second, and by the far the best, of George Miller's Mad Max trio is a tribute to the power of the s-f film to break free of its conventions and renew itself in a creative burst of ideas and images. On one level the ultimate road movie, *Max Max 2* is a compellingly reductive vision of post-industrial collapse. Here the end of the world is seen as a non-stop demolition derby, as gangs of motorized savages rove their desert wastes, bereft of speech, thought, hopes or dreams, dedicated only to the brutal realities of speed and violence.

Above all, *Mad Max 2* is an example of how sheer virtuosity can triumph in the film medium. A host of images wrench the retina – garish vehicles, fearful road armour and weird punk hairstyles, the sense of a world discarded after Judgement Day. In its raw power and vast scenic effects, *Mad Max 2* is punk's Sistine Chapel.

American Film
1987

Courting the Cobra

Projections 2
edited by John Boorman and Walter Donohue

The confidence of film directors, their zest and appetite for life, are nothing less than daunting, especially to the novelist, a gloomy soul sitting alone in the darkened auditorium of his own head and never certain that the lights will come on. Judged by the few grumbles in *Projections 2*, even a film director's lowest moments sound remarkably like a novelist's highs.

I once asked the veteran profile-writer Lynn Barber, who has interviewed hundreds of successful people in almost every profession, to name the happiest and most fulfilled of all. 'Film directors,' she promptly replied, a verdict amply confirmed here. Yet most filmmakers are unemployed at any moment, and reduced to peddling their latest projects from one unwelcoming office to the next. Film directors, as David Hare comments, are like deposed royalty, encountered in hotel lobbies as they wander the globe. They retain their titles, but lack a kingdom.

Launched last year by John Boorman and Walter Donohue, *Projections* is the best of the new series of film books, neither too popular nor too specialist, and free of the over-academic criticism that brings the entire paraphernalia of Marxism and psychoanalysis to the job of decoding John Ford westerns. *Projections* is packed with lively gossip and provocative ideas, underpinned by a shared passion for the medium of film. Directors, screenwriters and cinephotographers speak their minds with a frankness rarely seen in other professions.

In his introduction to *Projections 1*, John Boorman wrote wittily and ruefully of the difficulties he met in financing his recent films. He described the ordeal of making the sales pitch in a producer's office, a process that I have watched in Wardour Street over the years and which resembles the snake-charmer's courtship of the cobra, with the same plaintive little tunes, frozen immobility and fear of those bored, deadly eyes, swaying slightly from the effects of a large lunch. None the less, films are still made, and the most expensive dreams in the world are turned into light, and play against the silver wall of the planetary imagination. I hope that future numbers of *Projections* will look at the producer's creative contribution, always underestimated. The Hollywood of fifty years ago, its greatest era, was a producer's Hollywood where most directors were less important than the cameramen. Given the huge financial constraints, film may well be the least likely success story of the twentieth century.

One of the most interesting features in the new volume is a round-up of directors invited to predict the future of the cinema in the next millennium. Paul Schrader imagines the novelist and film director working in conjunction with the neuroscientist. 'The next version of *Ulysses* may well come in pill form,' he concludes, though many people already regard Joyce and Proust as the closest thing to a Valium. Even more apocalyptically, John Boorman guesses that not only the lens may become redundant, but also the eye and the camera, with electrical images fed directly into what I assume will be a kind of brain-bypass, something which we have already experienced in the form of television.

Other enjoyable features are long interviews with the maverick Robert Altman, director of *M*A*S*H* and *The Player*, and Hollywood's enduring one-man awkward squad, and with the British screenwriter Sydney Gilliat, who collaborated with Frank Launder on the script of Hitchcock's *The Lady Vanishes*. Gilliat offers his astute reflections on the curious and devious personality of Hitchcock, whom some have described as emotionally under-developed and little more than a grown-up schoolboy with a taste for lavatory humour. Gilliat knew him as a complex and scheming character, especially destructive of other people and determined to take all credit for himself.

Lucid and entertaining, Gilliat reminisces about the 1940s, the golden years of British film, and though now in his mid-eighties seems brimming with new ideas and as keen as ever to get behind a camera. His last words are typical of filmmakers as a whole, those hustlers, poets, bullies and mountebanks, every one a Cortez glimpsing an imaginary Pacific – 'Any offers?'

Daily Telegraph
1993

The Samurai of the Epic

The Warrior's Camera: The Cinema of Akira Kurosawa
Stephen Prince

In 1971 Japan's greatest filmmaker, Akira Kurosawa, director of *Rasho-mon* and *The Seven Samurai*, slashed his wrists with a razor, apparently in despair over the collapse of his career and failure to find commercial backing for his future films. Kurosawa's attempt to kill himself – a way out of his problems, incidentally, that he never allowed his samurai heroes – lies at the centre of *The Warrior's Camera*, an extended inquest into this would-be suicide and Kurosawa's motives. Suicide may well be an act perfected by the Japanese, but it is hard to imagine Billy Wilder walking stoically into the surf off Malibu after the failure of *Fedora*. Movies, even those as witty and brilliant as Wilder's, are not worth wetting one's toes for.

But Kurosawa was never a maker of movies. Film was his medium at a time – the forties and fifties – when the film was at least the equal partner of the movie, and the cinema had yet to separate into the art film, a species that may soon be extinct, and the entertainment movie that now swamps our imaginations. Some movies, like *Point Blank* and *Double Indemnity*, are intense and ruthless enough to count as films, but this was never a doorway open to Kurosawa.

Truffaut, in his published conversations with Alfred Hitchcock, compliments him on his good sense in going to Hollywood, and comments that there is something about England that is inherently uncinematic. Truffaut refers to the anti-dramatic nature of English life; our stolid routines and subdued manners, and even our weather, Truffaut claims, are anti-cinematic. At first sight, how much more these strictures would seem to apply to the notion of a Japanese cinema – especially the rain, which certainly drenches many of Kurosawa's films. Given the glacier-like rigidities of pre-war Japanese life, the total deference to authority and social consensus, and the suppression of the smallest gleam of individuality, it's plainly a miracle that a Japanese cinema ever emerged at all, let alone a maverick talent like Kurosawa's.

Stephen Prince suggests that Kurosawa only found the freedom to make his immensely personal films thanks to Japan's defeat in the Second World War. The shattered population, gazing at their fire-bombed, moonscape cities, realized where consensus and obedience had led and were prepared for a few years to visualize some kind of alternative. From the start of his career, making wartime propaganda films, Kurosawa believed in the power of cinema to bring about a national regeneration, and was convinced that the Japanese would find their salvation by thinking about themselves above all as individuals.

In 1950 he produced *Rashomon*, a masterpiece of subjectivity in which the murder of a warrior and the rape of his wife are seen from four conflicting viewpoints. As Stephen Prince points out, what is so tantalizing about *Rashomon* is its refusal to validate any of the witnesses' stories as the true account. In a world of absolute relativity, there is no way of knowing who is telling the truth. These same ambiguities prevail in Kurosawa's films with contemporary settings – *Drunken Angel* and *Stray Dog*, among others – bleak visions of post-war criminality that draw on the same sources as the Italian neo-realist cinema, and convey the unmistakable impression that the Japanese, more than any other people, enjoy being depressed.

His samurai epics, above all *The Seven Samurai*, show Kurosawa again subverting traditional views of Japan's historical past. The originality of the film, and an aspect that failed to translate into its Hollywood remake, *The Magnificent Seven*, was the unprecedented decision by the warriors, whose loyalty was to their feudal lord, to espouse the cause of the peasants – as strange as we would find the decision by a group of Grenadier Guards officers to set off for Yorkshire in the 1984 coal-strike and defend a village of striking miners.

Despite a long series of distinguished films, Kurosawa's career was already threatened by the sixties. With the triumph of television, Japanese cinema audiences stayed at home to watch formulaic samurai epics produced at a fraction of Kurosawa's lavish budgets. As well, a new kind of consensual thinking and corporate obedience had emerged with the rise of Japan Inc. The global victory won by Sony, Datsun and Matsushita Electric left no room for tortured self-doubt or moral relativities. The Japanese cinema fragmented into soft-porn and mass-entertainment industries, leaving behind a small group of art-film directors who loathed Kurosawa's sweeping epics and what they saw as his 'Hollywood' narratives.

Today Japanese cinema manages to produce an occasional oddball like *Tampopo*. But its great days seem to lie in the past, along with the great days of American and European film, a vanishing world that survives in cinematheques and the TV graveyard hours and, one step from oblivion, in the nearest that the consumer society comes to cultural nirvana, the video-rental classics shelf.

Guardian
1991

La Jetée

This strange and poetic film, directed by Chris Marker, is a fusion of science fiction, psychological fable and photomontage, and creates in its unique way a series of potent images of the inner landscapes of time. Apart from a brief three-second sequence – a young woman's hesitant smile, a moment of extraordinary poignancy, like a fragment of a child's dream – the thirty-minute film is composed entirely of still photographs. Yet this succession of disconnected images is a perfect means of projecting the quantified memories and movements through time that are the film's subject matter.

The jetty of the title is the main observation platform at Orly Airport. The long pier reaches out across the concrete no-man's-land, the departure point for other worlds. Giant jets rest on the apron beside the pier, metallic ciphers whose streamlining is a code for their passage through time. The light is powdery. The spectators on the observation platform have the appearance of mannequins. The hero is a small boy, visiting the airport with his parents. Suddenly there is a fragmented glimpse of a man falling. An accident has occurred, but while everyone is running to the dead man the small boy is looking instead at the face of a young woman by the rail. Something about this face, its expression of anxiety, regret and relief, and above all the obvious but unstated involvement of the young woman with the dead man, creates an image of extraordinary power in the boy's mind.

Years later, World War III breaks out. Paris is almost obliterated by an immense holocaust. A few survivors live on in the circular galleries below the Palais de Chaillot, like rats in some sort of abandoned test-maze warped out of its normal time. The victors, distinguished by the strange eye-pieces they wear, begin to conduct a series of experiments on the survivors, among them the hero, now a man of about thirty. Faced with a destroyed world, the experimenters are hoping to send a man through time. They select the young man because of the powerful memory he carries of the pier at Orly. With luck he will home on to this. Other volunteers have gone insane, but the extraordinary strength of his memory carries him back to pre-war Paris. The sequence of images here is the most remarkable in the film, the subject lying in a hammock in the underground corridor as if waiting for some inward sun to rise, a bizarre surgical mask over his eyes – in my experience, the only convincing act of time travel in the whole of science fiction.

Arriving in Paris, he wanders among the strange crowds, unable to make contact with anyone until he meets the young woman he had seen as a child at Orly Airport. They fall in love, but their relationship is marred by his sense of isolation in time, his awareness that he has committed some kind of psychological crime in pursuing this memory. As if trying to place himself in time, he takes the young woman to museums of palaeontology, and they spend days among the fossil plants and animals. They visit Orly Airport, where he decides that he will not go back to the experimenters at Chaillot. At this moment three strange figures appear. Agents from an even more distant future, they are policing the time-ways, and have come to force him back. Rather than leave the young woman, he throws himself from the pier. The falling body is the one he glimpsed as a child.

This familiar theme is treated with remarkable finesse and imagination, its symbols and perspectives continually reinforcing the subject matter. Not once does it make use of the time-honoured conventions of traditional science fiction. Creating its own conventions from scratch, it triumphantly succeeds where science fiction invariably fails.

New Worlds
1966

Blue Velvet

Blue Velvet is, for me, the best film of the 1980s – surreal, voyeuristic, subversive and even a little corrupt in its manipulation of the audience. In short, the perfect dish for the jaded palates of the 1990s. But a thicket of puzzles remains. First, why do the sensible young couple, played by Kyle MacLachlan and Laura Dern, scheme to break into the apartment of the brutalized nightclub singer (Isabella Rossellini) and risk involving themselves with the psychopathic gangster – Dennis Hopper in his most terrifying screen performance?

A curious feature of *Blue Velvet* is the virtual absence of the youngsters' parents, shadowy figures who take almost no part in the action. I assume the film is a full-blown Oedipal drama, and that the gangster and the nightclub singer are the young couple's 'real' parents. Like children hiding in their parents' bedroom, they see more than they bargained for. Playing his sadistic games with the singer, the gangster rants 'Mummy, mummy, mummy'; a useful pointer to David Lynch's real intentions. The young man longs to take the gangster's place in the singer's bed and, when he does, soon finds himself playing the same shocking games, a crisis that can only be resolved by killing his 'father' in the approved Oedipal fashion.

The second puzzle is the role of the severed ear found by the young man after he visits his father in hospital, and which sets off the entire drama. Why an ear rather than a hand or a set of fingerprints? I take it that the ear is really his own, tuned to the inner voice that informs him of his imminent quest for his true mother and father. Like the ear, the white picket fence and the mechanical bird that heralds a return to morality, *Blue Velvet* is a sustained and brutal tease, *The Wizard of Oz* re-shot with a script by Kafka and decor by Francis Bacon. More, more . . .

Time Out
1993

2 LIVES

Nancy Reagan, Elvis,
Howard Hughes and Hirohito . . .

The Chain-saw Biographer

Nancy Reagan: The Unauthorized Biography
Kitty Kelley

But why didn't the astrologers see this coming? The sunsets above Mulholland Drive must be an even more electric pink these days as the whole of Bel Air blushes for Nancy. By now everyone knows about her White House affair with Frank Sinatra, her legendary meanness as she recycled unwanted presents, her reckless spending of the tax-payer's money and Imelda Marcos-sized extravagance on designer clothes, her chilling relationships with her own children during the ruthless climb to success and, most damning of all, the astrologers who decided the dates of international conferences and determined those 'bad' days when Ronnie was not allowed to leave the White House at all.

Kitty Kelley is an exponent of the chain-saw school of biography, and through the blizzard of sawdust it is hard to make out the real woman within this devastating portrait. But the real was always a doubt-ful commodity in the case of the Reagans – so much of the President's image was manufactured, and so self-deluding his own notions of the world as he confused reality with the half-remembered movies of his youth, that it scarcely matters if the facts in this biography are true or not.

Observers of the Reagans often commented on 'the gaze', the look of rapt attention that Nancy turned upon the President whenever he spoke in public, but masks of various kinds had long been used by Nancy to screen her from anything she preferred to forget. Huge sections of her past had been freeze-dried and hidden away in a dark locker of her mind, never to be opened again. The daughter of an ambitious repertory actress and a failed car salesman – whom Nancy claimed to have been a Princeton graduate – she was brought up during her early childhood by her aunt and uncle when her parents divorced, a period of forced separation that seems to have numbed her for ever. In later life Nancy never contacted her natural father, transferring all her affection to Dr

Loyal Davis, a taciturn Chicago neurosurgeon whom her mother married when her career had ebbed.

This ultra-right wing and viciously racist man – he could never bring himself even to utter the word Jew – was later credited with shaping Ronald Reagan's political world-view and transforming him from a Democrat into a deep-blue Republican. Dr Davis had treated Spencer Tracy's crippled son, and after graduating from college the aspiring actress Nancy Davis (she had forced through her legal adoption against the wishes of her reluctant step-father while still a teenager) set off for Hollywood and an MGM screen test arranged by Tracy. Always rather old-fashioned, Nancy chose a traditional route to launch her career, opting for the casting couch when she began a long affair with Benny Thau, the MGM executive in charge of casting. A number of undistinguished films followed, in which she tended to play plucky housewives in maternity smocks, while off the set she enjoyed affairs with a succession of Hollywood's leading men, among them Robert Walker and Peter Lawford, who particularly prized her talents for oral sex.

But destiny finally dialled in the shape of another fading B-actor with an unhappy childhood, the president of the Screen Actors Guild, Ronald Reagan. Soon Hollywood was behind them, as the Reagans set their eyes on the governorship of California and, beyond that, the leading roles in the ultimate movie of them all, the presidency of the United States, in which he would star and she would direct, with a supporting cast of European monarchs, Russian statesmen and California millionaires.

Reading this wonderfully sleazy account of the Reagans' rise to power, of their relentless ambition and ruthless social climbing, one is still surprised by the confidence with which American politicians set about exploiting the fruits of office. Dissatisfied with the Sacramento governor's mansion, Nancy ordered another, a $1.4 million monstrosity that later stood empty for ten years. Once in the White House she began to amass a vast wardrobe of couture gowns and furs, all on indefinite 'loan' until the Internal Revenue Service panicked her into returning them. Tactlessly, she announced the purchase of a $200,000 china set on the same day that the President cut school lunches and declared that ketchup would be counted as a vegetable in the federally subsidized programme. She recycled inferior presents, and accidentally sent a gift-wrapped birthday present to her grandson of the teddy bear he had left in the White House. At the same time, Nancy's ruthlessness extended to herself. On hearing that she had a cancerous breast nodule, she demanded a total mastectomy against the advice of her doctors. But as one of the surgeons commented, the Reagans were not afraid of the knife. 'Both have had numerous facelifts. From the scars behind his ears, I'd say the President has had two lifts, and she's probably had three or four.'

Reagan's presidency was a mystery to Europeans, though Americans were happy to see this amiable if goofy former sportscaster on their TV screens rather than the moralizing Carter, and took him much more easily in their stride. But how could a man so intellectually third-rate, an empty stage-set of a personality across which moved cartoon figures, dragon ladies and demons of the evil empire, ever have become President of the world's most powerful nation? Was the image everything now, and who would be next – Colonel Sanders, Jimmy Osmond, Donald Duck? Is the USA so strong and so soundly constituted, so effectively ruled by its great bureaucracies, that politics and the presidency are an entertaining irrelevancy?

But the dream buckled with the Irangate-Contra affair and the revelation that summit meetings with Gorbachev were scheduled by Nancy and her $3,000-a-month astrologer. Since then the grey men have moved in again, led by George Bush ('Whiney' to Mrs Reagan). But perhaps the real lesson of the Reagan presidency is the sinister example he offers to future film actors and media manipulators with presidential ambitions and all too clearly defined ideas, and every intention of producing a thousand-year movie out of them.

Guardian
1991

Survival Instincts

Wild Swans
Jung Chang

The women of China must be among the most oppressed and, paradoxically, the most strong-willed in the world, as this harrowing account of three desperate lives proves on every extraordinary page. I can remember the bad-tempered amahs of my childhood, ruthless and hard-fisted little women darting about on their bound feet. At the other end of the social scale were the dragon ladies – tycoons' wives or successful businesswomen – in their long fur coats and immaculate make-up, who could petrify a small boy at fifty paces with their baleful stares.

Returning to China last summer, I was startled to find an advance guard of dragon ladies apparently waiting for me in the Cathay Pacific lounge at Heathrow. But there were none on the streets of Shanghai, and, fortunately, their places were taken by thousands of relaxed and cheerful young women in pretty frocks, strolling arm-in-arm with their husbands and friends. The sight would have warmed the hearts of Jung Chang's mother and grandmother, the two women whose tragically abused lives occupy the centre of this heart-rending book. Together they tell the story of China during the twentieth century, an epic of privation, cruelty and dashed hopes that makes one despair of politics as the answer to anything. China's greatest political leader and ideologue, Mao Zedong, brought an end to decades of devastation and civil war under the corrupt rule of Chiang Kai-shek, but in turn Mao, his wife and henchmen brought equally appalling cruelties to the Chinese people.

Jung Chang begins her memoir with Yu-fang, her grandmother, who at the age of fifteen, in 1924, became the concubine of an elderly Manchurian warlord. She herself was the daughter of a woman so unvalued, like all female children, that she had never been given a name and was known simply as 'number two girl' – like the servants of my own childhood whom I addressed for years as 'number two boy' and 'number two coolie'. Despite her bound feet, with their broken arches and crushed toes, Jung's grandmother was considered a beauty by her warlord general. Virtually a prisoner in a large harem, she bore a child, Jung's mother De-hong. After the general's death, when his wife might have sold her off to a brothel, she married a 65-year-old doctor, and enjoyed a brief happiness. However, Japan invaded Manchuria in 1931, and began to ransack the cities and countryside. Years of destitution followed, but somehow mother and daughter survived the deliberate brutalization of an entire people. At last, in 1944, American B-29s appeared in the sky, followed by a Russian occupation force who presided over yet another regime of terror and repression.

But the first Chinese communists also arrived. Ragged and ill-equipped, they looked poorer and scruffier than beggars. None the less, they soon restored order, restarted the economy and improved the food supply. When civil war broke out between Mao's forces and Chiang's Kuomintang armies, the teenage daughter threw in her lot with the communists, the only political group that promised an end to the barbarous treatment of women.

The late 1940s were a time of runaway inflation, when emaciated women pinned signs on their children: 'Daughter for sale for 10 kilos of rice.' Jung's mother became active in the underground, but was arrested by the Kuomintang. Miraculously, she survived a firing squad when the prisoner next to her was shot dead. Soon after, she fell in love with a romantic communist guerrilla who gave her Russian novels to read and – a point very much in his favour – knew the difference between Flaubert and Maupassant.

With Mao's conquest of the country, and the flight of Chiang to Formosa, a new and fairer China seemed waiting to be born. But the conservative peasant women, survivors of the Long March, resented the young and strong-willed students such as Jung's mother who attracted the communist menfolk. Mind-numbing sessions of public 'self-criticism' began to occupy much of the revolution's time. Everything was now politicized, as the regime suppressed the last vestiges of spirit and independence that had drawn Jung's mother to the communist cause in the first place. Suspected of bourgeois leanings, she and her husband were transferred to the remote western province of Sichuan, where they began to work their way up the party's administrative ladder. Even now their idealism still prevailed over the Orwellian logic of Maoist 'thought reform'. Cleanliness was regarded as unproletarian, ignorance was celebrated as freedom from bourgeois thinking, and constant meetings left no time for inward reflection, virtually eliminating the private sphere.

Jung was born in 1952, but she saw little of her mother, who was struggling to survive the successive purges of 'hidden counter-revolutionists, rightists and capitalist-roaders'. In this nonsense-world, grass, flowers and pets were deemed to be bourgeois. Red traffic-lights now signalled go, but the ensuing traffic chaos was merely a comical prelude to the sinister cruelties of the cultural revolution. Estranged from her husband, who feared that emotional support for her would be anti-party, Jung's mother, by now a senior education administrator, was forced to kneel on broken glass and parade with a dunce's cap on her head. The daughter was banished to the Himalayas to work as a barefoot doctor. At last, with the death of Mao, rehabilitation followed, but Jung's father died soon after, hounded to his grave by petty spite and envy.

As his daughter remarks, the hallmark of Maoism was the reign of ignorance and hatred, and I suspect that Mao's real achievement was to allow the Chinese, a supremely stoic and unemotional people, to express emotion fully for the first time. When Jung escapes to the West, a century-long nightmare seems to end. Immensely moving and unsettling, *Wild Swans* is an unforgettable portrait of the brain-death of a nation, and a tribute to the superhuman endurance of Chinese women. Sanity seems to have returned to China, but, as Jung reminds us, Mao's portrait still hangs in Tiananmen Square.

Sunday Times
1992

Fallen Idol

Elvis
Albert Goldman

The Hollywood cynic who commented, on hearing of Elvis Presley's death in 1977, 'Good career move,' might well have second thoughts after reading this ruthless exposé. Everyone watching Presley on television in his last years, as he swayed across the stage of the Las Vegas Hilton in his Prince Valiant suit, a bloated parody of himself who now and then treated his blue-rinsed audience to a canny leer, knew that something was wrong. But the memory of the young Presley remained, an electric charge that still pulls all the current out of the mains.

According to Albert Goldman, for at least the last decade of his life Presley was a hopeless drug addict, a walking pharmacopoeia of powerful stimulants and opiates that a coterie of compliant doctors injected into him at all hours of the day and night. Although the autopsy results were never published, it was probably a huge overdose that killed him during the long night of 17 August 1977, as he sat alone in his bathroom at Graceland, his stoned entourage asleep in their nearby bedrooms.

But by then, according to Goldman, the real Presley had been moribund for years, in effect since the death of his mother Gladys in 1958. Goldman clearly relishes his tale of Presley's slow and lurid decline, elaborating a long catalogue of those sins that seem particularly heinous to Americans. Mama's boy and bed-wetter, prude and glutton, voyeur and obsessive gun-fancier, Presley alienates his biographer's sympathies at every turn. In fact, almost everything about Presley is present in this biography except his enormous talent, and an influence on popular culture greater than that of any other musical performer this century.

Goldman makes much of the close relationship between Presley and his mother, lingering over their extreme physical intimacy – they slept in the same bed until his puberty. But despite her own well-developed taste for drugs and alcohol, Gladys seems to have offered Presley rock-like support throughout her short life. Again, Goldman reveals that Presley was a natural blond, and based his legendary black hairstyle on that worn by the young Tony Curtis in the 1949 film *City Across the River*. Does this diminish Presley, or show his astuteness in the way he assembled his potent stage image as that archetypal 1950s figure, the juvenile delinquent?

Goldman's attempt to demolish the Presley myth seems an attack on the whole popular culture of the period (he is now working on a book about John Lennon – watch out). Curiously Goldman seems obsessed with Presley's sexuality. In his first view of Presley, he describes him in his bedroom at Graceland towards the end, 'propped up like a big fat woman recovering from some operation on her reproductive organs'. He harps endlessly on Presley's voyeurism, his liking for two-way mirrors and closed-circuit TV through which he watched the Guys (the Tennessee buddies who formed his entourage) making it with their girls.

Still, not as wild or as sad as the end. By the age of forty, Presley had earned $100 million. He gave away Cadillacs to passing strangers, threw expensive jewellery to his audiences, once flew from Memphis to Denver in his private jet to buy a peanut butter sandwich. In a trance of drugs and terminal boredom, he fell asleep with his face in a bowl of chicken soup. He was constantly watched by his guards in case he choked on a piece of food, became incontinent and had to be carried to the lavatory and tied into diapers. At the end he was so obese that he used a golf cart to carry him from the elevator to the stage of the Hilton.

For some reason, though, I find myself admiring Presley all the more. That knowing smile, those savvy eyes and that talent transcend everything, even this book.

Guardian
1981

The Killing Time

The Executioner's Song
Norman Mailer

Ours is a season for assassins. How far does our fascination with Oswald and Charles Manson, Gary Gilmore and James Earl Ray play on the edgy dreams of other lonely psychopaths, encourage them to gamble their trigger fingers on a very special kind of late twentieth century celebrity? Will everyone in the future, to adapt Warhol, be infamous for fifteen minutes? Given the immense glare of publicity, a virtual deification by the world's press and television, and the remarkable talents these rootless and half-educated men can show for manipulating the mass media, their actual crimes soon seem to sink to a lower, merely human realm.

Lee Harvey Oswald, had he not been shot by Jack Ruby, would presumably now be up for parole, ready to play his part – as TV anchorman, or special assignment writer for *Guns and Ammo*? – in the election of yet another Kennedy. With luck any would-be assassins in the future will give themselves away haggling with their agents for the biggest film advance and the right prime-time TV coverage.

The Executioner's Song is Norman Mailer's account of the crimes, trial and execution in 1977 of Gary Gilmore, the first convicted murderer to be put to death in the United States after a ten-year moratorium. Dedicated to Mailer's agent, at first sight the book is off-putting, perhaps the last chapter in the very system of exploitation that Mailer criticizes. Mailer never met Gilmore, and the 1,000-page text is based on a mass of extended interviews by Lawrence Schiller, an ex-*Life* photographer turned Hollywood entrepreneur. The result is a vast cast of largely minor characters and an excess of parallel narration never properly fused together, which makes nonsense of Mailer's attempt to call it a novel.

But in fact the repetitions and the flat documentary style allow Mailer to build up a masterly portrait of the murderer – Gilmore might well have been one of the morose GIs in *The Naked and the Dead*. By the time of his release from an Illinois penitentiary at the age of thirty-five,

Gilmore had spent eighteen of the previous twenty-two years in prison and reform school. The illegitimate son of a sometime convict and a mother who resented him from earliest childhood, Gilmore had already tasted celebrity. During a prison riot in Illinois the local TV crew 'selected' him as one of the leaders and put him on television to say a few words. His looks and the way he spoke attracted attention and the first fan mail from women admirers.

Returning to Provo, Utah, and a life of drugs, beer-drinking and petty theft, he cold-bloodedly murdered a gas station attendant and a motel clerk for little more than the equivalent of £50, and was arrested almost immediately by the police. Sustained by his girl-friend, Nicole, a remarkable young woman who would stand outside the jail, bellowing 'Gary Gilmore, I love you!' he accepted his death penalty and settled down to await his execution. The police psychiatrists diagnosed Gilmore as a psychopathic personality, and he seems to have felt no anger or hostility towards the men he murdered, regarding them with the same total blankness that he felt for himself. Already in the death cell he was planning both Nicole's suicide and his own execution – he wanted to be shot in the dark with tracer bullets, so that he could watch them coming towards him. Even the horrendous conditions on Death Row, a long way from Cagney and George Raft, hardly affected him. Mailer vividly describes this depraved zoo, a bedlam of cries and rage, the condemned men exposing their genitalia through the bars, hurling cups of urine into the faces of any intruders.

Gilmore's refusal to appeal against his death penalty soon made him a local celebrity. The first curious journalists interviewed him, the advance guard of an army of hustlers and agents, veteran wheeler-dealers from the Manson and Ruby cases, film and TV executives who swarmed in from all over the world. Gilmore's own lawyer, who doubled as his literary agent, defended his right to die, claiming: 'I think executions should be on prime-time TV.' The first hard cash, $500, was paid by the *Daily Express* ('When the British are here en masse,' said one excited newsman, 'the stamp is on the meat').

In a strange but impressive way, Gilmore expanded to fill the roles assigned him. One journalist noted that there was racist Gary, Country and Western Gary, artist manqué Gary, self-destructive Gary, Karma Gary and Gary the movie star. He quoted Shelley and Hermann Hesse, and would ask visitors 'Are you familiar with Nietzsche?'

The end came as he wanted it. The climax, and greatest set-piece in the book, is Mailer's account of the last night before the execution, a virtuoso description of the deranged prison party held around the drugged Gilmore, wearing a comical Robin Hood hat and brandishing pornographic photos of his girl-friend, while a huge TV and press encampment waited outside the prison.

Soon after dawn the party ended. To the tune of 'Una Paloma Blanca', Gilmore was taken to the execution yard in the prison cannery. As a TV commentator bawled: 'You'll be able to hear the shots, I promise!' Gilmore was tied to a chair in front of the concealed firing squad. After the shots, in the first silence since Gilmore's arrest, the only sound was the blood dripping on to his tennis shoes below the seat. Perhaps not surprisingly, only one witness managed to be sick.

Guardian

1979

Mob Psychology

Little Man: Mayer Lansky and the Gangster Life
Robert Lacey

Americans cherish their gangsters, Robert Lacey remarks in this entertaining biography of Meyer Lansky, one of the most mysterious criminal figures of the past fifty years. At times that fascination seems to extend to the entire world of crime, itself an inverted image of the American Dream, with its violence, energy and pursuit of the fast buck. Only serial killers, presidential assassins and out-and-out psychos – none of whom are interested in money – are excluded from the gallery of glamorized rogues.

The small-town bank-robbers of the 1930s were rapidly mythologized into a band of punk Robin Hoods, from Dillinger and Pretty Boy Floyd to Baby-Face Nelson and Ma Barker, a proto-feminist heroine if I saw one, who died beside son Fred, firing her Thompson in a final gun-battle with the G-men. But none of them could match the sinister charm of the big city crime-bosses who emerged from the Prohibition years. As the American economy boomed during the Second World War, the public imagination seemed to insist that crime too be conducted on a corporate basis, matching the giant scale of the steel, oil and automobile industries.

With the invention of the Mafia, whose existence many US law enforcement officers deny to this day, the endemic corruptions and venalities of American life were explained away at a stroke. Capone had died in prison of syphilis after being convicted of tax evasion, and he was followed by a financially more savvy group of New York criminals, above all Lucky Luciano, who broke away from traditional Sicilian practices into more expansive and profitable underworld activities.

Although associated with these mobsters, who were deeply involved in drugs, extortion and labour racketeering, Meyer Lansky was a very different figure, as Robert Lacey points out, and his elevation to the pantheon of criminal fame is in many ways surprising. But if the American public demanded that crime be put on a corporate basis, someone had to be found with the brains and administrative skills to run the corporation, and Lansky seemed to play the part to perfection. The American press called him the Chairman of the Board, and the brains behind the Mafia. He was claimed to have a personal fortune of $300 million, to have financed Bugsy Siegel in the creation of Las Vegas and to have teamed up with Batista to run the great Havana casinos. 'We're bigger than US Steel' was his most quoted remark, and he achieved the ultimate in popular fame by being portrayed by Lee Strasberg as the Mafia chief Hyman Roth in *The Godfather II*.

A few years ago I drove along Miami Beach where Lansky had retired, past the luxury condos with their washed gravel drives that looked as if they were delivered fresh from the quarry each morning, past the stretch limos guarded by large-shouldered men in black suits and shades. I imagined Lansky in a duplex apartment under the sky, manipulating the Mafia's vast cash reserves on a terminal linked to Wall Street as he gazed at his fleet of cocaine-running speedboats. But I couldn't have been more wrong, and the luxury condos, if not the cocaine boats, were almost certainly owned by Miami dentists and heart surgeons. As Robert Lacey reveals, the image of Lansky created by American newspapers and television was a complete myth, partly sustained by the failure of the US Justice Department to convict him of any serious crime, a failure that only reinforced the belief in Lansky's all-embracing power.

In fact, before his death he was living in a poorly furnished one-bedroom apartment, and left so little money to his heirs that his crippled son was soon reduced to existing on welfare. After the overthrow of Batista, and the loss of the Riviera hotel-casino in Havana that Lansky had built, he lived for years in a modest bungalow north of Miami, whose only expensive equipment was the elaborate bugging device which the FBI secretly installed. Unlike the New York crime bosses, Lansky was never involved in drugs, prostitution or labour racketeering, despite his childhood friendship with a real crime-tsar, Luciano. Born in eastern Poland in 1902, Lansky arrived in America with his parents at the age of four. A clever child with a flair for mathematics, he was small but aggressive, and as a teenager became a lookout and strong-arm man for the Jewish and Italian gamblers on New York's lower east side. His quick mind and organizational skills were invaluable to Luciano during the bootlegging years, and with the repeal of Prohibition Lansky turned his skills towards that other great American pastime, illicit gambling.

Robert Lacey makes the point that, far from being one of the architects of modern organized crime, Lansky in the post-war years was primarily a casino operator, inside and outside the law. He helped to devise the concept of the big Las Vegas resort hotel, which offered glitz along with first-class service and is now the dominant style of the international hotel. The illegal skimming of the take which he organized for the gangster owners of the Vegas hotels is the main charge against him, but like many a corrupt book-keeper he led a frugal private life, subscribing to the Book of the Month Club and worrying about his unhappy children, who were clearly unable to cope with the manufactured image that the US media had foisted upon their father.

By the time he died at the age of eighty he seems to have wearied of his reputation as the mastermind of American crime. As the nurses struggled to resuscitate him he thrashed away at them, crying out his last words: 'Let me go!' The Las Vegas hotels he helped to run have long since been sold to legitimate international corporations, and one wonders where the American imagination will turn to next in its search for a criminal superhero.

Guardian
1991

Closed Doors

The Hughes Papers
Elaine Davenport, Paul Eddy and Mark Hurwitz

A strongly punitive note sounds through this investigation into Howard Hughes's final years, as through so many recent books and news-magazine exposés, particularly those of American origin. Clearly Hughes's sometimes bizarre though often merely eccentric behaviour during the last twenty years of his life still profoundly irritates his fellow-citizens, destroying far too many cherished fantasies. Great-grandson of a Confederate general, son of the millionaire inventor of the world's most efficient oil-drilling bit, aviation pioneer and Hollywood man-about-town who 'escorted' its greatest leading ladies, Howard Hughes bought and sold airlines and film studios, personally designed a brassiere for Jane Russell and helped to introduce that unique cultural institution, the in-flight movie.

How galling, then, that this embodiment of so many potent national myths should slam the door on it all at the age of fifty and opt for exile, silence and cunning, and even more so that his quest for absolute privacy should be conducted in such a tantalizingly public way. If Hughes had retired to some impregnable mock-Xanadu or an exclusive Long Island sanatorium, no one would have minded; but he doubled the offence by sealing himself into the penthouse of the Desert Inn Hotel above the one national fantasy he had so far left alone – Las Vegas.

Unlike *The Hughes Papers*, a compilation of Hughes's confused financial shenanigans, mild political bribery and muddled efforts to take over the whole of Nevada, the one book about Hughes which might have refurbished the myths has not yet been published – Clifford Irving's fake biography. This imaginary account of Hughes's secret life during his purported exile – the big-game hunting expeditions, meetings with Hemingway, conversations with Schweitzer, etc. – would have safely restored the hero to his pedestal. Had Hughes, who was seventy-one when he died, in fact died two or three years earlier, before he could have issued his denial, Irving's biography would not only have been published but its authenticity, for powerful psychological reasons, could never have been seriously challenged.

The Hughes Papers exhaustively analyses the possible involvement of the Hughes empire in political and financial corruption. But the present state of the art as revealed by Watergate and the Lockheed scandals suggests that Hughes's activities in the fifties and sixties amounted to little more than discreet tinkering, and would barely be of interest except for his increasingly eccentric behaviour. I admire Hughes, above all for the casual way in which he closed the door on the world. Lying back on a couch with the blinds drawn, popping pills and worrying about fad diets while watching the 170th re-run of *Ice Station Zebra*, reminds me in many ways of life today in the Thames Valley. Hughes may well have been more in touch with reality than one assumes.

New Statesman
1977

Last of the Great Royals

Hirohito
Edward Behr

Asked in 1986 for his thoughts on Halley's Comet, which had visited our skies after an interval of seventy-five years, the Emperor Hirohito remarked: 'It's nice to see it again.' The reply accords in every way with the popular image of this remote and unworldly sovereign, dedicated to marine biology, that most endearing of sciences, who knew little or nothing of Japan's preparations for the Second World War and bore no responsibility for the appalling atrocities his armed forces committed. Hirohito's finest hour, by this reckoning, was his surrender speech on 14 August 1945, a few days after Hiroshima and Nagasaki, calling on his forces to lay down their arms and reminding them, in a felicitous phrase that has its own dotty charm, 'that the war situation has developed not necessarily to Japan's advantage'.

General MacArthur, an almost preposterously imperial figure, was one of the first to accept the now traditional view of Hirohito. At their meeting in September 1945 the trembling Hirohito expected to be arrested on the spot – already there had been calls for his indictment as a war criminal. But MacArthur was affability itself, offering the Living God a Lucky Strike and putting him at his ease. Their meeting was in private, though Mrs MacArthur was listening to every word behind a curtain, and it is hard to know what convinced MacArthur that Hirohito was 'a sincere man and a genuine liberal'. At any event Hirohito, after publicly renouncing his godliness, then embarked on the rest of his immensely long and undisturbed reign. He resumed his state visits to foreign countries and was courteously received by Queen Elizabeth and President Ford. By the time of his death Japan had become one of the world's economic superpowers, and the Japanese monarchy was almost alone in having retained its dignity intact – by comparison our own scrambling royals might be auditioning for *EastEnders*. Hirohito's funeral was attended by the President of the United States and a host of kings, heads of state and prime ministers. The hunger-strike mounted in protest by a British ex-serviceman seemed little more than a quaint anachronism.

Edward Behr's biography is a cool and convincing attempt to dismantle the myths that constitute one of the most successful public relations exercises of our century. Above all, he sets out to expose Hirohito's true role in the 1930s and 1940s – a formidable undertaking, given the maze-like complexity of Japanese imperial and political life, and the uniquely strange upbringing of Hirohito himself. Behr portrays the wartime Hirohito as a cunning prevaricator and opportunist, who exploited his own wavering diffidence in dealing with his military chiefs. However, spontaneity and personal choice were qualities the future Emperor had never been allowed to cultivate. At the age of ten weeks he was taken away from his seventeen-year-old mother, the Empress Sadako, and brought up by a retired admiral. He was provided with no childhood friends or games, and had to submit to grim routines to improve his posture and eyesight. One of the few respites came at the age of fifteen, when his father, the Emperor Taisho, sent one of his concubines to Hirohito's quarters. She reported back that the Crown Prince 'had displayed a certain scientific curiosity in sex, leading in time to a perfectly normal conclusion'. So was born, perhaps, the future marine biologist.

This apart, Hirohito's only real pleasure in his entire life was his visit to Britain in 1921. He was captivated by the Royal Family's friendliness and informality, and returned to Japan with a set of bagpipes, a lifelong dedication to English breakfasts and plus-fours, and a determination to be the first monogamous Emperor. By all accounts he made a happy marriage, though his bride received from the Empress Sadako what must be the ultimate mother-in-law's wedding gift – an illustrated pillow book of advice on sex techniques and ways of ensuring a male heir.

On ascending the throne Hirohito reduced the size of the court and put an end to the custom of being presented, on important occasions, with gifts of dead fish. But his meals were first sampled by food-tasters, and there was a daily examination of the royal faeces. More importantly, he had earlier established a privately subsidized think-tank, the University Lodging House. This was a select and secretive club where bright young bureaucrats mingled with up-and-coming military men, and became a sounding-board for various right-wing and ultra-nationalist ideas.

Edward Behr points out that Hirohito was exceptionally methodical and industrious, read everything to which he put his seal, and was aware of whatever took place within the Supreme War Command and the cabinet. Despite certain vague reservations, he supported the invasions of Manchuria in 1931 and China in 1937, promoted those responsible and was well aware of the preparations for the attack on Pearl Harbor. Behr believes that he envisaged a short, sharp war with the United States and Britain, which would be followed by a peace treaty guaranteeing Japan's future dominance over East Asia. All too soon the American counter-attacks in the Pacific and a series of devastating naval defeats cooled his ardour. His aides noticed that he spoke increasingly of his friendship with the British Royal Family, harping on his blessed days at Balmoral.

Meanwhile, of course, British prisoners were being worked to death on the Burma railway. By the time the B-29 raids had begun to lay waste entire Japanese cities, a growing air of unreality had settled over court life. Between visits to the palace air-raid shelter there were lectures on calligraphy and Chinese culture. At last, after the dropping of the A-bombs, Hirohito decided to save what was left of Japan, and made his famous broadcast ending the war. But as General MacArthur remarked, it is hard to understand how someone powerful enough to end the war could not have prevented it in the first place.

After defeat he entered the last phase of his rule. He attended poetry competitions and became a keen TV fan and addict of sumo wrestling. Forever shy, he was said to be at ease only with marine biologists of his own height. However, his role in the war was not completely forgotten. In 1972 one of his former soldiers, Corporal Yokoi, returned to Japan after holding out for twenty-eight years in the jungles of Guam. Japanese TV audiences were baffled by the corporal's insistence on carrying out his military duties to the last, determined to return his rifle, still in working order, to his Imperial Majesty. Hirohito commented: 'I hope he gets a good rest.'

But as Edward Behr asks in his epilogue, had there ever been, in the Japanese eye, the notion of surrender? Nowhere in Hirohito's speech is surrender, or defeat, specifically mentioned, and many Japanese are now convinced that Japan was the war's prime victim. Whatever else, this total inversion of the truth may be the greatest achievement of this astute, devious and mysterious man.

Observer
1989

Sinister Spider

Dragon Lady: the Life and Legend of
the Last Empress of China
Sterling Seagrave

Of all the maligned women in history – a richly stocked sisterhood that stretches from Eve to Mrs T – the most unfairly treated may well have been the last Empress of China, Tzu Hsi, who ruled from 1861 to her death in 1908. Sterling Seagrave's scrupulously researched exposé of the insults to her reputation makes one wonder how false our images of the great and famous probably are. Were Cleopatra and Catherine the Great anything like the figures that historians have described? Even in the era of the telephoto lens and the satellite interview our impressions of Nancy Reagan and Imelda Marcos may reflect our needs rather than their reality.

Contemporary reports, apparently so reliable, can lead to enormous injustice, and around Tzu Hsi the most scurrilous gossip solidified into instant history. During my Shanghai childhood in the 1930s I listened spellbound to strange tales about the Dowager Empress told by old China hands who had lived in Peking during the last years of her reign. Virtually entombed within the Forbidden City for fifty years, she had presided like a sinister spider over the Manchu empire. Only her closest courtiers had ever set eyes on her, and even her doctors were never allowed to see or touch her. Whenever she was ill, so the story went, silken cords were tied to her wrists and unwound to a curtained ante-room, where the royal physician would make his diagnosis from the faintest tremblings. I was deeply impressed, though years later in England I learned of fashionable Harley Street doctors who diagnosed the maladies of their rich women patients, and prescribed the desired stimulants and tranquillizers, entirely over the telephone – a not too dissimilar kind of silken line.

What I was not told as a child was that Tzu Hsi was widely believed to be a monster of depravity, a vicious oriental Messalina who presided over orgies of sexual perversion, poisoned her own son and was responsible for China's humiliation during the Opium Wars and the Boxer Rebellion. This wholly false picture was only revised in 1975 when Hugh Trevor-Roper exposed its principal creator in his *Hermit of Peking: the Hidden Life of Sir Edmund Backhouse*. An Oxford graduate who spoke fluent Chinese, Backhouse arrived in Peking in 1899 and became unofficial editor and adviser to Dr George Morrison, local correspondent of *The Times*, who spoke no Chinese at all.

Prompted by the poisonous republican propaganda of Chinese revolutionaries campaigning against the Manchu dynasty, Backhouse concocted a stream of fabricated despatches about the Empress and the Imperial Court that satisfied the western appetite for tales of eastern corruption, and fixed the image of China as a haunt of dragon ladies, cruel and inscrutable mandarins and generally devilish behaviour (how I searched for it, in vain) that has lasted in large part to the present day.

As Trevor-Roper revealed, Backhouse supported himself by forging the court papers and court diaries that confirmed his malicious portrait of Tzu Hsi. Shortly before his death in Peking in 1943, during the Japanese occupation, he compiled the last of his fictions, an account of his long love affair with the lewd and elderly Empress and the weird orgies that she organized for her entertainment.

Sterling Seagrave sets the record straight. He draws on long-suppressed reports (which Backhouse denounced as forgeries) by western visitors who had met the Empress and found her to be a genial and kindly woman of quirky disposition but great strength of character. A former concubine of the Emperor Hsien Feng, she became the Dowager Empress when she was still in her mid-twenties and a complete novice in matters of state. Despite the immense handicaps of being a woman and almost never leaving the Forbidden City for the next fifty years, she did her best to steer China through the dangerous decades of confrontation with the west.

But fiction, though not as strange as truth, can be far more potent and self-justifying, and the Dowager Empress's supposed depravity seemed retrospectively to vindicate the gunboats and raiding parties of the European powers as they set about their ruthless exploitation of her nation.

Daily Telegraph
1992

Lipstick and High Heels

Deng Xiaoping and the Making of Modern China
Richard Evans

Deng Xiaoping is widely rumoured to be dying, but it would be a mistake to write off this feisty little man before the grave is cold, as Sir Richard Evans, Our Man in Peking from 1984 to 1988, makes clear in his shrewd biography of the most important Chinese leader since Mao Zedong. It could be said of China that for forty centuries nothing happened and, then, in a single century, everything happened. The feudal agricultural society that had moved through the millennia at an almost geological pace burst into the modern age with the overthrow of the Manchu dynasty in 1912. A new China soon emerged – urban, industrializing and, in due course, fiercely Marxist – and with it arrived a new kind of Chinese man and woman, as many Westerners found to their cost.

In 1949 my father was trapped in Shanghai after the communist take-over and, like all old China hands, confidently expected the ideological purity of the invading armies to last as long as it took them to climb down from their tanks and stroll into the bars and brothels of downtown Shanghai. In fact, their puritan zeal only intensified, and my father found himself on trial, accused of various anti-communist misdeeds. Fortunately he was able to quote enough Marx and Engels to convince the magistrates that he had seen the error of his ways. He was acquitted and a year later escaped to Hong Kong, aware that the old China of 'squeeze' and corruption had gone for good, a transformation that I still find hard to grasp and which was due in large part to men such as Deng Xiaoping.

Deng was born in 1904, the son of a prosperous landowner in Sichuan province, and at the age of sixteen travelled to France as a worker-student, where he laboured at a series of menial jobs, developed a life-long taste for croissants and met Zhou Enlai, who introduced him to Marxism. After five years he returned to China a committed communist. He survived the Long March in 1934–5, served as a political commissar during the war against Japan, and after the defeat of Chiang Kai-shek helped to drive through the programme of land reform, when hundreds of thousands of landowners and rich peasants were killed in what Sir Richard calls the greatest social revolution in the history of the world. These numberless deaths, like those in Tiananmen Square in 1989, cast a shadow over this apparently likeable man, whose talent for friendship frequently saved his life.

As Sir Richard points out, Deng's years in France inoculated him against the sinocentrism that marred the vision of Mao Zedong, who never went abroad except to visit Russia. Early in his career Deng realized that China could develop into a modern state only if it was willing to learn from the outside world. In 1958 he spoke publicly of the day when Chinese women would be able to afford lipstick and high-heeled shoes, a more revolutionary notion, given the extreme poverty of the peasant population, than anything dreamed of in the Communist manifesto. Inevitably he became a victim of the Cultural Revolution, and was persecuted by Mao's vicious wife, Jiang Qing, and the Red Guards, who accused Deng of being a 'capitalist-roader' and humiliated him by forcing him to kneel in the 'airplane' position with his arms outstretched behind his back. After years of exile in a remote province Deng was restored to office upon Mao's death in 1976. As China's leader during the 1980s he launched the immense programme of economic and political reform that opened the country to foreign investment and transformed its landscape in a way that must have dismayed the old guard.

In 1991, during a visit to Shanghai, I had dinner in the restaurant on the top floor of the television tower with the affable director of the TV foreign news service. He asked me what I thought of the new Shanghai. Looking out at the forest of skyscrapers that reared from the crumbling streets of the old International Settlement, I tactlessly said that it reminded me of New York. He stared at me in a deeply depressed way, slowly exhaling the cigarette smoke from his lungs, as if the same thought had crossed his own mind more than once.

Summarizing Deng's achievements, Sir Richard speculates about the future facing China after his departure. He predicts that the present collective leadership will give way to the rule of one dominant figure, in accord with Chinese tradition, and that China's educated class, despite its appetite for social and cultural freedom, will doubt the wisdom of abandoning one-party rule. This combination, it seems to me, of a paramount leader, one-party rule and phenomenal economic and industrial growth (a yearly average of 10 per cent, a potential for mischief-making on a global scale that thankfully was denied to Mao) will make China's future a matter of vital concern to all of us, and we can only hope that the country is led by someone with the hard-headed pragmatism displayed by Deng Xiaoping.

Daily Telegraph
1993

3 THE VISUAL WORLD

Warhol, Hockney, Dali
and the Surrealists . . .

The Spectre at the Feast

The Andy Warhol Diaries
edited by Pat Hackett

Said hello to lots of people, who said hello to me . . . This entry in November 1976 virtually sums up the entire contents of the diaries which Warhol kept for the last ten years of his life. The endless parties and gallery openings drift by in a dream of Manhattan, touched by movie stars and pop celebrities. Mick and Bianca, Jack Nicholson and Jackie O, Madonna and Yoko flare briefly through a prose as soft and depthless as his screen prints of car crashes and electric chairs. As he moves through the New York dusk with his white wig and ashen pallor, Warhol resembles a spectre at the feast, a role in which he seems literally to have cast himself. In June 1968 he had been shot and critically wounded by Valerie Solanas, founder of SCUM, the Society for Cutting Up Men, who had played a small part in his film *Bike Boy*. Semi-conscious, Warhol heard his doctors say that he had died, and from then on considered himself 'officially back from the dead'.

Sadly, Warhol's creative imagination failed to join him on the return journey, and the gun-shots in the Factory sounded the effective end of his remarkable career. Was Warhol the last important artist to emerge since the Second World War? The works of his fellow pop-artists, the comic-strip blow-ups of Roy Lichtenstein and the billboard murals of James Rosenquist, seem as dated as half-forgotten advertisements. By contrast, Warhol's silk-screened soup-cans and celebrities, criminals and race riots are now even more vivid than their original sources, exposing the eerie banality of the world that modern communications have created. The multiple images mimic the mass-produced news photographs that swamp our retinas, and make an unsettling judgment on our notions of fame and success.

What sets Warhol apart is his effortlessly assumed naivety, a wide-eyed innocence that recalls an earlier filmmaker. In many ways Warhol is the Walt Disney of the amphetamine age. In his silk-screen images there is the same childlike retelling of the great fairy-tales of our time, the mythic lives of Elvis and Marilyn, Liz and Jackie. Presented in cartoon form, the replicated frames resemble film strips, their colours hand-painted by a studio of assistants.

Like Disney, he then moved on to wildlife documentary films, *Flesh*, *Trash* and *Bad*, his camera lens observing the mating rituals and repro-ductive cycles of the canyon-life of Manhattan. And Warhol, of course, was for ever his own greatest creation, a Valium-numbed Mickey Mouse in a white fright-wig. His dead-pan comments on his own work show a teasing astuteness. 'If you want to know about Andy Warhol, just look at the surface of my paintings. There's nothing behind it . . . I want to be a machine . . . Everybody's plastic. I want to be plastic . . .'

Inevitably, his dream came true. Why did this brilliant and gifted man – after Warhol, remember, came Schnabel with his wall-loads of broken crockery and the lurid twilight of Gilbert & George – lose his inspiration and devote himself for his last twenty years to commercial portraits and the cocktail party circuit described in his diaries?

As a child Warhol was a keen reader of movie magazines, and all his life remained star-struck by the rich and famous. Together, his paintings and films constitute the ultimate fan-magazine devoted to celebrity. The multiple images of Marilyn Monroe and Jackie Kennedy drain the tragedy from the lives of these desperate women, while the Day-Glo palette returns them to the innocent world of the child's colouring book. The same banalization of celebrity seems to have affected Warhol himself, ensnaring him in the reductive process he had once observed in the glitterati around him. He records in July 1983: 'There was a party at the Statue of Liberty, but I'd already read publicity of me going to it so I felt it was done already.'

So the diaries unroll, recording the endless parties (nine, I counted, in one evening alone) and not a single interesting conversation. He notes the impossible arrogance of Jane Fonda and reflects without envy on the astronomical prices paid to his fellow-artists Rauschenberg and Jasper Johns – he himself was having to get by on $25,000 portraits of bankers and their wives. Neutral to the last, he confirms his Valium addiction and lists the deaths of his friends from Aids, a fear of which may have led to the slight social ostracism he seems to have suffered. People avoid him, fail to invite him to parties, seat him at remote tables. One assumes that his unexpected death in 1987 after gall-bladder surgery would not have unduly surprised him. By then he was almost as cele-brated as the stars he so thrillingly admired, his imagination fixed for ever in those carefree days in New York ten years earlier, when 'it was wall-to-wall everybody rich and famous, and you couldn't understand how they were all in town because it was August, and then you know it is a great city'.

Guardian
1989

Escape into the Seraglio

Hockney on Photography:
Conversations with Paul Joyce

Affable and engaging, his Yorkshire savvy filtered through the warmest shades of California sunshine, David Hockney wears his celebrity more casually than any post-war artist. Neither Warhol, with his eerie, death's-head stare, nor Dali, too often coming on like a hallucinating speak-your-weight machine, ever achieved the comfortable rapport with his audience that Hockney has been able to take for granted since the 1960s.

Together, Hockney's life and work sum up exactly what the public today asks of its artists. Cannily, Hockney has saved his real waywardness for his life-style – the gold lamé jacket and dyed blond hair, once so outrageous, and the pool-boys high in the Hollywood Hills – while his paintings have remained wholly acceptable to his Sunday supplement admirers. The playgroup palette reminds them of the kindergarten paint-boxes with which they dabbled as toddlers, while the images of Los Angeles offer a romanticized vision of that latter-day Samarkand among the freeways. In many respects, Hockney performs the role today which Alma-Tadema played for his Victorian audience. Both artists have satis-fied the public's need for exotic, far-away lands filled with graceful houris and sybaritic dreams. Both specialized in swimming-pools, but where Alma-Tadema, depicting the seraglios of a wholly mythical east, sur-rounded his marble grottos with pretty girls, Hockney furnishes the pools of his equally mythical west with a parade of pretty boys.

Anyone who has spent even five minutes in Los Angeles can see that this city of dreadful night is nothing like the sanitized realm invented by Hockney in his paintings of the 1960s. Hockney's Los Angeles resembles the real terrain of dingbats and painted glue, stretching as far as forever under a tangle of overhead wires, only in the sense that Rick's Café resembles the real Casablanca. Needless to say, Hockney's vision is all the better for that, and I for one wish that he had stayed with his houris in the Hollywood Hills, painting ever bigger and bigger splashes. But the great period of the swimming-pools had passed with the end of the 1970s, at about the time when the first British visitors arrived en masse and discovered the reality of his imaginary city.

By then Hockney had himself begun to discover reality in the form of photography, a long-standing enthusiasm which seems to have seized the centre stage of his imagination during the 1980s. *Hockney on Photography* is a lavishly illustrated guide to the series of photo-collages he has made in the last six years. These, he believes, pose a fundamental challenge to the 'one-eyed' tradition that has always dominated photography since its birth.

In his interviews with the filmmaker Paul Joyce, Hockney describes his first experiments with the Polaroid camera and the significance for the future of photography of what he calls his 'joiners'. He ranges widely over the history of western painting, contrasting its single-point perspective with the generalized perspective of eastern art, and discusses his attempts in the photo-collages to enlarge the dimension of time and infuse a greater degree of realism. Hockney speaks with all his customary wit and intelligence, though he is frequently pushed over the top by an immensely subservient interviewer. 'I wonder whether you are going almost beyond art itself,' he gushes. 'Photography is no longer the same after this work of yours . . .'

'Picasso and others then took off from Cézanne, and now I'm trying to take off from Picasso in an even more radical way,' Hockney rejoins. He disdains the ignorant viewpoint of 'people who think they know about art, or write for the *Guardian*'.

Suitably chastened, I none the less feel that Hockney's ambitious claims suffer severely when placed against the actual photo-collages. The overlapping rectangular prints form a mosaic of sharp angles and unintegrated detail that soon irritates the eye. Hockney maintains that the joiners are 'much closer to the way that we actually look at things' but the human eye is not faceted, and the only people who see like this are suffering from brain damage. Gazing at these jittery panoramas one sees the world through the eyes of a concussed bumblebee rather than, as Hockney hopes, through the visionary lens of some future Rembrandt of the Rolleiflex. There is no sense of when the separate photographs were taken, and the collages could equally have been shuffled together from cut-up copies of the same snapshot. A masterpiece of still photography such as Cartier-Bresson's 'The Informer', reproduced in the book, showing the revenge of concentration camp inmates, resonates with a richness of meanings that transcends the single image and the moment of time it records.

These resonances are missing from the photo-collages, which work, if at all, only as still lives or landscapes. Hockney himself gives the game away when he admits that his technique would be unsuitable for a serious subject like the tragic image·of a napalmed child on a Vietnam highway, also reproduced. I hope Hockney returns to his swimming-pool near Mulholland Drive, shuts his eyes to the city below and once again brings us the candied dreams of his mythic west.

Guardian
1988

In the Voyeur's Gaze

This August, 300 yards from our apartment in Juan-les-Pins, the pleasant park of eucalyptus and fir trees between the RN7 and the sea had unexpectedly vanished, along with the old post office and the tabac selling the Marseille edition of the *Guardian*. In their place was an immense bare-earth site, exposed soil raked by bulldozers, for the moment occupied by an air-conditioned pavilion fit for some latter-day caliph resting en route from Nice Airport to his summer palace in Super-Cannes.

Cautiously entering the pavilion, we found ourselves in a property developer's showroom, filled with promotional displays and a huge model of the new Côte d'Azur, 'truly the French California'. An attractive guide took us on a tour of this visionary realm, a multilingual Scheherazade who swiftly spun her 1,001 tales of the world in waiting. Here, at the newly named Antibes-les-Pins, will arise the first 'intelligent city' of the Riviera. Outwardly, the pitched roofs supported by dainty classical columns, the pedestrian piazzas and thematic gardens suggest something to calm the fears of our uneasy heir to the throne, but behind the elegant façades everything moves with the speed of an electron.

The 10,000 inhabitants in their high-tech apartments and offices will serve as an 'ideas laboratory' for the cities of the future, where 'technology will be placed at the service of conviviality'. Fibre-optic cables and telemetric networks will transmit data banks and information services to each apartment, along with the most advanced fire, safety and security measures. To cap it all, in case the physical and mental strain of actually living in this electronic paradise proves too much, there will be individual medical tele-surveillance in direct contact with the nearest hospital.

I've no doubt that Antibes-les-Pins, to be completed by 1999, will be a comfortable, pleasant and efficient place in which to live and work.

Claire, my girl-friend, couldn't wait to move in. While I dozed on the balcony with Humphrey Carpenter's *Geniuses Together*, an enjoyable memoir of the 1920s Paris of Gertrude Stein, Joyce and Hemingway, Claire had discovered a piece of the twenty-first century under my nose.

The next day, as we drove to Marseille to see the Edward Hopper exhibition at the Musée Cantini, police helicopters raced overhead along the high-speed auto-route, while Canadair flying boats water-bombed the blazing hillsides a few miles from the city. The endless marinas and highways of the Côte d'Azur, and the fibre-optic vision of Antibes-les-Pins, reminded me of how technologically obsessed the French have always been. The future, which in Britain has been dead for decades, still thrives in the French imagination and gives its people their strong sense of get up and go. Prince Charles may be doing his best to propel the British into a nostalgic past where, in due course, he will feel more comfortable under an ill-fitting crown, but the French are still living in the future, far more fascinated by high-tech office blocks, electronic gadgets and Minitels than they are by Escoffier and Saint-Laurent.

Walking around the Edward Hopper paintings in the quiet gallery near the Old Port, we had entered yet another uniquely special world, that silent country of marooned American cities under a toneless, depression-era sky, of entropic hotel rooms and offices where all clocks have stopped, where isolated men and women stare out of one nothingness into the larger nothingness beyond. It was ironic to see the French visitors to the exhibition, residents one day, perhaps, of the California of the new Côte d'Azur, enthusing over Hopper's images of a stranded US. They seemed to show the same appreciation for these pictures of a vanished American past that an earlier generation of Americans had felt for the Impressionist painters and their evocation of the Paris of the belle époque. Presumably, too, they saw Hopper's close links with Degas and Monet, and recognized that in a sense this American painter was the last of the French impressionists.

Surprisingly, for a painter who seems so completely of his own country, Hopper's ties to France are strong. To British eyes Hopper's melancholy bars and hotel rooms sum up the America of the 1930s and 1940s, the antithesis of the folksy and sentimental *Saturday Evening Post* covers of Norman Rockwell. Hopper depicts that hidden and harder world glimpsed in the original *Postman Always Rings Twice*, and many of his paintings could be stills from some dark-edged James M. Cain thriller.

Yet Hopper's imagination was formed across the Atlantic, above all by the three visits to France which he made before the First World War. Born in Nyack, New York State, in 1882, Hopper was a life-long francophile. In the catalogue of the Marseille exhibition Gail Levin, curator of the Hopper collection at the Whitney Museum of American Art, points out that Hopper's passion for all things French extended far beyond painting to take in poetry and the novel, theatre and cinema. During their long marriage he and his American wife, Josephine Nevison Hopper, frequently wrote to each other in French, although they were never to visit France together.

At the New York School of Arts his teachers lectured Hopper enthusiastically on Courbet, Degas, Renoir and Van Gogh, and Hopper later spoke of the 'vital importance of the French art of the nineteenth century for American painting'. In 1906, when he arrived on his first visit to France, he was consummating an already intense love affair. After the money-driven tumult of New York he found Paris elegant and unhurried. He particularly liked the way the Parisians seemed to live their entire lives in the street, and spent his time sketching them in the boulevards and cafés.

Among these drawings a figure appeared who would dominate the paintings of Hopper's maturity – a nude woman standing by an open window, hand to her face in a meditative pose. In spite of Hopper's strict Baptist upbringing, or perhaps because of it, as Gail Levin comments, Hopper was especially fascinated by the prostitutes who plied their trade in the streets of Paris, and the sight of these women seems to have unlocked the door of his sexual imagination. In his sketches, the prostitutes sit in their cafés, indifferent to the stares of the passers-by, marking out for the first time the voyeuristic space that separates Hopper from the mysterious and impassive women who dominate his paintings.

Nearly forty years later, in 'Morning in a City' (1944), we see the same woman by her open window, standing naked by an unmade bed as she stares into the street below. She appears again and again, in 'Night Windows' of 1928 and 'Hotel Room' of 1931, as if glimpsed from a passing elevated train or through an open hotel-room door. This voyeur's eye bereft of emotion, in which all action is suspended, all drama subordinated to the endless moment of the stare, seems to be the key to Hopper's paintings. Even the isolated houses and office buildings that form a large part of his subject matter are depicted as if they too are the object of a voyeur's gaze.

In 1909 and 1910 Hopper made two further journeys to France. On his return he married Josephine Nevison, and when she asked him why she attracted him he replied: 'You have curly hair, you know a little French, and you are an orphan.' Curiously, Josephine Hopper, to whom he remained happily married for the rest of his life, served as his model for almost all the solitary women whom Hopper poses in their tired hotel rooms.

He never again crossed the Atlantic. He and Josephine bought a car and embarked on a series of long drives across the United States, to Colorado, Utah and California. Hopper's paintings depict an archetypal America of small cities and provincial towns, late-night bars embalmed in the empty night, airless offices and filling stations left behind by the new highway, but seen through an unfailingly European eye. The mysterious railway lines that cross many of his paintings are reminiscent of Chirico's, and his steam locomotives might pull the carriages that Delvaux left stranded in their sidings, while his strange nudes sleep-walk in the evening streets.

Out of sympathy with the art of his American contemporaries, he protested publicly in 1960 against what he felt was the excessive attention given to the abstract expressionists. In a sense he had bypassed the American art of the twentieth century, and his own roots went back to the Paris he had known before the First World War. Still at work after the deaths of Bonnard, Leger and Matisse, Hopper may arguably be not only the last impressionist, but the last great French painter. Hopper's 'New York Movie' of 1939 might easily have been painted by Degas had the latter lived on into the age of the great picture palaces. In a gloomy side-chapel the usherette stares into the carpeted darkness, lost in her own dreams while a larger dream fills the distant screen. Degas remarked that he painted his women subjects as if he was seeing them through a keyhole, catching them in their most intimate and unselfconscious moments. Degas' women are precursors of Hopper's, but in painting the depression America of the 1930s Hopper brings his eye to bear on the alienation of the twentieth-century city.

His women expose themselves to a far more public gaze than a keyhole. They stand by their open windows as if no one can see them, as if the anonymity of the modern city renders them invisible to the passengers of a passing train. They expose everything but reveal nothing. In a late-night bar, in the 'Nighthawks' of 1942, a couple sit like characters on a theatre stage, but no drama is communicated to the audience. Hopper's gaze is far removed from that of Hitchcock's *Rear Window*. He is uninterested in whatever banal mystery surrounds his solitary men and women, or in whatever pointless business is transacted in their provincial offices.

Leaving this powerful but unsettling exhibition, we set off for the Old Port and a necessary drink at a quayside café. Beyond the white picket fence which I had last seen in *The French Connection* was moored the life-size replica of a square-rigged sailing ship from Polanski's ill-fated *Pirates*, a masterpiece of fibre-glass that towers above the fishing-boats in the harbour. Two years ago it was moored at Cannes, as if taking its revenge on the film festival where it came unstuck, but has now moved down the coast to Marseille, and it was ironic to see the natives of the great seaport paying their 30 francs to inspect this cathedral of floating kitsch.

But for once kitsch was reassuring. As the Côte d'Azur of Matisse and Picasso gives way for the last time to the fibre-optic, telemetric California of Antibes-les-Pins, to English language radio stations and the science park of Sophia-Antipolis, Hopper's marooned hotel rooms appear positively inviting, as his French admirers may have realized. In the context of the future unwrapping itself on our doorsteps Hopper's voyeurism and undisguised loneliness seem almost like intimacy. Penned in their high-security apartments, constant medical tele-surveillance linking them to the nearest hospital, a generation of even more isolated women will soon stare across their bedrooms. But this time there will be no keyholes through which others can observe them, no half-open doorways or windows on to the watching night.

Guardian
1989

A Humming-bird for
Salvador Dali

Edward James
John Lowe

Poeted: The Final Quest of Edward James
Philip Purser

Scurrying from continent to continent in his surrealist search for a quarry he never identified, Edward James led his life as if he had forever mislaid his invitation to the Mad Hatter's tea party. The highest compliment one can pay this spoilt and eccentric man, who must have been one of the most tiresome people imaginable, is to say that no one else so deserved to sit beside Alice and the March Hare at that magical table.

During the dark days of the late 1940s, when I was first discovering surrealism for myself, the name of Edward James began to appear in catalogues and reference books. Who was this mysterious collector, all the more strangely an Englishman, for years the patron of a group of artists regarded as little more than charlatans? A tantalizing clue appeared in Magritte's 'Not to Be Reproduced', a double portrait of the back of James's head as he stood beside a mirror with Lautréamont's *Song of Maldoror*, the black bible of surrealism, and gradually a few facts about James began to emerge. He had been active in surrealist circles in the 1930s, and had financed a ballet season for George Balanchine. Dali described him as 'my little humming-bird' and, on the family estate near Chichester, James had furnished a house with Dali's sofa in the shape of Mae West's lips, and a stair carpet into which were stitched the bath-time footprints of his wife, the dancer Tilly Losch.

Apart from these details, there was little more to go on, and James himself seemed to vanish until Philip Purser's *Where Is He Now? – The Extraordinary Worlds of Edward James*, published in 1978, and now revised and enlarged as *Poeted: The Final Quest of Edward James*. In his lively detective story, Purser describes how he tracked James down to a remote hillside in Mexico, where he was building a jungle Xanadu among the snakes and parrots. Unhappily for his long-time admirers,

James turned out to be a shrill and eccentric old man pottering about in an Old Etonian blazer, who talked and twittered but had nothing interesting to say. Yet this was the man who had opened his purse so generously to the surrealists, and whose judgements had been tested by time, in a way that those of the Saatchis, and the New York bankers at present buying warehouses of Manhattan kitsch, are never likely to be.

Fashions in biography change, as they do in the novel. Ruthless documentation of frailty is now the vogue, a fashion set off in the 1970s by American academic biographers who funded teams of PhD students eager to scan ancient hotel receipts and discover exactly how many whiskey sours Zelda and Scott Fitzgerald drank on a dull afternoon in Atlanta in 1928. Richard Ellmann's much praised biography of Oscar Wilde took frankness a stage further. Scarcely any sense of Wilde appears in this massive account – he comes across as flawed but vaguely presidential, rather like Goering – but the book is filled with details of sheet stains at the Savoy, Wilde's symptoms and pus-filled diseases, the exact daily distance he was forced to climb on the prison treadmill and, above all, the money he made, details which fascinate us but may strike future readers as prurient or irrelevant.

Now John Lowe, the former principal of West Dean College – the arts and crafts foundation which James set up before his death in 1984 – has written a full-scale biography in what may be a new mode, of portraits composed by biographers who actively dislike their subjects. He describes himself as a friend of James and 'a kind of enemy . . . my feelings towards him varied from amused affection to a black loathing. There were moments when I thought him an evil man.' But James was always unexpected, and if he was boring, at least he was boring in a new way. Both these biographies are shrewd and entertaining accounts of this monster of egotism, who seems to have made up for an empty childhood by paying the adult world to pretend to be a huge indulgent nursery.

He was born in 1907 to a wealthy Edwardian family which had made its fortune in American mining and railways. His mother was a society beauty and court favourite, and James was long rumoured to be the illegitimate son of Edward VII. In later life James, who loathed his mother (once, when calling for a child to accompany her to church and asked which one, she snapped: 'Whichever one goes with my blue gown!') suggested that in fact she was the King's illegitimate daughter – it's tempting to speculate on the dynastic possibilities of a surrealist monarch ascending to the English throne, though this may well be about to happen . . .

At Oxford he was an intimate of Betjeman and Randolph Churchill, hung his rooms with silks and black velvet, and became a poet. Soon after he inherited both his father's and his uncle's fortunes, and decided to leave the university and serve as an honorary attaché at Rome. The surrealist impulse was already well developed. In a secret report he astounded the Foreign Office by informing them that Mussolini was laying down the keels of 300 submarines (in fact, three, but someone as rich as James could scarcely be expected to count). By the early 1930s he had established himself as a patron of the avant-garde, underwriting Balanchine's Ballet 1933 and befriending Dali and Magritte at a time when they needed help. Although a lifelong homosexual, he became infatuated with Tilly Losch, who saw him as little more than a hyper-trophied cash-till. On their honeymoon night, crossing America by train, he tried to enter her cabin and was greeted with 'Edward, don't be a fool. Everyone knows you're homosexual. That's why I agreed to marry you.'

In most upper-class English families this would have been the recipe for a long and happy union, but all his life James was driven by an intense restlessness. In 1939 he abandoned England and settled in America, staying first with Frieda Lawrence in Taos, and then moving to Los Angeles, drawn by Aldous Huxley and the Vedanta movement. But the Hollywood intellectuals were only interested in him as long as he picked up the bill, and by the late 1940s James was already developing certain Howard Hughes-like symptoms of separation from reality – he moved from one LA hotel to another, obsessed with the cleanliness of the bedlinen, covering every surface in the rooms with layers of tissue paper.

At last, presumably in a final attempt to create some kind of concrete dream for himself, he moved to a remote jungle village in northern Mexico and began to build a strange palace for the birds. This homage to Max Ernst, on which he spent some $10 million, was unfinished at his death, and is already being undermined by a nearby stream.

Guardian
1991

The Artist at War

Images of War
edited by Ken McCormick and Hamilton Darby Perry

Our images of war today come almost entirely from the combat newsreel and photograph, their visual impact bought at a certain cost in reflection and insight. Goya's 'Disasters of War' and Picasso's 'Guernica' scarcely match for sheer horror the Vietnam newsreel of a naked girl, skin stripped from her back, stumbling along a road from a napalmed village, or the first film footage of Belsen and Dachau. Satellite television now brings the realities of the Gulf War not just into our living rooms but deep into our brains, with scarcely known effects on the imagination.

The Falklands and Vietnam newsreels gave us a convincing idea of what it was like to be a soldier, but the TV reports from the Gulf incite our imaginations in a wholly new way, urging us to become a cruise missile. Breathtaking super-technologies confirm every Rambo-like fantasy of battlefield omnipotence. The nose-cameras mounted on the laser-guided smart bombs plunge us through doorways and ventilation shafts, every hit a bull's eye, stored away for future reference in the viewer's memory. Before anyone is hurt we are back to General Schwarzkopf, the P. T. Barnum of Desert Storm, jovially commenting on what some lucky Iraqi driver saw in his rear-view mirror as he crossed a bridge disintegrating behind him.

Already one can visualize the combatants in a future war returning from their sorties and fire-fights to scan the evening rushes, and perhaps planning the next day's tactical strike in terms of its viewer potential. Even now the shoulder-holsters worn by officers of the British Armoured Brigade look suspiciously like a glamour accessory – with its chest-hugging harness, the shoulder-holster has always been the male brassiere, a heavy-duty 375 Magnum holster the equivalent of a loaded 44 D cup. If the war gets rougher, the shoulder-holsters will presumably jut more aggressively, like the corsetry of barmaids in a tough roadhouse . . .

Can the old-fashioned war artist with brushes and paint-box ever hope to match this electronic video-game? The artists of the Second World War found themselves competing with the newsreel and photograph, but these were recorded for the most part by men and women in the field of battle, who shared the danger and panic, and had no time to construct a reflective frame around their camera lenses.

Looking through the huge collection of paintings and drawings that make up *Images of War*, produced by some 200 artists from twelve countries, one has a sense that a process is taking place far closer to dreaming than direct reportage – an oblique and restorative working through of experience, of repair and renewal, a coming to terms with violent action and its aftermath. Together they form a powerful and moving record, not only of World War II, but of the effects of battle on the artists who were present. Many of the paintings were commissioned by governments or armed forces, but others, like the poems and drawings found on the body of a Japanese officer, were the responses of individuals who probably never expected to share them. It would be tempting to say that national characteristics emerge intact – the British artists do show the nuggety courage of the ordinary tommy and civilian enduring the blitz, while the American artists have a graphic sweep and scale that reflect the determination and emotional needs of a great military power flexing its strength for the first time.

But the German artists seem unremarkably muted, with none of the visual and ideological fervour of Waffen SS recruitment posters, though it is hard to tell how far this is governed by the process of selection. Without exception, the Russian front is pictured as a hell of cold and desolation. Franz Eichhorst's *Soldiers* shows ill-clad Wehrmacht troopers huddling in blankets in a frozen ditch, and it is no surprise that the painting was never exhibited.

The Russian paintings are the most impressive of all, and for once the conventions of state-sanctioned social realism – tractor art, at its crudest – come together to evoke the overwhelming national crisis that summoned the will of the peasants, soldiers and factory workers who saw their country turned into a sea of fire and death. The Homeric scale of their stand against German barbarism comes through these paintings more strongly than in any others in *Images of War*, and suggests that the notion of heroism had already died in the west.

But what separates these paintings and drawings is not the nationality of the artists so much as the theatre of war. The images of air combat, sadly, rarely rise above the level of Airfix art, while those of the sea war, such as several vast panoramas of the Dunkirk evacuation, tend to stay within the conventions of the wartime *Illustrated London News*, compelling though those sepia vistas of great battles often were. The most moving paintings are those of the land war, expressed in a series of often small but telling images – the deadening boredom of railway stations where the ordinary soldier or sailor spent so much of the war; the eerie golden emptiness of an Italian cornfield through which an allied tank moves like a sinister harvester, as if death has lost its way; the shrinking of the infantryman's world to the ground under his feet, the ever-present cold and his mug of tea.

Wholly absent from this selection is any sense of triumphalism. A reader knowing nothing of the Second World War would find it hard to decide who had won the war and who had lost. None the less, endurance and pride shine through, as they do in what is, for me, the most stirring image in the book, painted in 1985, of a group of elderly Russian ladies, medals heavy on their ample bosoms, posing at a reunion before a mural painted of them forty years earlier when they were Red Army pilots. The distance crossed between the young women and the old, between the clear-cheeked, eager youngsters and their wise and determined older selves, is the distance covered by the paintings in this remarkable book.

Guardian
1991

The Culture of the Comic Strip

The Encyclopaedia of American Comics
edited by Ron Goulart

The International Book of Comics
edited by Denis Gifford

Invisible literatures proliferate around us today – faxes and electronic mail, press releases and office memoranda, obscure genre fictions wrapped in metallized jackets that we scarcely notice on our way to the duty-free shop. One day in the near future, when the last corporate headquarters has been torn down and we all earn our livings at the domestic terminal, anthologies of twentieth-century inter-office memos may be as treasured as the correspondence of Virginia Woolf and T. S. Eliot.

If this seems unlikely, it may be worth noting that the originals of 10 cent comic books published in the 1930s are now worth thousands of pounds, far exceeding in value the first editions of most literary writers of the period. The separation between high and popular culture is now virtually complete, probably to the former's loss. None of the artists in either of these encyclopaedias would ever have won the Turner Prize, but the influence of the comic strip on film, advertising and the iconography of everyday life has been vastly greater than that of any Arts Council favourite collecting his cheque from the Prince of Wales. In the past fifty years only Dali, Magritte and Warhol have matched the influence of the anonymous artists who inked their splash-panels in the King Features Syndicate 'bull-pen', creating the images of a popular culture that range from the Prince Valiant suit in which Elvis Presley romanced the Las Vegas matrons to the Superman clones endorsing a car battery or lavatory cleaner.

Yet, for a form still rarely admitted to polite society, the comic strip had surprisingly classy beginnings. *The Comic Magazine*, first published, appropriately, on 1 April 1796, contained a Hogarth print in every monthly issue, which together formed the series 'Industry and Idleness' and could be regarded as an early form of comic strip. During the nineteenth century, particularly in Britain and the United States, a host of caricature magazines and comic sheets were published, though the first recurring character in his own comic strip only appeared in 1895.

The circulation wars between the American press barons, and advances in the technology of colour printing, led William Randolph Hearst to introduce the first comic strip supplements to his Sunday papers. Humour was still the dominant subject on both sides of the Atlantic, and a huge range of scatty and eccentric characters began to form the folk culture of the twentieth century, from Little Orphan Annie to Popeye and Mutt and Jeff. Together they created a genuinely weird and baroque world that occasionally, as in Little Nemo in Slumberland, produced a dreamlike masterpiece that transcends the limits of the popular medium and has rarely been matched since.

By the 1930s, perhaps in response to the Depression, crime and detective strips were well established, led by Chester Gould's Dick Tracy, and in America the comic book was now openly aimed at an adult readership. In Britain, which lacked the necessary social and geographical mobility, the comic strip was virtually monopolized by children's humour, of a peculiarly warped and introverted kind, from which I'm glad to have been saved – though as a boy in Shanghai I had my own problems trying to find the exotic world of Terry and the Pirates, an oriental farrago of inscrutable mandarins, dragon ladies and sinister pagodas, among the department stores and art deco cinemas of the real city in which the strip was set.

Unquestionably, the biggest influence on the evolution of the comic strip, and on popular culture generally, was science fiction. Buck Rogers and Flash Gordon embarked on still credible interplanetary adventures, but soon gave way to an army of superheroes, led by Superman and Batman, who stayed home on Earth, battling crime, international terrorism and the Nazi menace. Both had everyday selves with whom the reader could identify, those of newspaper reporter and thoughtful playboy. The superheroes who followed them, Captain Marvel and Captain America, moved beyond the constraints of time and space in their defence of the nation at war. By the 1960s, America's immense selfconfidence and the overheating imagination of the Marvel Comics artists gave birth to a race of god-like figures who existed on the astral plane alone. Among these were the Incredible Hulk, the Amazing Spiderman and, strangest of all, the Silver Surfer, an emissary from the stars sent to warn the people of Earth of their impending doom, a noble and tragic figure who became trapped within our atmosphere. Given to flights of agonized and poetic moralizing, he was one of the few to break the rule that the more advanced the super-science surrounding the hero, the less intelligent and articulate he becomes.

None of these comic strips, I have to admit, has ever held much charm for me, at least since childhood, and the depth psychology of the entire comic book universe I happily leave to others. But it's impossible to deny the immense visual energy of the comic book artists, with their zooming angles of attack, sudden close-ups and crane-shots. Many of the greatest strips, from Batman to the Fantastic Four, are cinematic tours de force that have strongly influenced contemporary film. The *Star Wars* series, Sylvester Stallone's entire career, and recent movies such as *Die Hard* and *Total Recall* are little more than imitation comic strips, patterned on the same compensation fantasies and paranoid view of the world. The success of Arnold Schwarzenegger makes sense if one accepts that his grotesque physique and hesitant approach to speech and thought exactly mimic the steroidal musculature and bearing of the comic-book superhero.

It is even more depressing to reflect that American comics are read by virtually the entire US population well into adult life, and have probably been the dominant force in shaping the American imagination, a sobering thought for any British novelist hoping to sell his introverted crochet-work to an American audience. For good or bad, one can see the comic book's influence not only on film but on the present-day American novel, with its constant foregrounding of action, avoidance of the passive tense and dislike of explanatory matter, its narrative equivalent of a visual climax every four frames, and dialogue that would be more comfortable in capital letters inside a balloon. Tom Wolfe's journalism and fiction show the process already well developed. Like it or not, the contour lines of our culture have long since side-stepped Bloomsbury and the Left Bank and run back to those anonymous offices in Manhattan and Los Angeles where an exclamation mark is an understatement.

Guardian
1991

A Still Life

Learning to Look
John Pope-Hennessy

Sir John Pope-Hennessy, sometime director of the V & A and the British Museum, is the last of the arts grandees, a rare and now endangered species that will become extinct at his death. Their triumph in the age of the common man is one of its minor and more intriguing mysteries. Along with Bernard Berenson, Kenneth Clark, Anthony Blunt and, arguably, Diana Vreeland of *Vogue*, Sir John has helped to shape the way we respond to the visual arts. If, as is often claimed, our great museums and galleries are the cathedrals of a new secular religion, then Sir John has been one of its greatest pontiffs, presiding over its highest altars with a fastidiousness so rarefied as to be ionospheric. 'Works of art have always seemed to me to have a supernatural power,' he writes in this autobiography, and one feels that between Sir John and eternity there now lies nothing but the radiant ether of his exquisite sensibility.

Needless to say, the grotesque over-valuation of the visual arts which Sir John has helped to achieve has been translated into the commodity beloved of all religions in their decline. If the Mona Lisa, entombed in her glass-fronted bunker at the Louvre, were ever to come to market, every brush stroke would probably be worth a million dollars, an estimate implicitly underwritten by Sir John and his fellow grandees.

But a sea-change seems under way, and the great temples of the visual arts are under siege from a new generation of curators, many of them showmen and theme-parkers of a type repellent to Sir John, but who may bring the top-heavy edifice of the fine arts a great deal closer to the ground. Shortly before he left the V & A to become director of the British Museum, Sir John was visited by the secretary of his successor, Dr Roy Strong. She announced that his office would be redecorated by a firm named Supertheatricals Ltd. When asked why this was necessary, she replied: 'Because Dr Strong will be receiving members of the aristocracy.' Sir John comments: 'This was the beginning of a thirteen-year regime that reduced the museum and its staff to a level from which it will not recover for many years.' Later he is even more scathing about Roy Strong's successor, 'a capable librarian named Mrs Elizabeth Esteve-Coll, who embarked on policies of a brainless vulgarity . . .'

However, the gallery arrangement of which he is most proud, the impressionist collection at the Metropolitan Museum in New York, with its vast open-plan display of scores of paintings, seems to me to be an example of the airport concourse approach to exhibitions, closer in spirit to the Motor Show than to the scholarly isolation he so values.

To be fair to Roy Strong, he was merely paying Sir John the compliment of trying to imitate him. The opening chapters of this autobiography, unrolling the purple carpet of Sir John's distinguished ancestry, are a parade of establishment figures who served in the highest echelons of the British army and the Colonial Office – governors, generals, governor-generals, and enough titled ladies to outstare Debrett. As for Supertheatricals Ltd, the name might well describe the endless galleries of renaissance art with which Sir John had begun to redecorate the office of his mind from the earliest age. A major-general's son, he was sent to Downside at the age of nine, his aesthetic sensibilities already well developed. Of his fellow boys and playground adventures he tells us nothing, and recalls only 'a passable library', the Medici prints in the corridors, and his reading of Tacitus, Ovid and Juvenal.

His adolescence, like his life as a whole, is experienced exclusively in terms of the works of art he travels endlessly to admire. Human relationships appear to have been erased from his life long before he went up to Oxford. Physical passion, the realm of the senses, the discovery of sex, seem never to have troubled him. He describes himself as 'a lifelong celibate', and seems to have passed his entire Oxford years in the Ashmolean museum. He sets off on his first visit to Italy, which is a procession of frescoes, predellas and altarpieces. We learn nothing of Italian food, women, landscape or even its architecture, of any quickening of the blood and awareness of the charged pleasures of life.

This avoidance of feeling has left an empty heart in this autobiography and, one guesses, in its author's life. Time and again he introduces us to remarkable and extraordinary people, and then tells us nothing about them. He frequently visits Bernard Berenson, then at the height of his fame, but draws no portrait of BB and fails to comment on his dubious dealings with Duveen. In the entire biography, spanning some eighty years, he never once meets a living twentieth-century painter, though he admires Picasso, Matisse and, surprisingly, the Pop Artists.

In 1938 he joined the V & A, whose walls closed around him for thirty-five years. The Second World War passes in half a dozen pages, and he remembers little more than the 'fetid smell' of people sleeping in Holland Park tube station during the blitz. He served in RAF intelligence, and once, bizarrely, found himself inspecting sentries in St James's Park, of which he remarks: 'I had never met ordinary people before.' To his amazement, he finds them 'congenial and interesting'.

But ordinary people never played much part in Sir John's life. He has now retired to Florence, where he poses in his apartment wearing a dark, pin-striped suit and tie, the curator of a very rare private collection, himself. As for the outside world, at which he stares in such steely fashion, he refers in the first paragraph of his book to 'the sweaty tourists' on the Ponte Vecchio (the next time I dare to set off for the Uffizi I will remember to shower twice and keep a wary eye open for a pair of hypersensitive nostrils), though it is the taxes of those over-charged tourists which have paid Sir John's salary all these years. But for Sir John, Sir Kenneth, (Sir) Anthony and, even, Sir Roy, the Ponte Vecchio would be far less crowded than it is.

It seems a curious paradox that a man so bereft of human experience, who has never by his own admission enjoyed a physically intimate relationship, who has never seen a child born or, one assumes, a woman naked (shades of Ruskin) should be considered an authority on those masterpieces of western art that celebrate the most impassioned and most mysterious of human experiences.

How does he assess, one is curious to know, Titian's luscious and ambiguous Venus of Urbino, which hangs only a few hundred yards from his apartment, let alone the legion of annunciations, nativities and agonies in the garden that he spent his life observing? More interestingly, what vacuum of the human spirit have Sir John and fellow grandees been able to fill so deftly as the impresarios of the British Museum, the Louvre and the Metropolitan, with their dreaming pharaohs, crucifixions and resurrections, the ultimate in supertheatricals waiting for a second de Mille?

Guardian
1991

The Last Real Innocents

Children of War, Children of Peace,
Photographs by Robert Capa

Few of these children smile. Some are wounded, and many are clearly starving, holding out their hands to the camera or raising an empty bowl to a passer-by. They wander around the debris of war, and sit astride a tank turret or the fuselage of a downed bomber as if these were the commonplace furniture of everyday life. Even those playing their games in peacetime seem wary of the sky over their heads, as if watching for a flight of approaching enemy aircraft. Nevertheless, they are clearly children, in the sense that most are small and under ten years old, but they have the look of crushed adults, with eyes far sharper than any one can see today in a suburban playground or shopping mall. Above all, they seem aware that they exist outside time, and have only a confused and not-to-be-remembered past and a future on which they can never rely.

In *Children of War, Children of Peace*, Robert Capa's extraordinary images, selected from the 70,000 negatives he left behind at his death in 1954, remind us of how far the world has moved away from the Europe and Asia he began to photograph nearly sixty years ago. Television has glamorized war for us, whether the movie-drenched jungle palette of the Vietnam newsreel or the sinister black-and-white film relayed to our living rooms from the nose-cone cameras of Desert Storm's smart bombs, which almost incite the television viewer to become a cruise missile.

Meanwhile, the consumer society has turned our cities into extended video arcades, with competing levels of unreality laid down like the strata of an electrographic Troy. Turning the pages of this moving book, one is virtually looking at the last generation of real children, standing silently like witnesses to the last real world. Today's children, across a large part of the planet, are dressed in trainers and Day-Glo track suits, and they have voices and a body language to match or mimic their television culture heroes. A bored and indulgent adult world has foisted on to its offspring the image of a kind of dandified super-infant, adept at computerspeak by the age of four, tuned in to the latest consumer fads and canny in its reading of its parents' psychology.

By contrast, Capa's children, photographed in the China and Spain of the 1930s and in Europe during the 1940s, seem to show no understanding at all of the world around them. They gaze in an undemonstrative way at passing parades, stare up at approaching bombers or trudge with their small suitcases along the refugee road to the nearest frontier, unaware of the significance of the events that have shattered their lives. So powerful are Capa's images of war that they shape one's perception of even the most innocent settings. Only Pablo Picasso, photographed in 1948 on the French Riviera at Golfe-Juan as he romps with his baby son, projects an uninhibited joy in the young life between his hands. For the most part, though, Capa tended to photograph peace as if it were another kind of war, and managed to make Europe, and certainly Britain, resemble the third world. As they play their games in the streets of post-war Europe, Capa's children seem to wait for the sound of tanks or the footsteps of men with guns. Only the few pictures taken in the United States are set in a country that has not known war within its borders this century – though Hemingway's Idaho, where he is photographed with his son Gregory, surrounded by guns, perhaps qualifies as a kind of honorary war zone.

Given the ever-present background of stress and upheaval, culminating in the photograph of a French Army halftrack taken a few hours before Capa himself was killed by a land mine in Vietnam, it may seem surprising that none of the children show any fear. But children, as long as they are with their parents or adults they trust, can feel touched by war even during the most violent and terrifying times. Bearing in mind the tragic events Robert Capa's subjects must have witnessed, and the probability that most would grow up to become adults, one can be grateful for even this small measure of innocence preserved.

New York Times
1991

The Coming of the Unconscious

Surrealism
Patrick Waldberg

The History of Surrealist Painting
Marcel Jean

The images of surrealism are the iconography of inner space. Popularly regarded as a lurid manifestation of fantastic art concerned with states of dream and hallucination, surrealism is the first movement, in the words of Odilon Redon, to place 'the logic of the visible at the service of the invisible'. This calculated submission of the impulses and fantasies of our inner lives to the rigours of time and space, to the formal inquisition of the sciences, psychoanalysis pre-eminent among them, produces a heightened or alternate reality beyond that familiar to our sight or senses. What uniquely characterizes this fusion of the outer world of reality and the inner world of the psyche (which I have termed 'inner space') is its redemptive and therapeutic power. To move through these landscapes is a journey of return to one's innermost being.

The pervasiveness of surrealism is proof enough of its success. The landscapes of the soul, the juxtaposition of the strange and familiar, and all the techniques of violent impact have become part of the stock-in-trade of publicity and the cinema, not to mention science fiction. If anything, surrealism has been hoist with the petard of its own undisputed mastery of self-advertisement. The real achievements of Ernst, Tanguy and Magritte have only just begun to emerge through the mêlée of megaphones and manifestos. Even in the case of a single painter, such as Salvador Dali, the exhibitionistic antics which the press have always regarded as 'news' have consistently obscured the far more important implications of his work.

These contradictory elements reflect the dual origins of surrealism – on the one hand in Dada, a post-World War I movement not merely against war and society, but against art and literature as well, out to perpetrate any enormity that would attract attention to its mission – the total destruction of so-called 'civilized' values. The rise of Hitler, a madman beyond the wildest dreams even of the Dadaists, shut them up for good, although the influence of Dada can still be seen in 'happenings', in the obscene tableau-sculptures of Keinholz and in the critical dictats of André Breton, the pope of surrealism, that 'surrealism is pure psychic automatism.' Far from it.

The other, and far older, source of surrealism is in the symbolists and expressionists of the nineteenth century, and in those whom Marcel Jean calls 'sages of dual civilization' – Sade, Lautréamont, Jarry and Apollinaire, synthesist poets well aware of the role of the sciences. Sade's erotic fantasies were matched by an acute scientific interest in the psychology and physiology of the human being. Lautréamont's *Song of Maldoror*, almost the basic dream-text of surrealism, uses scientific images: 'beautiful as the fleshy wattle, conical in shape, furrowed by deep transverse lines, which rises up at the base of the turkey's upper beak – beautiful as the chance meeting on an operating table of a sewing machine and an umbrella'. Apollinaire's erotic-scientific poetry is full of aircraft and the symbols of industrial society, while Jarry, in 'The Passion considered as an Uphill Bicycle Race', unites science, sport and Christianity in the happiest vein of anti-clerical humour.

This preoccupation with the analytic function of the sciences as a means of codifying the inner experience of the senses is seen in the use surrealism made of discoveries in optics and photography – for example, in the physiologist E. J. Marey's Chronograms, multiple-exposure photographs in which the dimension of time is perceptible, the moving figure of a man represented as a series of dune-like lumps. Its interest in oceanic art, in the concealed dimensions hinted at by Rorschach tests, culminated in its discovery of psychoanalysis. This, with its emphasis on the irrational and perverse, on the significance of apparently random associations, its concept of the unconscious, was a complete mythology of the psyche which could be used for the exploration of the inner reality of our lives.

Something of the ferment of ideas that existed by 1924, when André Breton issued the First Surrealist Manifesto, can be seen from both these histories. What seems extraordinary is the sheer volume of activity, the endless stream of experimental magazines, pamphlets, exhibitions and congresses, films and absurd frolics, as well as a substantial body of paintings and sculpture, all produced by a comparatively small group (far smaller, for example, than the number of writers in science fiction here and in the USA).

Equally, the movement is noted for the remarkable beauty of its women – Georgette Magritte, demure sphinx with the eyes of a tamed Mona Lisa; the peerless Meret Oppenheim, designer of the fur-lined cup and saucer; the mystic Leonora Carrington, painter of infinitely frail fantasies; and presiding above them all the madonna of Port Lligat, Gala Dali, ex-wife of the poet Paul Eluard, who described her before his death as the one 'with the look that pierces walls'. One could write a book, let alone a review, about these extraordinary creatures – nymphs of another planet, in your orisons be all my dreams remembered.

In so far as they have a direct bearing on the speculative fiction of the immediate future, the key surrealist paintings seem to me to be the following.

Chirico: 'The Disquieting Muses'

An undefined anxiety has begun to spread across the deserted square. The symmetry and regularity of the arcades conceal an intense inner violence; this is the face of catatonic withdrawal. The space within this painting, like the intervals within the arcades, contains an oppressive negative time. The smooth, egg-shaped heads of the mannequins lack all features and organs of sense, but instead are marked with cryptic signs. These mannequins are human beings from whom all time has been eroded, and reduced to the essence of their own geometries.

Max Ernst: 'The Elephant of Celebes'

A large cauldron with legs, sprouting a pipe that ends in a bull's head. A decapitated woman gestures towards it, but the elephant is gazing at the sky. High in the clouds, fishes are floating. Ernst's wise machine, hot cauldron of time and myth, is the benign deity of inner space.

Magritte: 'The Annunciation'

A rocky path leads among dusty olive trees. Suddenly a strange structure blocks our way. At first glance it seems to be some kind of pavilion. A white lattice hangs like a curtain over the dark façade, and two elongated chess-men stand to one side. Then we see that this is in no sense a pavilion where we may rest. This terrifying structure is a neurological totem, its rounded forms are a fragment of our nervous systems, perhaps an insoluble code that contains the operating formulae for our own passage through time and space. The annunciation is that of a unique event, the first externalization of a neural interval.

Dali: 'The Persistence of Memory'

The empty beach with its fused sand is a symbol of utter psychic alienation. Clock time here is no longer valid, the watches have begun to melt and drip. Even the embryo, symbol of secret growth and possibility, is drained and limp. These are the residues of a remembered moment of time. The most remarkable elements are the two rectilinear objects, formalizations of sections of the beach and sea. The displacement of these two images through time, and their marriage with our own four-dimensional continuum, has warped them into the rigid and unyielding structures of our own consciousness. Likewise, the rectilinear structures of our own conscious reality are warped elements from some placid and harmonious future.

Oscar Dominguez: 'Decalcomania'

By crushing gouache between sheets of paper, Dominguez produced evocative landscapes of porous rocks, drowned seas and corals. These coded terrains are models of the organic landscapes enshrined in our central nervous systems. Their closest equivalents in the outer world of reality are those to which we most respond – igneous rocks, dunes, drained deltas. Only these landscapes contain the psychological dimensions of nostalgia, memory and the emotions.

Ernst: 'The Eye of Silence'

This spinal landscape, with its frenzied rocks towering into the air above the silent swamp, has attained an organic life more real than that of the solitary nymph sitting in the foreground. These rocks have the luminosity of organs freshly exposed to the light. The real landscapes of our world are seen for what they are – the palaces of flesh and bone that are the living façades enclosing our own subliminal consciousness.

The sensational elements in these paintings reflect their use of the unfamiliar, their revelation of unexpected associations. If anything, surrealist painting has one dominant characteristic: a glassy isolation, as if all the objects in its landscapes had been drained of their emotional associations, the accretions of sentiment and common usage. What they demonstrate is that the most commonplace elements of reality – for example, the rooms we occupy, the landscapes around us, the musculatures of our own bodies, the postures we assume – may have very different meanings by the time they reach the central nervous system. Surrealism is the first systematic investigation of the most unsuspected aspects of our lives – the meaning, for example, of certain kinds of horizontal perspective, of curvilinear or soft forms as opposed to rectilinear ones, of the conjunction of two apparently unrelated postures.

The techniques of surrealism have a particular relevance at this moment, when the fictional elements in the world around us are multiplying to the point where it is almost impossible to distinguish between the 'real' and the 'false' – the terms no longer have any meaning. The faces of public figures are projected at us as if out of some endless global pantomime, and have the conviction of giant advertisement hoardings. The task of the arts seems more and more to be that of isolating the few elements of reality from this mélange of fictions, not some metaphorical 'reality', but simply the basic elements of cognition and posture that are the jigs and props of our consciousness.

Surrealism offers an ideal tool for exploring these objectives. As Dali has remarked, after Freud's explorations within the psyche it is now the *outer* world which will have to be eroticized and quantified. Surrealism offers a neutral zone or clearing house where the confused currencies of both the inner and outer worlds can be standardized against each other.

At the same time we should not forget the elements of magic and surprise that wait for us in this realm. In the words of André Breton: 'The confidences of madmen: I would spend my life in provoking them. They are people of scrupulous honesty, whose innocence is only equalled by mine. Columbus had to sail with madmen to discover America.'

New Worlds
1966

The Touchstone City

Paris and the Surrealists
George Melly

For two decades, from 1920 to 1940, Paris and surrealism conducted a passionate affair, broken off when the more fickle of the partners fled to the United States during the Second World War, only to find the door slammed in its face when it returned with the GIs in 1945. As George Melly remarks in his introduction to this enchanting book, it is surprising that an artistic movement so avowedly international in its aims should have identified itself so closely with a single city. Dada, the rumbustious godfather at the movement's birth, had first appeared during the Great War in, of all places, Zurich. Delvaux and Magritte rarely strayed from Brussels, and Dali, when not at Port Lligat, painted in hotel rooms on both sides of the Atlantic. Most of Max Ernst's masterpieces, those calcinated landscapes like 'Europe after the Rain' that are pre-visions of the third world war, were painted in the Arizona desert they so closely resemble.

None the less, Paris was the great forcing house of surrealism and its theoretical centre, in part because André Breton, surrealism's 'Pope' and one-man think-tank, chose to live there. When Breton left Paris for America, at the outbreak of the Second World War, surrealism died, and never really managed to resuscitate itself. Had Breton remained in Paris, perhaps to work for the resistance, surrealism might have fought off the post-war challenge to its authority posed by Sartre and the existentialists. After the war the movement lost its bearings, though the consumer society of the past forty years, and the creation of a TV monoculture dissolving the last barriers between fantasy and reality, is a surrealist domain in its purest form.

George Melly has long been identified with the English wing of surrealism, first as E. L. T. Mesens's assistant at the London Gallery, which specialized in surrealist art, and then as one of surrealism's most intelligent collectors and fuglemen. Recalling his first visit to Paris in 1946 – he had hoped to meet the surrealists, but nearly had his wallet stolen by two prostitutes whose bed he shared – he had the happy notion of revisiting the city and collaborating with a sympathetic photographer on a book about the countless Parisian locales forever associated with the surrealists. The result is the tastiest little feast of wit and pleasure. Michael Wood's photographs brilliantly complement Melly's urbane commentary, and without any expressionist or surrealist camera-work illustrate just what inspired the surrealists' infatuation with Paris. Through his self-effacing camera lens this touchstone city of charm and elegance becomes increasingly eerie, filled with strange passageways and arcades like sets from a remake of *The Cabinet of Dr Caligari*. A forest of curious monuments and obelisks rises into the air, there are restless stone lions that seem to have strayed from a Magritte canvas, and art nouveau Métro stations whose metal railings and canopies seem to be evolving into vegetal forms. Above all, as Melly points out, Paris is filled with a profusion of statuary, resembling the pumice-like figures of a population fossilized by the lava of a nearby Vesuvius.

Melly identifies Paris as feminine, London as strongly, even oafishly, masculine. He wonders why surrealism never took root in England, and cites our Protestantism, our intolerance of ideas and, perhaps most important of all, the absence of café life. Certainly, surrealism failed to take root in New York for the same reason, and only Warhol, with his endless round of parties, found a substitute for the Parisian café.

As soon as Melly's feet touch the Paris pavements his spirits rise, and he makes an entertaining and amiable guide, retracing the path of his first visit to André Breton in 1952. Breton spoke no English, and Melly struggled with his modest French, but afterwards he had the strong sense that both had talked in English. The best compliment I can pay to this romantic and seductive book is to say that for an hour or two, turning its pages of calm and mysterious photographs, I was quite convinced I had been reading in French.

Guardian
1991

The Innocent as Paranoid

The art of Salvador Dali is a metaphor that embraces the twentieth century. Within his genius the marriage of reason and nightmare is celebrated across an altar smeared with excrement, in an order of service read from a textbook of psychopathology. Dali's paintings constitute a body of prophecy about ourselves unequalled in accuracy since Freud's *Civilization and its Discontents*. Voyeurism, self-disgust, biomorphic horror, the infantile basis of our dreams and longings – these diseases of the psyche which Dali rightly diagnosed have now culminated in the most sinister casualty of the century: the death of affect.

This demise of feeling and emotion has paved the way for all our most real and tender pleasures – in the excitements of pain and mutilation; in sex as the perfect arena, like a culture-bed of sterile pus, for all the veronicas of our own perversions; in our moral freedom to pursue our own psychopathology as a game; and in our ever-greater powers of abstraction – what our children have to fear are not the cars on the freeways of tomorrow but our own pleasure in calculating the most elegant parameters of their deaths.

Dali's paintings not only anticipate the psychic crisis that produced this glaucous paradise, but document the uneasy pleasures of living within it. The great twin leitmotifs of the twentieth century – sex and paranoia – preside over his life, as over ours. With Max Ernst and William Burroughs he forms a trinity of the only living men of genius. However, where Ernst and Burroughs transmit their reports at midnight from the dark causeways of our spinal columns, Dali has chosen to face all the chimeras of his mind in the full glare of noon. Again, unlike Ernst and Burroughs, whose reclusive personalities merge into the penumbra around them, Dali's identity remains entirely his own. Don Quixote in a silk lounge suit, he rides eccentrically across a viscous and overlit desert, protected by nothing more than his furious moustaches.

For most people, it goes without saying, Dali is far too much his own man. Although the pampered darling of jet-set aristocracy, many of whom, like Edward James and the Vicomte de Noailles, have done their intelligent best by him, forking out large amounts of cash when he most needed it, the general response to Dali is negative – thanks, first, to the international press, which has always encouraged his exhibitionist antics, and second, to the puritanical intelligentsia of Northern Europe and America, for whom Dali's subject matter, like the excrement he painted in 'The Lugubrious Game', reminds them far too much of all the psychic capitulations of their childhoods.

Admittedly Dali's chosen persona – part comic-opera barber, part mad muezzin on his phallic tower crying out a hymn of undigested gobbets of psychoanalysis and self-confession (just the kind of thing to upset those bowler-hatted library customs clerks), part genius with all its even greater embarrassments – is not one that can be fitted into any handy category. Most people, even intelligent ones, are not notably inventive, and the effort of devising a wholly new category, and one at that to be occupied by only one tenant, demoralizes them even before they have started.

At the same time it seems to me that the consistent failure to grasp the importance of Dali's work has a significance that extends far beyond any feelings of distaste for his personal style, and in many respects resembles the failure of literary critics to come to terms with science fiction. Already one can see that science fiction, far from being an unimportant minor offshoot, in fact represents one of the main literary traditions of the twentieth century, and certainly its oldest – a tradition of imaginative response to science and technology that runs in an intact line through Wells, Aldous Huxley, the writers of modern American science fiction, and such present-day innovators as William Burroughs and Paolozzi. One of the conventions of the past thirty years has been that the so-called Modern Movement – i.e., the literary tradition running from Baudelaire and Rimbaud through Joyce and Eliot to Hemingway and Camus, to name a few landmarks – is the principal literary tradition of the twentieth century. The dominant characteristic of this movement is its sense of individual isolation, its mood of introspection and alienation, a state of mind always assumed to be the hallmark of the twentieth-century consciousness.

Far from it. On the contrary, it seems to me that the Modern Movement belongs to the nineteenth century, a reaction against the monolithic philistine character of Victorianism, against the tyranny of the paterfamilias, secure in his financial and sexual authority, and against the massive constraints of bourgeois society. In no way does the Modern Movement have any bearing on the facts of the twentieth century, the first flight of the Wright brothers, the invention of the Pill, the social and sexual philosophy of the ejector seat. Apart from its marked retrospective bias, its obsession with the subjective nature of experience, its real subject matter is the rationalization of guilt and estrangement. Its elements are introspection, pessimism and sophistication. Yet if anything befits the twentieth century it is optimism, the iconography of mass-merchandizing, and naivety.

This long-standing hostility to science fiction, and the inability to realize that the future provides a better key to the present than does the past, is reflected in a similar attitude to surrealism as a whole. Recently, as part of a general rejection and loss of interest in the past, both science fiction and surrealism have enjoyed a sudden vogue, but Dali still remains excluded. He is popular as ever only with the rich – who presumably feel no puritan restraints about exploring the possibilities of their lives – and a few wayward spirits like myself.

Dali's background was conventional. Born in 1904, the second son of a well-to-do lawyer, he had a permissive childhood, which allowed him a number of quasi-incestuous involvements with governesses, art masters, old beggar women and the like. At art school he developed his precociously brilliant personality, and discovered psychoanalysis. By this time, the late 1920s, surrealism was already a mature art. Chirico, Duchamp and Max Ernst were its elder statesmen. Dali, however, was the first to accept completely the logic of the Freudian age, to describe the extraordinary world of the twentieth-century psyche in terms of the commonplace vocabulary of everyday life – telephones, wristwatches, fried eggs, cupboards, beaches. What distinguishes Dali's work, above everything else, is the hallucinatory naturalism of his renaissance style. For the most part the landscapes of Ernst, Tanguy or Magritte describe impossible or symbolic worlds – the events within them have 'occurred', but in a metaphoric sense. The events in Dali's paintings are not far from our ordinary reality.

This reflects Dali's total involvement in Freud's view of the unconscious as a narrative stage. Elements from the margins of one's mind – the gestures of minor domestic traffic, movements through doors, a glance across a balcony – become transformed into the materials of an eerie and overlit drama. The Oedipal conflicts we have carried with us from childhood fuse with the polymorphic landscapes of the present to create a strange and ambiguous future. The contours of a woman's back, the significance of certain rectilinear forms, marry with our memories and desires. The roles of everything are switched. Christopher Columbus comes ashore having just discovered a young woman's buttocks. A childhood governess still dominates the foreshore of one's life, windows let into her body as in the walls of one's nursery. Later, in the mature Dali, nuclear and fragmentary forms transcribe the postures of the Virgin, tachist explosions illuminate the cosmogony of the H-bomb, the images of atomic physics are recruited to represent a pietist icon of a Renaissance madonna.

Given the extraordinary familiarity of Dali's paintings, it is surprising that so few people seem ever to have looked at them. If they remember them at all, it is in some kind of vague and uncomfortable way, which indicates that it is not only Oedipal and other symbols that frighten us, but any dislocation of our commonplace notions about reality. The latent significance of curvilinear as opposed to rectilinear forms, of soft as opposed to hard geometries, are topics that disturb us as much as any memory of a paternal ogre. Applying Freud's principle, we can see that reason safely rationalizes reality for us. Dali pulls the fuses out of this comfortable system. In addition, Dali's technique of photographic realism and the particular cinematic style he adopted involve the spectator too closely for his own comfort. Where Ernst, Magritte and Tanguy relied very much on a traditional narrative space, presenting the subject matter frontally and with a generalized time structure, Dali represents the events of his paintings as if each was a single frame from a movie.

Although he is now famous for his paintings of the late 1920s and early 1930s, such as 'The Persistence of Memory', at the time Dali was close to penury. Picasso, Braque and Matisse held a monopoly of the critics' attention; the great battle being fought then, older than any Uccello painted, was between a philistine public and the cubist painters. Faced with this position, Dali, assisted by his ruthless and ambitious wife Gala, set out to use that other developing popular art of the twentieth century – publicity, then shunned by intellectuals and the preserve of newspapers, advertising agencies and film companies. Dali's originality lay in the way he used the techniques of publicity for private purposes, to propound his own extremely private and conceptual ideas. Here he anticipated Warhol and a hundred other contemporary imitators.

Applying himself to a thousand and one stunts, he soon achieved the success he needed. At the start of World War II he moved to America, and his autobiography *The Secret Life of Salvador Dali* was written in the New England home of one of his first American patrons. Here Dali reveals his mastery as a writer, and invents a completely new alphabet, vocabulary and grammar of ideas, rich in psychoanalytic allusions but freighted also with an immense weight of reference to geology, aesthetic theory, metaphysics, metabiology, Christian iconography, haute couture, mathematics, film criticism, heraldry, politics – melded together into a unique alloy. This new language, which few people seem willing to read, just as they refuse to look at his paintings, allowed him to enlarge verbally on his visual subject matter, and was formalized above all in his so-called paranoic-critical method, i.e., the systematic and rational interpretation of hallucinatory phenomena.

Some idea of the richness and seriousness of this language can be seen in the titles of Dali's paintings:

'Gala and the Angelus of Millet immediately preceding the arrival of the conic anamorphosis'

'Suburbs of the Paranoic-Critical town: Afternoon on the outskirts of European history'

'The flesh of the décolleté of my wife, clothed, outstripping light at full speed'

'Velazquez painting the Infanta Margarita with the lights and shadows of his own glory'

'The Chromosome of a highly coloured fish's eye starting the harmonious disintegration of the Persistence of Memory'

Although comic masterpieces at first sight, each of these titles, like dozens of others, exactly describes the subject matter of the painting. More than that, each illuminates its painting. To describe the landscapes of the twentieth century, Dali uses its own techniques – its deliberate neuroticism, self-indulgence, its love of the glossy, lurid and bizarre. Behind these, however, is an eye as sharp as a surgeon's. Dali's work demonstrates that surrealism, far from being a gratuitous dislocation of one's perceptual processes, in fact represents the only reasonable technique for dealing with the subject matter of the century.

The Paintings

1 *The classic Freudian phase.* The trauma of birth, as in 'The Persistence of Memory', the irreconcilable melancholy of the exposed embryo. This

world of fused beaches and overheated light is that perceived by the isolated child. The nervous surfaces are wounds on the cerebral cortex. The people who populate it, the Oedipal figures and marooned lovers, are those perceived through the glass of early childhood and adolescence. The obsessions are: excrement, the flaccid penis, anxiety, the timeless place, the threatening posture, the hallucinatory over-reality of tables and furniture, the geometry of rooms and stairways.

2 *The metamorphic phase.* A polyperverse period, a free-for-all of image and identity. From this period, during the late 1930s, come Dali's obsessions with Hitler (the milky breasts of the Führer compressed by his leather belt) and Lenin's buttocks, elongated like an immense sexual salami. Here, too, are most of the nightmare paintings, such as 'The Horrors of War', which anticipates not only Hiroshima and the death camps, but the metamorphic horrors of heart surgery and organ transplants, the interchangeability and dissolving identities of our own organs.

3 *The Renaissance phase.* Dali's penchant for a wiped academic style, Leonardoesque skies and grottoes, comes through strongly during the 1940s and 1950s in paintings such as his 'Hypercubic Christ'. These images of madonnas and martyred Christs, quantified by a formal geometry, represent a pagan phase in Dali's art.

4 *The Cosmogonic-religious phase.* In the fifties Dali embarked on a series of explicitly religious paintings (most of them apparently on secular topics), such as those using the central figure of Christopher Columbus. Here the iconography of nuclear physics is used to invest his religious heroes with the unseen powers of the universe.

5 *The phase of Analytic Geometry.* The masterworks of this period, among the greatest in Dali's art, are the famous 'Young Virgin auto-sodomized by her own chastity', and 'Goddess leaning on her elbow'. Here the quantification of time and space is applied to the mysterious geometry of our own morphology and musculature.

6 *Nuclear phase.* Dali's marriage with the age of physics. Many of his most serene paintings, such as 'Raphaelesque Head Exploding', date from this recent period.

Notwithstanding the immense richness and vitality of this work, Dali still invites little more than hostility and derision. All too clearly one can see that polyperverse and polymorphic elements, acceptable within, say, automobile styling, are not acceptable when they explicitly refer to the basic props and perspectives of our consciousness.

At the same time, other factors explain this hostility, above all the notion of the naive. Too often, when we think of the naive, we shed a sentimental tear for the Douanier Rousseau or the Facteur Cheval (the eccentric country postman who built with his own hands a dream palace in pebbles and cement that rivals Ankor). Both these men, naives of genius, for the most part lonely, ignored and derided during their lifetimes, fit conveniently into our idea of the naive – amiable simpletons with egg on their ties. We can reassure ourselves that Jarry, Apollinaire and Picasso laughed at Rousseau, and admit that we too might laugh faced with so odd a departure from the accepted norm.

What we fail to realize is that science fiction, like surrealism, provides just this departure, and is an example of an art of the naive in mid-twentieth-century terms. None of us have egg on our ties (more likely crepe suzette, given *Playboy* prices), nor are we particularly amiable, but like Dali we may well be simpletons. I regard Dali, like Wells and the writers of modern science fiction, as true naives, i.e. those taking imagination and reality at their face value, never at all sure, or for that matter concerned, which is which. In the same category I place many other notable originators, such as William Burroughs – certainly a naive, with his weird delusions, possibly correct, that *Time* magazine is out to subvert our minds and language – and Andy Warhol, a faun-like naive of the media landscape, using the basic techniques of twentieth-century mass communications, cinema and colour reproduction processes, for his own innocent and child-like amusement.

Dali is a good example of the sophisticated naive, with an immense vocabulary of ideas and imagery, taking the 'facts' of psychoanalysis at their face value and applying them like a Sunday painter to the materials of twentieth-century life – our psychopathology, our switchboards of emotion and orgasm. Rousseau's enchanted botanical forests have been replaced by flyovers and production lines, but Dali's paintings still remain a valid image of the interior landscape of our minds.

That other naive, Henri Rousseau, a minor customs official, died alone and in poverty in 1910. His friends who had laughed at him then realized his true worth. Two years later he was reburied in a decent grave. The great sculptor, Brancusi, became a simple engraver and inscribed on the tomb an epitaph written by Apollinaire: 'Dear Rousseau, can you hear us? . . . let our luggage pass through the doors of heaven without paying duty . . .' Let us hope that on Dali's death a suitable epitaph is written to celebrate this unique and undervalued genius, who has counted for the first time the multiplication tables of obsession, psychopathology and possibility.

New Worlds
1969

Archetypes of the Dream

Salvador Dali: The Surrealist Jester
Meryle Secrest

Alone among the great surrealists, Salvador Dali has remained faithful to their historic mission, now almost impossible to fulfil, of shocking the bourgeoisie. Sooner or later, respectability embraced Max Ernst, Tanguy and Magritte. The pioneers of Dada and psychic revolution, who so detested commerce, academia and the cash nexus, died laden with honours and prestige, their paintings traded for millions, their pedestals secure in the critical pantheon. Dali alone remains beyond the pale, still greeted with a shudder by the bureaucracy of the art world. Yet, if surrealism is the greatest imaginative venture of the twentieth .century, its course has in large part been set by Dali.

For over fifty years, Dali has incarnated the spirit of surrealism. His luminous beaches with their fused sand, his melting watches, marooned lovers and exploding madonnas have become the popular archetypes of the dream and unconscious, images so familiar from film and stage design, paperback jackets and department store windows that it is easy to forget their source in this single extraordinary mind. None the less, Dali's critical reputation remains that of a purveyor of sensational and lurid kitsch. As Meryle Secrest points out in her well-researched biography, this is almost wholly due to his exhibitionist antics and hunger for material rewards (summed up in André Breton's cruel anagram, 'Avida Dollars') and to his marked flair for the wrong kinds of publicity, with which he seems to have deliberately subverted his own seriousness.

The key to the Dali riddle, the author believes, lies in the painter's earliest childhood. Some nine months before Dali's birth his parents had been devastated by the death of their first son, Salvador. With Dali's arrival they were convinced that their lost son had been reborn, christened him Salvador and lavished on him the most tolerant affection. The young Dali found himself saddled with this double burden – of never being wholly convinced that he existed in his own right, while being encouraged by his doting parents in every precocity. Given this combustible mix, success was guaranteed. 'At the age of six I wanted to be a cook,' Dali has said. 'At seven I wanted to be Napoleon. And my ambition has been growing ever since.'

Meryle Secrest charts the rise to celebrity of this remarkable and in many ways monstrous personality, at once brilliant and egocentric, witty, callous and engaging, and his domination of international surrealism. For all his pranks, Dali became utterly serious in front of his easel. He was prepared to accept the logic of psychoanalysis and brave enough to enter areas where many of the surrealists became squeamish: castration, voyeurism, onanism and coprophilia. This complete frankness and readiness to exploit himself mark Dali out as a true modern. His surrealist masterpieces of the 1930s, with their eerie light that is more electric than solar, seem like elegant but sinister newsreels filmed inside our heads.

His greatest support, as Meryle Secrest shows, was his wife Gala, his lifelong model and muse, whom almost everyone appears to have detested, this mysterious Russian with 'the look that pierces walls' (or bank vaults, as George Melly commented). After Gala's death in 1982 Dali lapsed into extreme melancholy and was seriously injured in a mysterious fire, but has now recovered.

Guardian
1986

Fools and Innocents

Stanley Spencer
Kenneth Pople

Part holy fool and part unholy innocent, Stanley Spencer led his life as if every passing second was literally the first moment of existence, to be greeted with open-mouthed wonder, unstinted praise for the Creator, and a sharp eye to every visionary chance. Like a street urchin scampering after a visiting parade, Spencer saw everything from knee height, astounded by the crowds and the brass band but only too eager for a glimpse up the carnival queen's skirts.

Reading this rich and authoritative biography, one is repeatedly struck by Spencer's good fortune in living and working at the time he did. Today he would be an intimate of Wogan and Paloma Picasso, be painting murals for the Playboy mansion and co-hosting a New York chat-show with Quentin Crisp, while an army of lawyers exploited the merchandizing rights to his latest Resurrection or Crucifixion. Few artists can have been so confined, and so liberated, by the constraints of that innocent world before the coming of the mass media.

Small Thames-side towns have a special magic, each an island waiting for its Prospero. Cookham, where Spencer was born in 1891, is more self-contained than most, enclosed by water meadows that often flood in winter, isolating the town in a way that must have forced the young Stanley to peer doubly hard at the precious ground under his feet. In the later years of his fame, Spencer affected an eccentric and almost bumpkin manner, trundling his easel and paints around Cookham in a dilapidated pram. In fact, he was born into a respectable and high-minded Victorian family, the ninth child of Annie Spencer, a former soprano, and her husband William, a master-builder turned church organist and amateur astronomer. The family were inveterate talkers, a trait Spencer displayed all his life, exhausting his wives, friends and patrons with monologues that lasted half the night. But his Cookham childhood, with its Bible-reading, love of Ruskin and abhorrence of idleness, its fierce discussions of politics, poetry and philosophy, must have generated a pressure-cooker atmosphere where the smallest talent was stretched and encouraged – a regime fairly typical then but vanished today except, perhaps, in Japan; one looks forward to a comparable flowering of philosophers, artists and statesmen from the Tokyo–Osaka mega-conurbation, though youngsters there show a disappointing tendency to commit suicide, a possible Japanese design flaw . . .

Eager to become an artist from his early teens, Spencer entered the Slade, where his remarkable draughtsmanship soon revealed itself. His prize-winning Nativity, painted while a 21-year-old student, virtually set out the entire prospectus of his imagination and life's work. Here we find the familiar Pre-Raphaelite panorama of tranquil village lanes, curiously warped as if by a defective fish-eye lens. The isolated embracing couples, and the biblical myth domesticated by the garden railings and placid harvest field, are charged with a barely concealed sexuality that expresses itself in the clumsy gestures and askew glances soon to become Spencer's most distinctive trademark.

Spencer's childhood in Cookham so shaped his life that his biographers have searched every surviving record for a crucial early experience. Spencer was a tireless writer, maintaining an immense correspondence with himself, composing long essays in his notebooks, eventually adding up to millions of words, stored in trunks through which he would rummage, re-reading and annotating.

As an example of Cookham's magical hold over the small boy, Kenneth Pople cites Spencer's description of himself listening to the maid alone in her attic bedroom, talking to an invisible person. In fact, she was talking to her counterpart on the other side of the party wall, but Spencer was convinced that 'a sort of angel' had kept her company. On another occasion, when one of his older brothers caught pneumonia, the womenfolk sitting around the bed despatched the young Stanley with a message that the crisis had come, duly reported by Spencer as 'Christ has come.' For Spencer, Cookham was a paradise in which all the world's ills could be cured. By placing his great religious tableaux among its calm lanes and thatched houses he was in no way trying to follow the long tradition of setting the Crucifixion on a Tuscan hillside or the Annunciation in a lavish Florentine villa, and satisfying the spectator's sense of dignity and occasion against a familiar backdrop. Spencer's intention, in his 'Betrayal' and 'Crucifixion', was to enlist Cookham in an attempt to assuage the pain of these terrible events. Spencer's entire life's work as a painter was a single-minded quest to redeem the world through this Thames-side town.

Few people can have had higher expectations of sex than Spencer, and few can have been so led astray by their obsessions. Dogmatically strait-laced about the sanctity of marriage, he was still a virgin when he met Hilda Carline, a fellow painter and Christian Scientist who was the second inspiration of his life. His first sexual experience with her probably prompted his greatest painting, the 'Resurrection in Cookham Churchyard'. Spencer and Hilda appear several times in this huge canvas, along with their many friends and relatives, reborn into the wonder of Cookham not from the dead but from the previous moment of existence.

It is ironic that the scene of his most famous triumph should soon have become the cockpit of personal disaster – Spencer's unhappy relationship with Patricia Preece, who lived with her lesbian companion, Dorothy Hepworth, in a nearby cottage. The two women, both struggling artists, clearly saw Spencer as a rabbit waiting to be snared and skinned. Patricia confided to a friend that 'she would have to marry that dirty little Stanley Spencer.' They were married soon after his divorce from Hilda. For the honeymoon Patricia and Dorothy left for Cornwall together, sharing a room while Spencer was told to follow them later. Considerate to a fault, they even invited Hilda to join them. On their return to Cookham, Spencer was expelled for ever from the marital home. All this he accepted without complaint. Hilda remained the love of his life, and he was with her during her final illness. After her death he continued to write letters to her until the end of his own life ten years later. The suggestion sometimes made that this was a means of sexually exciting himself in no way diminishes his devotion to her.

Guardian
1991

Desperate Humours

Ronald Searle
Russell Davies

In many ways Ronald Searle's world reminds me of Max Wall – his twitchy clubmen and crazed headmistresses reveal the same ferocious impotence, and a desperate humour that has nothing to do with comedy. This is tragedy that has opened the wrong door and found itself on a burlesque stage with a few baffling props – a samurai sword, a school-girl's gymslip and a bottle of Lemon Hart rum. Out of these materials Searle has created a unique graphic universe, intensely English – though he might dislike anyone saying so – but enormously deepened by his years as a Japanese prisoner, and by a certain single-mindedness and detachment of character at which this biography can only hint.

I remember coming across his prison-camp drawings within a few months of leaving my own camp, and thinking how exactly he had caught the squalor of camp life (rather like Gatwick airport during a peak-travel baggage strike), and the peculiar impassivity of the Japanese soldiers, for whom their prisoners had already ceased to exist, so that cruelty and violence meant no more than a few practice flourishes of the kendo sword. Superficially, Searle's touch lightened when he launched his post-war career as a humorous cartoonist and illustrator, but even then, in the barbed wire profiles of Russian militia-men and New York cops, and especially in St Trinian's – Holloway on speed – one still senses somewhere in the background the perimeter wall of Changi Jail.

Inevitably, biographies of the living are partial portraits – most of the principal figures in this one are still alive, including both wives, and many of his fellow artists and commissioning editors – but Searle's Cambridge childhood seems to have been uneventful, though the university town's curious mix of the preposterous and the banal, the grandiose assumptions forever held down by the low fenland skies, may have given the future moralist and humorist a useful start.

He was born in 1920, the son of a former World War I infantry sergeant and a remarkably beautiful mother, and by his mid-teens had already shown a well-developed will. After leaving school at fifteen, when the family were unable to afford any further education, he became a solicitor's clerk, financing his evening art-school classes out of his own earnings. His confident and strongly drawn cartoons soon began to appear in the *Cambridge Daily News*, and in 1938 he won a full-time scholarship to a local art school. He contributed to *Granta* and held two exhibitions of his work. But for the war, the young Ronald Searle might have launched himself on a conventional English career, in due course becoming editor of *Punch* and a pillar of Fleet Street and the Garrick.

Then, in April 1939, a few months before the outbreak of war, Searle enlisted in the Territorial Army, for reasons which Russell Davies never fully explores. He was mobilized into the Royal Engineers and stationed, first in Norfolk, and then in Kirkcudbright in Scotland, where the girls of a progressive Edinburgh academy, St Trinnean's, had been evacuated. Transformed by Searle's imagination, the school became St Trinian's and his most famous creation, from which in later years he tried to escape, with mixed success. Before setting off overseas in his troopship, Sapper Searle posted the original St Trinian's cartoon to the assistant editor of *Lilliput*, Kaye Webb, not realizing that he was writing to his future wife.

He first saw the published cartoon on the streets of Singapore during the Japanese artillery bombardment. Searle's harrowing drawings made during his captivity, at Changi Jail and the Selarang Barracks, and then on the Siam–Burma Railway, constitute one of the greatest graphic records of the Second World War. Searle endured repeated beatings, starvation and malaria, and the deaths of his friends, all the while sketching on pages torn from books, and bartering, in Russell Davies's quaint term, 'orgiastic' drawings with the Japanese guards in return for precious supplies of paper.

After liberation there was a banquet in Singapore laid on by Mountbatten and his press attaché Tom Driberg. The next year, at the Labour Party conference, the latter shared a bedroom with Searle, and after urinating in the wash-basin asked: 'Ronnie, are you a masochist?' But Searle had coped with far greater terrors, and the publication of his wartime drawings soon made him a celebrity. The St Trinian's series followed, a nightmare preview of women's lib, and eerily prophetic in other ways – 'Fair play, St Trinian's, use a clean needle,' a teacher admonishes two girls nobbling a rival before an inter-school track event.

Whether suffocated by *Punch*, or needing to break away from the little England of the pre-Beatles sixties, Searle suddenly packed his bags and left for Paris in 1961, leaving behind his wife and children. It seems a pity that he missed London in the sixties, which were tailor-made for his caustic line. In the last thirty years he has rarely returned to England and, after a happy second marriage, now lives in Provence. By dropping *Punch* in favour of *Holiday* and the *New Yorker* he widened his subject matter and was able to show his mastery of colour, creating some of the most striking covers in the history of those magazines. His humour is as strong and quirky as ever, but the horizon lines in his drawings get ever deeper – the deepest since Dali's – and the shadows reaching towards the feet of his harassed tourists and executives seem to have their sources far beyond the margins of the page.

Guardian
1990

4 WRITERS

Scott Fitzgerald, Henry Miller,
the Marquis de Sade
and William Burroughs . . .

Legend of Regret

Some Sort of Epic Grandeur: The Life of F. Scott Fitzgerald
Matthew J. Bruccoli

Few writers have so identified themselves with their own work as Scott Fitzgerald. With some – Ernest Hemingway or Evelyn Waugh – it is difficult enough to separate the man from the legend, but in Fitzgerald's case one often feels that there was only the legend in the first place. Jazz-age darling, spoiled genius and alcoholic writer romantically dying the slow Hollywood death, Fitzgerald played these parts as if they were roles in the movies whose scripts he later found himself forced to write.

Matthew Bruccoli's elaborately researched biography goes some way to disinterring the real Fitzgerald, though perhaps his warts-and-all portrait is yet another romantic fiction, and one that happens to be closer to our own taste. All the same, Fitzgerald's extraordinary charm, and that touching determination to be a success, to run faster than the dream and to enfold it, come through as strongly as ever.

The son of a failed furniture manufacturer in St Paul, Fitzgerald felt an outsider from the start. Desperate for admiration, he struggled to reach the school football team, but was labelled a show-off. At Princeton, which he regarded as a rich young man's country club, he found his first social success. However, his academic record was a disaster, and already he was rationalizing this into a potent myth of romantic failure. His poems and stories in the college magazine sound many of the themes in his later fiction – the gifted man ruined by a selfish woman, the hero half-consciously seeking destruction, and the strong strain of masochism.

He soon set about satisfying his own obsessions. Fitzgerald's service in the army was another partial failure. He was considered an unreliable officer and was not sent overseas. The captain in charge of his training platoon was Dwight D. Eisenhower, and though, sadly, Ike's opinion of Fitzgerald is unrecorded his fellow officers disliked Fitzgerald and played elaborate practical jokes on him. But while he was stationed at Montgomery, Alabama, he met Zelda Sayre, his future wife and a destructive force beyond all his dreams.

The last of the southern belles, Zelda was beautiful, daredevil and exhibitionist, a brilliant and racy talker. She smoked in the street, flirted outrageously and had scandalized entire states. To win her, and the money he needed to satisfy her own demands for success, Fitzgerald wrote his first novel, *This Side of Paradise*. Its publication in 1920 was a critical and commercial triumph, launched the Jazz Age and locked Scott and Zelda into a legend that only ended with her death thirty years later in an asylum fire.

Fitzgerald was always puritanical about sex, and his views on marriage were surprisingly conventional. 'Just being in love is work enough for a woman. If she . . . makes herself look pretty when her husband comes home in the evening, and loves him and helps him with his work and encourages him – oh, I think that's the sort of work that will save her.'

Given her entirely opposite nature, Zelda must have been a powerful spur to Fitzgerald, touching his deepest dreams of romantic rejection. It is hard to imagine him writing his masterpiece of nostalgia and regret, *The Great Gatsby*, without the aid of this tragic but extraordinary woman. Her first mental breakdown in 1929, like the Crash itself, marked the end for Fitzgerald, and his imagination never recovered. Between 1920 and 1929, according to Bruccoli, Fitzgerald earned $244,967, at least six times its present value, but from then on his income sharply declined. If the twenties had spoiled and encouraged Fitzgerald, the thirties ignored him.

Fitzgerald's best work is about the failure to recapture past emotions, and one feels that the series of calamities that form his later life was almost consciously set up to provoke that poignant regret. During the endless champagne party of the twenties this seemed touching and romantic, but far less so in the thirties against a background of real failure and despair.

His last three years in Hollywood, contrary to popular myth, were modestly successful. But he died, in the words of John O'Hara, 'a prematurely old little man haunting bookshops unrecognized'. His last royalty statement in 1940 from Scribners reported sales of forty copies for all his books, including seven copies of *The Great Gatsby*, for a total royalty of $13.

A Working-class Proust

Henry Miller
Robert Ferguson

Henry Miller bursts into the twentieth-century novel like a reprobate uncle gate-crashing an over-sedate party, scandalizing the company with a string of off-colour stories before slipping away with the two prettiest wives, but leaving behind him the strong sense that for a few minutes everything has become a great deal more fun. Reading this lively and entertaining biography, I was struck by Miller's charm, amiability and irrepressible good nature, qualities (none too prevalent among writers) which most people who met him instantly recognized. I can still remember reading *Tropic of Cancer* when I first went to Paris after the war, and being stunned by the no-nonsense frankness of Miller's language and by the novel's sheer zest and attack. The ozone of sex rushed through Miller's pages, and his prose had a life-hungry energy that made Molly Bloom's soliloquy at the close of *Ulysses* seem contrived and mannered.

Miller was never a commercial pornographer (well, hardly ever), but the new puritanism of our day has helped to devalue his reputation in recent years. The sexual imagination needs every encouragement to remain in the daylight where we can see it, rather than plunge again into the subterranean world of repression and taboo from which Miller helped to free us. Feminist critics like Kate Millet have castigated Miller, in effect for seeing sex from the viewpoint of an eighteen-year-old stoker on his first shore-leave, rushing down the gangway towards a welcoming party of good-time girls, but that, alas, is how most eighteen-year-old males see sex, certainly those from Henry Miller's background. Miller, it seems to me, was the first proletarian writer to create a pornographic literature based on the language and sexual behaviour of the working class, and this was the source of his appeal to the American servicemen whose elbows jostled mine in the Paris bookshops of the forties.

Another problem Miller poses for the reader is that of knowing who exactly he is. Henry Miller is the hero of his fiction and his own greatest creation, so much so that, as Robert Ferguson remarks, he became a hybrid of man and book. This conflation of author and text is anathema at present, given our desperate need to demystify the writer and shoulder aside any claims he may make to the ownership of his own text. Irritatingly for the deconstructionists, Miller's novels, like his life, only make sense in terms of the mythic illusions he managed to weave around them.

Since Miller was his only real subject matter, it is not surprising that he waited until his forties before becoming a writer. Only then had he amassed enough material to make himself the hero of his own imagination. He was born in 1891 into the immigrant German community in Brooklyn, the son of a hard-drinking tailor and a doting mother who must have given him his lifelong self-confidence, so much so that the young Henry developed what Robert Ferguson terms a reverse paranoia, in which he suspected others of plotting secretly to find ways of increasing his happiness. His mother urged him to read aloud to his playmates, and Henry made the interesting discovery that while this tended to put the boys to sleep, the girls very much enjoyed it, a phenomenon visible at poetry readings today.

After leaving school Miller worked briefly at his father's tailor's shop, where one of the customers was Frank Harris, who scandalized everyone at his fittings by revealing that he wore no underwear. At the age of nineteen Henry began a long-standing affair with a sympathetic widow in her mid-thirties. He spent his spare time roaming around Brooklyn, his head full of Walt Whitman, probably the greatest influence on Miller with his plain man's stance, emotional humanitarianism and notoriety. Miller dreamed of becoming a writer, but already suffered from intense writer's block long before penning a word.

He married Beatrice, the first of his five wives, in 1917 in order to avoid being conscripted, but the marriage soon faded and a few years later in a Manhattan dance-hall he met a taxi-dancer, June Smith, who talked to him about Strindberg and Pirandello. She became his second wife and the great inspiration of his fiction for the next forty years. This erotic but remote woman, who shared his passion for Dostoevsky and was probably the only woman whom Miller really loved, later prompted Anaïs Nin to comment: 'The more I read Dostoevsky the more I wonder about June and Henry and whether they are imitations ... are they literary ghosts? Do they have souls of their own?' Together they opened a speak-easy, exploited gullible businessmen who became infatuated with June, and immersed themselves in Greenwich Village bohemia. Smarting from his wife's lesbian friendships, Miller was still unable to write, until June gave him a volume of Proust and the idea struck him that he could become a working-class Proust, a notion that formed the basis of his entire career.

Needing to place some kind of distance between himself and his Brooklyn subject matter, he set off for Paris in 1930, where he soon established a reputation as a starving artist but astutely worked out a rota system by which he dined every evening at the home of a different friend, a traditional rite of passage for so many aspiring writers. He helped to found a group called the New Instinctivists (they were against admirals but for rear-admirals, against prostitutes but for whores, against the photographing of hands – particularly poets' hands – and, of course, against the New Instinctivism) and began a heady, ten-year affair with Anaïs Nin. She saw him as the Mellors to her Lady Chatterley, but was surprised to find 'a gentle German who could not bear to let the dishes go unwashed'. Inspired by Nin's exotic and hyperventilating persona, every bit as self-created as his own, and excited by her moods and what he described as her singing in 'a sort of monotonous, inharmonic Cuban wail', Miller at last began to write what was to become his first and greatest novel, *Tropic of Cancer*. The title was his nickname for one of June's breasts, Tropic of Capricorn for the other.

Celebrity followed its publication in France in 1934, though it was not until 1961, nearly thirty years after it was written, that it was at last published in the United States. By then Miller had long since moved to Big Sur on the California coast, where he became one of the gurus of the sixties, a venerated sage and cosmic tourist who dipped his feet into Scientology, Christian Science, white witchcraft and Ramakrishna.

He lived to an immense old age, his charm and optimism intact, delighted by his long-delayed success, enjoying his fame and his ping-pong and the succession of beautiful women like Brenda Venus, a *Playboy* gatefold model, who happily befriended him. Thinking of the morose and ungenerous glare which our own most famous 'old devil' turns upon the world, it is refreshing to be reminded of Miller's warmth, love of women and rapscallion good humour.

Independent on Sunday
1991

Magical Seas

In Search of Conrad
Gavin Young

Armchair travellers who happily sailed with Gavin Young aboard his *Slow Boats to China* should dust down their oilskins and sou'westers, settle themselves comfortably by the winter fireside and prepare to set off on another enchanted voyage. *In Search of Conrad* is the most pleasurable book I have read this year, and far more than a collection of traveller's tales, though any travel book by Young exists in a class of its own.

Part mariner's log and part detective story, it brilliantly evokes the Far-Eastern landscapes fixed for ever in our imaginations by Conrad's novels. But above all Young makes us realize that the world Conrad described nearly a century ago is still there, far from our marinas and airports and international hotels, waiting for the determined traveller among the archipelagos of the South China and Java Seas, still haunting the secret rivers of Borneo and the Celebes.

Thanks in part to Francis Coppola's *Apocalypse Now*, Conrad is chiefly identified with his short novel, *Heart of Darkness*, the story of a European trader deranged by the cruelties of the then Belgian Congo. But much of Conrad's greatest fiction – in particular *Lord Jim* and *Almayer's Folly* – is set on the other side of the world, among the islands of the East Indies through which he had sailed as a merchant marine officer during most of the 1880s and as master of the barque *Otago*, his first and last command.

A newspaper correspondent and war reporter for many years, Young had often visited Bangkok, Borneo and Singapore, places well known to Conrad and familiar settings for his novels and stories. Many of the characters and incidents in his fiction are a complex blend of the real and imaginary, so much so that Young decided to retrace Conrad's journeys around the East Indies and try to discover the sources of the events that had inspired the great mariner-novelist. His quest begins, fittingly, in Singapore, now a high-rise enclave of late twentieth-century commerce, but a hundred years ago the home port of the character who dominates Young's book, Capt. William Lingard. This daring privateer and owner-captain had found a secret route up the dangerous Berau River in east Borneo and was the original of Capt. Tom Lingard, played with such panache by Ralph Richardson in Carol Reed's *An Outcast of the Islands*.

William Lingard had employed a Eurasian book-keeper named Charles Olmeijer to represent him in his Berau office, and he too appears, as Kaspar Almayer, in *Almayer's Folly* and *An Outcast of the Islands*. Young follows both the true and fictional trails from Singapore to the Berau River, by way of Jakarta, Makassar and Surabaya, outposts of the exotic that come alive under the author's affectionate gaze, like so many tropical Samarkands. He takes ship in a series of small trading vessels of the kind he described in *Slow Boats to China*, manned by gregarious and charming crews who seem to have responded whole-heartedly to the romantic dream that impelled this obsessed and affable Englishman.

More vividly than most novelists could manage, Young lovingly describes these eccentric boats, rusty hulks dipping top-heavy through these magical seas, skippered by eccentric captains happy to enrol themselves for a few hours or days in the author's quest. No one can evoke so subtly the pregnant mystery of a strange estuary or shoreline, or bring alive the scents and colours of a nondescript port that suddenly detaches itself from the background jungle and is to be one's dubious home for the next ten days.

And overlaying this feast is the spirit of Conrad, and the ghosts of his characters who still haunt these remote trading stations. Olmeijer died in Surabaya, and Young tracks down his remarkable grave, and that in Singapore of A. P. Williams, the disgraced first officer of the *Jeddah*, who urged his captain to abandon 950 pilgrims to their deaths in a storm and was the original of Lord Jim – in fact, the pilgrims and the *Jeddah* survived, astounding Williams and Captain Clark when they were towed into Aden three days later.

William Lingard vanished mysteriously when Arab traders cracked the navigational riddle of the Berau and took away his trade, but his ghost still sails through the secret archipelagos of the Java Sea and into the pages of Young's bewitching book.

Daily Telegraph
1991

Sermons from the Mount

Fates Worse Than Death
Kurt Vonnegut

Novelists are not the nicest people. Touchy, unloved and aware that the novel's greatest days lie back in the age of steam, we occupy a rung on the ladder of likeability somewhere between tax inspectors and immigration officials, with whom all too many of us share an unworthy interest in money and social origins. The one great exception is Kurt Vonnegut, whose sheer amiability could light up all the cathedrals in America – where, in fact, many of the homilies and lay sermons that make up this collection were originally delivered. Vonnegut's heart, by now a prized American totem, is at least as big as Mount Rushmore, and in his latest photographs he looks as if he is already up there, a huge man, craggy and serene, slightly eroded by the winds of fate, but admired for his rugged kindliness.

Reading these essays and speech-day addresses, one senses that Vonnegut, against all the odds, has forgiven us everything. Only plague, famine and Richard Nixon seem to lie beyond the reach of his vast compassion. He rambles away in his affable, cracker-barrel fashion, intoning his trade-mark 'so it goes', spinning a cocoon of the sweetest sugar around our failings and foibles. Yet all this sentimentality is surprisingly bracing – it's a challenge in itself to find someone who has looked the world straight in the eye and never flinched.

Is it an act? Or, at least, a desperate stratagem that the young Vonnegut devised after witnessing the destruction of Dresden? 'I didn't give a damn about Dresden,' he remarks here. 'The fire-bombing of Dresden explains absolutely nothing about what I write and what I am.' But this is scarcely borne out by his endless references to Dresden and his obvious qualms over his German ancestry, a sense of unease that I suspect is the main engine of his imagination. For a sometime science-fiction writer whose subject was the future, Vonnegut is unusually obsessed with his own past. He talks frankly about his Indianapolis childhood, marred by his unhappy father, who eventually killed himself, and by his mother, who loathed her husband and later became insane. A self-described depressive from a family of depressives, Vonnegut concludes that 'you cannot be a good writer of serious fiction if you are not depressed.'

Fortunately for his readers, he began his career on a cheerier note. He comments that American humorists tend to become unfunny pessimists if they live past a certain age, which he estimates to be sixty-three for men and twenty-nine for women, though the reverse seems true to me – Imelda Marcos and Vanessa Redgrave have yet to reach their hilarious prime, while Vonnegut, now sixty-eight, is droller than ever. His early s-f novels, *Player Piano* and *The Sirens of Titan*, are far less sentimental than his later work, and are filled with irony and black humour, though in *God Bless You, Mr Rosewater* a woozy bonhomie was already breaking through. Vonnegut's alter ego, Kilgore Trout, addresses his fellow American s-f writers with the resonant words, 'I love you sons of bitches', a generous tribute to one of the most mentally shuttered groups in existence.

With *Slaughterhouse Five*, based in part on his wartime experiences as a prisoner of war in Dresden, Vonnegut broke away from s-f into the mainstream novel and, his greatest test, international celebrity. Success often destroys American writers, or at least derails them – Hemingway, Kerouac and Truman Capote never lived up to the popular images of themselves – in a way difficult to grasp on this side of the Atlantic. Americans may not read but, like the French, they take books and writers seriously, whereas the British view their writers in a vaguely adversarial way and success usually comes with a live round still in the chamber.

One feels that for Americans fame is always unexpected, whereas British writers have thought of nothing else from the first rejection slip, like people I have known whose choice of Desert Island Discs has been fixed for twenty years before the producer's telephone call. Anyone who has done the classic book-promotional tour of American cities, and stood in those vast shopping malls in the anonymous suburbs of Chicago or Seattle, has sensed the planetary loneliness of America and wondered how one would then cope with success, an even more demanding challenge than failure.

Vonnegut's sensible and savvy response was to become his country's itinerant preacher and pin-pricker, dispensing folksy wisdom along with a strong dose of purgative. As in these lectures, he mixes fortune-cookie philosophizing with acid satire. God, or at least our notions of God, he finds a constant provocation. 'The more violent picture of Him you create, the better you'll do ... any God you create is going to be up against Miami Vice and Clint Eastwood and Sylvester Stallone. And stay clear of the Ten Commandments – those things are booby-trapped.'

He scorns people who get divorced because they no longer love each other. 'That is like trading in a car because the ash-trays are full.' Or is it because the battery is flat, or the CD player has been stolen? Either way, Vonnegut insists that life is unserious. However, he himself has a long memory for a slight – after Salman Rushdie's hostile review of *Hocus Pocus*, he writes: 'I was so upset I considered putting a contract out on him', an example of mafia humour at its most awesome.

Objecting to the line in the requiem mass, 'let light perpetual shine upon you', he visualizes his dead sister trying to fall asleep in her grave with the lights on, and devises a rival mass with the words, 'Let not light disturb their sleep', which a composer friend sets to music. Some time after its Buffalo premiere Vonnegut's wife bumps into Andrew Lloyd Webber, and informs him that her husband has also written a requiem, to which Lloyd Webber, sensing that he has started a fad, retorts with the best line in this book: 'I know. *Every*body is writing requiems ...'

Sunday Times
1991

The Bear of Little Brain

The Brilliant Career of Winnie-the-Pooh
Ann Thwaite

The spell cast by the bear of little brain is as powerful and mysterious as ever. Ann Thwaite's lavishly illustrated tribute to A. A. Milne and the affable Pooh describes the transformation of a charming children's fantasy into a worldwide cultural phenomenon, a process that tells its own intriguing story about the rest of us. Winnie-the-Pooh may well be one of the three most successful characters that English fiction has created this century, taking his place beside Peter Pan and James Bond, juvenile heroes who also made the sensible decision never to grow up.

The real Christopher Robin became a West Country bookseller and endured an agonizing struggle to free himself from the fictional character who threatened to overwhelm him. One can easily imagine the strain on a shy middle-aged man of being approached by the thousandth child as its mother pipes: 'Now, dear, meet the real Christopher Robin.' But the rest of the world embraced Milne's creation with a fondness that never wavered. Ann Thwaite traces Pooh's origins to a black bear cub which Henry Colebourn, a Canadian army officer, bought in 1914 at White River, Ontario, from the hunter who had killed its mother. The bear, which Colebourn named Winnie after his home town of Winnipeg, was donated to London Zoo when his regiment embarked for France, and was a popular attraction until its death in 1934. Pooh, Thwaite claims, was the Milnes' name for a swan they knew, and has migrated across the species gap with happy results.

The bear's absent-minded nature and bumbling adventures were perfectly complemented by E. H. Shepard's evocative drawings. Sales of the English editions still average half a million copies a year, and the Pooh books have been translated into twenty-five languages, among them Chinese, Serbo-Croat, Esperanto and Latin. Soft-toy versions of Pooh and his companions first appeared in the 1930s, and there were endless merchandizing spin-offs – Pooh bookends, garden ornaments, a Hollywood film and, the nearest thing to deification our century offers, giant effigies at Disneyland. In 1947 Christopher Milne's original toys made a triumphant tour of America, and now reside in the New York Public Library, where they will one day occupy a climate-controlled case. Already one may confidently guess it will become a shrine.

Standing back from all this, if one can, how does one explain the appeal of what is, after all, a stuffed toy? Dorothy Parker may have detested the bear, ending a caustic review of *The House at Pooh Corner* with 'Tonstant Weader fwowed up', but I have never known anyone who remembered Pooh with less than total affection, something rare in children's fiction. I still dread even thinking about those versions of the Grimms' fairy tales with their eerie and threatening coloured plates.

But then childhood is not the happy idyll we choose to remember, and part of the appeal of the Pooh stories is that they describe the world of childhood as if it had been happy. Over the years there have been psychoanalytic interpretations of Pooh (repressed fears of puberty), Marxist readings (Pooh and company as members of a decadent *rentier* class), and even a Taoist version (Pooh as the all-accepting philosopher prince). Matching the vast scope of the Pooh phenomenon, I see the Pooh world in geo-political terms, as a parable of the British Empire in its last two declining decades, with Christopher Robin as the embattled young District Commissioner trying to control his wayward colonial charges. But whatever the interpretation, the magic endures, which Ann Thwaite's fascinating history amply proves. As she reflects, echoing Milne, somewhere a boy and his bear will be playing for ever.

Daily Telegraph
1992

Babylon Revisited

The Day of the Locust
Nathanael West

Few novelists today dream of emigrating to Hollywood, following the shadows of Scott Fitzgerald and Aldous Huxley to the writers' building on the studio lot and scripting popular adaptations of *The Magic Mountain* or *The Brothers Karamazov*. Jet travel, the fax machine and the demise of the studio system mean that British novelists write their commissioned scripts at home in Maida Vale or Holland Park, which may say something about the sorry state of today's cinema. Forty years ago, as I mused over my first rejection slips, working as a Hollywood scriptwriter seemed the sweetest way for a novelist to sell his soul, and a vast literature already existed about the moral agonies of being paid $3,000 a week to do so. I couldn't wait to be summoned to that city of man-made sunsets, where the twentieth century created its greatest myths, even if I ended face down in a swimming pool in Beverly Hills, a small price to pay for true celebrity.

Nathanael West's *The Day of the Locust*, first published in 1939, remains the best of the Hollywood novels, a nightmare vision of humanity destroyed by its obsession with film. West, the author of *Miss Lonelyhearts* and *A Cool Million*, had worked as a scriptwriter in Hollywood for five years, but wisely made the hero of his novel a painter rather than a writer, accepting that in film, if not everywhere else, the image mattered more than the word. His young hero, Tod Hackett, is a promising artist who has been brought to Hollywood to work in the design department of a major studio. The novel opens as he watches a rehearsal of the Battle of Waterloo, taking place on a studio lot crowded with stuffed dinosaurs, Egyptian temples and Mississippi steamboats. The costumes of the hussars and grenadiers, thanks to his scrupulously researched designs, are authentic replicas, but beyond the studio, in the streets of Los Angeles, absolutely nothing else is real.

His apartment building in the Hollywood Hills is surrounded by luxury homes that resemble Rhineland castles, Swiss chalets and Tudor mansions, built not of stone or brick, but of plaster, lath and paper. Yet crowds of sightseers are drawn to Los Angeles from all over America, and for them the spectacle provides the only reality in their stunted lives. Hackett watches them as they loiter on Hollywood Boulevard, waiting for even the briefest glimpse of their screen idols. He notices that their eyes are filled with envy and a sullen hate, as if they are aware that their dreams are as insubstantial as the painted glue around them. Having nothing else in their lives, they are desperate to seize the sources of their dreams and even, perhaps, destroy them.

In his spare time, Hackett is at work on a visionary painting, 'The Burning of Los Angeles', which will portray the destruction of the city by this alienated horde. Throughout the novel, West brilliantly counterpoints scenes from Hackett's apocalyptic canvas with events that he observes in the Hollywood demi-monde and its cast of weird and shiftless characters. Among them are a drugstore cowboy who makes a modest living in westerns; a lonely accountant, Homer, who has abandoned his job in Iowa; a failed vaudeville performer reduced to selling polish door to door; and his beautiful daughter Faye, a part-time film extra. Faye bears a resemblance to the young Marilyn Monroe that is uncannily prophetic. With her platinum hair and affected little-girl wisdom, her nights spent as a call-girl and her determined dreams of becoming a serious actress, Faye is a remarkable portrait of the young Monroe during her first unhappy years in Hollywood.

Powerful set-pieces fill the pages, like the brutal but enthralling cockfight staged in Homer's garage, which not even Hemingway could have bettered, and the filmed Waterloo that turns into a catastrophic rout of collapsing scenery and injured stuntmen. Most impressive of all is the final chapter when Hackett is trapped and nearly killed by a crowd outside a Hollywood premiere. This delirious and vengeful mob seems to have stepped straight from his painting of Los Angeles in flames. The fury of the crowd, unable to find an enemy and so turning on itself, is chillingly conveyed in West's spare and unemotional prose. Much of the novel's force stems from the reader's sense that, fifty years later, Hollywood's power over our imaginations is undiminished, and that his vacant and restless sightseers are proxies for all of us.

Sadly, West and his wife died in a car crash in 1940. One wonders what he would have made of Hollywood Boulevard today – tacky and faded, the haunt of hookers, drug dealers and edgy tourists, waiting for

Tod Hackett's great fire to surge up from the wastelands of central LA and at last destroy the city of dreadful night.

Sunday Times
1993

The Divine Marquis

Marquis de Sade
Maurice Lever

The whip whistles through almost every page of this bracing biography, against a background of the heaviest breathing since Bram Stoker's *Dracula*. The Marquis de Sade is the spectre at the feast of European letters, the prodigal son invited in from the cold only to leave footprints of human blood on the welcome-mat. Coping with his wayward genius is like digesting the news that a distant relative ran the torture chambers in a death camp. Do his warped genes, these demented dreams of sodomy and the lash, also thread themselves through our lives?

'Should we burn Sade?' asked a worried Simone de Beauvoir during the post-war reassessment of Sade. I suspect that the jury will always be out, unable to weigh his deviant imagination against the countless massacres of our century. Sade's novels have been the pillow-books of too many serial killers for comfort, but the 'divine Marquis' refuses to go away, and may well have an important message for us.

Almost forgotten during the nineteenth century, Sade was rediscovered in the 1930s after the publication of his lost masterpiece, *The 120 Days of Sodom*. The surrealists embraced him eagerly, hailing him as a precursor of Freud who revealed the infinite perversity of the human mind. Others saw him as a political revolutionary, the ultimate rebel against the bourgeois order, constructing a self-sufficient anti-society from his elaborate hierarchies of torturers and willing victims. But the horrors of the Third Reich shut the surrealists up for good and forced even Sade's keenest admirers to wonder if his psychopathic imagination had paved the way for Hitler and helped to write the script of the Holocaust.

Both his writings and sexual behaviour led to Sade's imprisonment for decades in the Bastille and the Charenton asylum. Yet, as Maurice Lever points out in his scrupulously neutral biography, Sade's brutal treatment of prostitutes and peasant girls during his sexual games was commonplace among the aristocracy of his day. What condemned him was his refusal to disavow himself.

Lever comments that Sade's early life contains all the ingredients of his novels. At the age of four he was taken from his mother, who immured herself in a convent, and was brought up by his uncle, a libertine priest, in a gloomy palace surrounded by debauched women. Sade developed what Lever terms a negative Oedipus complex, forming an alliance with his adulterous father and dreaming of the cruellest revenges on his absent mother. He took a long-suffering wife, Renée-Pélagie de Montreuil, who helped him to stage his orgies, but his devotion to the whip led his strong-willed mother-in-law, known as la Présidente, to have him committed to prison, where he remained for thirteen years until the Revolution.

Prison only spurred Sade's sexual imagination, and in the Bastille he produced his greatest work, *The 120 Days of Sodom*, penned in microscopic handwriting on a strip of paper forty feet long. Sade harangued the insurgent crowds from his cell window, using as a megaphone the funnel with which he emptied his chamber-pot into the moat – a perfect example of the medium fitting the message – and he was moved from the Bastille a few days before its fall. He was heartbroken over his lost manuscript, though it surfaced more than a century later and was first published by a German psychiatrist.

Freed by the Revolution, Sade became a judge on a popular tribunal, but the guillotine sickened him and he began a second career as a playwright. Condemned by Napoleon for immorality, he was interned in the Charenton asylum, where he staged plays with a cast of lunatics. Fashionable audiences flocked from Paris, a foretaste of the uneasy admirers his writings would attract in the twentieth century.

Meanwhile his sinister presence endures, subverting any wistful notions of literature as a moral repository and testing-ground. During his days as a journalist, Joseph Goebbels wrote a third-rate novel, *Michael*, which can be dismissed out of hand and never compels us to reconsider the career of the Nazi leader and the cruelties he helped to perpetrate. The problem posed by Sade is that *The 120 Days of Sodom* is a masterpiece, a black cathedral of a book forcing us to realize that the imagination transcends morality and that anything can serve as the raw material for a compelling work of art, even those whistling whips and flowering bruises.

Daily Telegraph
1993

Myth Maker of the
Twentieth Century

Naked Lunch
William Burroughs

In *Finnegans Wake*, a gigantic glutinous pun, James Joyce brought the novel up to date, circa 1940, with his vast cyclical dream-rebus of a Dublin publican who is simultaneously Adam, Napoleon and the heroes of a thousand mythologies. William Burroughs takes up from here, and his fiction constitutes the first portrait of the inner landscape of the post-war world, using its own language and manipulative techniques, its own fantasies and nightmares, those of

> Followers of obsolete unthinkable trades doodling in Etruscan, addicts of drugs not yet synthesised, investigators of infractions denounced by bland paranoid chess players, officials of unconstituted police states, brokers of exquisite dreams . . .

The landscapes are those of the exurban man-made wilderness:

> swamps and garbage heaps, alligators crawling around in broken bottles and tin cans, neon arabesques of motels, marooned pimps scream obscenities at passing cars from islands of rubbish.

Whatever his reservations about some aspects of the mid-twentieth century, Burroughs accepts that it can be fully described only in terms of its own language, idioms and verbal lore. Dozens of different argots are now in common currency; most people speak at least three or four separate languages, and a verbal relativity exists as important as any of time and space. To use the stylistic conventions of the traditional oral novel – the sequential narrative, characters 'in the round', consecutive events, balloons of dialogue attached to 'he said' and 'she said' – is to perpetuate a set of conventions ideally suited to a period of great tales of adventure in the Conradian mode, or to an over-formalized Jamesian society, but now valuable for little more than the bedtime story and the fable.

Burroughs begins by accepting the full implication of his subject matter:

> Well these are the simple facts of the case – There were at least two parasites one sexual the other cerebral working together the way parasites will – And why has no one ever asked 'What is word?' – Why do you talk to yourself all the time?

Operation Rewrite, Burroughs's own function as a writer, defines the subject matter of *The Ticket that Exploded*:

> The Venusian invasion was known as 'Operation Other Half,' that is a parasitic invasion of the sexual area taking advantage, as all invasion plans must, of an already existing mucked up situation – The human organism is literally consisting of two halves from the beginning, word and all human sex is this unsanitary arrangement whereby two entities attempt to occupy the same three-dimensional coordinate points giving rise to the sordid latrine brawls which have characterised a planet based on 'The Word'.

Far from being an arbitrary stunt, Burroughs's cut-in method is thus seen as the most appropriate technique for this marriage of opposites, as well as underlining the role of recurrent images in all communication, fixed at the points of contact in the webs of language linking everything in our lives, from nostalgic reveries of 'invisible passenger took my hands in dawn sleep of water music – Broken towers intersect cigarette smoke memory of each other' to sinister bureaucratic memos and medicalese. Many of the portmanteau images in the book make no sense unless seen in terms of this merging of opposites, e.g. the composite character known as Mr Bradly Mr Martin, and a phrase such as 'rectums merging' which shocked the reviewer in *The London Magazine* to ask 'how?' – obviously the poor woman hadn't the faintest idea what the book was about.

In turn, Burroughs's three novels are a comprehensive vision of the individual imagination's relationship to society at large (*Naked Lunch*), to sex (*The Soft Machine*), and to time and space (*The Ticket that Exploded*). In *Naked Lunch* (i.e., the addict's fix), Burroughs compares organized society with its extreme opposite, the invisible society of drug addicts. His implicit conclusion is that the two are not very different, certainly at the points where they make the closest contact – in prisons and psychiatric institutions. His police are all criminals and perverts, while his doctors, like the egregious Dr Benway of Islam Inc., are sadistic psychopaths whose main intention is to maim and disfigure their patients. Most of them, of course, are not aware of this, and their stated intentions may be the very opposite. Benway, a manipulator and co-ordinator of symbol systems, whose assignment in Annexia is TD – Total Demoralization – makes it his first task to abolish concentration camps, mass arrest, and 'except under certain limited and special circumstances' the use of torture. When out of a job he keeps himself going by performing cut-rate abortions in subway toilets, 'operating with one hand, beating the rats offa my patients with the other'. Likeable and insouciant, Benway is full of ingenious ideas for uncovering the spies who infest every nook and cranny:

> 'An agent is trained to deny his agent identity by asserting his cover story. So why not use psychic jiu-jitsu and go along with him? Suggest that his cover story is his identity and that he has no other. His agent identity becomes unconscious, that is, out of control . . .'

However, questions of identity are highly relativistic. As one spy laments: 'So I am a public agent and don't know who I work for, get my instructions from street signs, newspapers and pieces of conversation . . .'

By contrast, the addicts form a fragmentary, hunted sect, only asking to be left alone and haunted by their visions of subway dawns, cheap hotels, empty amusement parks and friends who have committed suicide. 'The fact of addiction imposes contact,' but in their relationships with one another they at least take no moral stand, and their illusions and ambitions are directed only at themselves. But for its continued comic richness – for much of the way it reads like the Lenny Bruce show rewritten by Dr Goebbels – *Naked Lunch* would be a profoundly pessimistic book, for Burroughs's conclusion is that the war between society and individual freedom, a freedom that consists simply of being *individual*, can never end, and that ultimately the only choice is between living in one's own nightmares or in other people's, for those who gain control of the system, like Benway and the Nazi creators of the death camps, merely impose their own fantasies on everyone else.

What appear to be the science fictional elements in *The Soft Machine*, and to a greater extent in *The Ticket that Exploded* – there are Nova Police, and characters such as the Fluoroscopic Kid, the Subliminal Kid, the delightful Johnny Yen, errand boy from the death trauma, heavy metal addicts, Green boy-girls from the terminal sewers of Venus – in fact play a metaphorical role and are not intended to represent 'three-dimensional' figures. These self-satirizing figments are part of the casual vocabulary of the space age, shared by all people born after the year 1920, just as Mata Hari, the Mons Angel, and the dirty men's urinal to the north of Waterloo form part of the semi-comical vocabulary of an older generation. The exploding ticket, i.e., the individual identity in extension through time and space, provides Burroughs with an endless sour.. f brilliant images, of which 'the photo flakes falling' is the most moving in the book – moments of spent time, each bearing an image of some experience, drifting down like snow on all our memories and lost hopes. The sad poetry of the concluding chapter of *The Ticket*, as the whole apocalyptic landscape of Burroughs's world closes in upon itself, now and then flaring briefly like a dying volcano, is on a par with Anna Livia Plurabelle's requiem for her river-husband in *Finnegans Wake*.

> And zero time to the sick tracks – A long time between suns
> I held the stale overcoat – Sliding between light and shadow
> – Cross the wounded galaxies we intersect, poison of dead
> sun in your brain slowly fading – Migrants of ape in gasoline
> crack of history, explosive bio-advance out of space to neon
> . . . Pass without doing our ticket – Mountain wind of Saturn
> in the morning sky – From the death trauma weary goodbye
> then.

For science fiction the lesson of Burroughs's work is plain. It is now nearly forty years since the first Buck Rogers comic strip, and only two less than a century since the birth of science fiction's greatest modern practitioner, H. G. Wells, yet the genre is still dominated by largely the same set of conventions, the same repertory of ideas, and, worst of all, by the assumption that it is still possible to write accounts of interplanetary voyages in which the appeal is to realism rather than to fantasy. Once it gets 'off the ground' into space all science fiction is fantasy, and the more serious it tries to be, the more naturalistic, the greater its failure, as it completely lacks the moral authority and conviction of a literature won from experience.

Burroughs also illustrates that the whole of science fiction's imaginary universe has long since been absorbed into the general consciousness, and that most of its ideas are now valid only in a kind of marginal spoofing. Indeed, I seriously doubt whether science fiction is any longer the most important source of new ideas in the very medium it originally created.

However, Burroughs's contribution to science fiction is only a minor aspect of his achievement. In his trilogy, William Burroughs has fashioned from our dreams and nightmares the authentic mythology of the age of Cape Canaveral, Hiroshima and Belsen. His novels are the terminal documents of the mid-twentieth century, scabrous and scarifying, a progress report from an inmate in the cosmic madhouse.

New Worlds
1964

Hitman for the Apocalypse

Literary Outlaw: The Life and Times of

William S. Burroughs
Ted Morgan

Hitman for the apocalypse in his trench coat and snap-brim fedora, William Burroughs steps out of his life and into his fiction like a secret agent charged with the demolition of all bourgeois values. More than in the case of almost any other writer, Burroughs's life merges seamlessly into his work. Hemingway and Evelyn Waugh were never for a moment convincing as big-game hunter and country gentleman, two of the least likely roles that writers, bundles of nerves and indecision, can ever have asked themselves to play. Had they swapped roles, both might have been more comfortable. One can see Hemingway presiding over a *finca* near Pamplona, breeding bulls rather than skewering them, and Waugh contentedly blasting apart every wildebeest in the Serengeti.

Genet, living out his last days in the tiny hotel rooms that reminded him of his prison cells, consciously turned his back on the world and returned himself to the realm of his own pages, while Burroughs has never left them. Reading Ted Morgan's rich and authoritative biography, one constantly feels that Burroughs's fiction, however extreme, is a milder version of his life. In the late 1970s Burroughs rented a windowless apartment, soon nicknamed the Bunker, in a converted YMCA in the Bowery. The concrete space, with its white porcelain urinals, had once been a changing-room, and Burroughs was pleasantly at home there, surrounded, as he liked to say with a touch of his death-rattle humour, by the heavy psychic traces of naked boys.

This strange scene seems to spring straight from the pages of *Naked Lunch*, from that dank world of subway dawns, cheap hotels and empty amusement parks, and it is this unity of life and vision that gives Burroughs's fiction its enormous charge. At a time when the bourgeois novel has triumphed, and career novelists jet around the world on Arts Council tours and pontificate like game-show celebrities at literary festivals, it is heartening to know that Burroughs at least is still working away quietly in Lawrence, Kansas, creating what I feel is the most original and important body of fiction to appear since the Second World War.

As the contemporary novel transforms itself into a regional or even provincial form, Burroughs's fiction remains international in its scope and subject matter. Surprisingly, those novelists like Snow or Malraux who rose to senior posts in the political establishments of their day left only minor works of fiction about their privileged subject matter. By contrast Burroughs, the professional outsider, sometime petty criminal and drug addict, has produced an unmatched critique of the nature of modern society and the control and communication systems that shape our view of the world.

For all his heroic rebellion against the convention-bound middle class, Burroughs was born in 1914 on one of its most comfortable slopes. His paternal grandfather had invented what was to become the Burroughs adding machine, and the young Burroughs enjoyed a well-to-do child-hood in St Louis – though already, at his private school, the father of a schoolmate remarked of him: 'That boy looks like a sheep-killing dog.'

Sensing that he was a misfit, and aware of his homosexuality from an early age, Burroughs began to experiment with drugstore chloral hydrate when he was sixteen, his first steps in the exploration of states of altered consciousness that was to become a secondary career. He graduated from Harvard with a dose of syphilis and a low view of formal education, but unsure where to point his life. His parents gave him a monthly allowance of $200, which arrived regularly for the next twenty-five years.

Few research funds have been put to better use. The allowance gave him the chance to go down the hard way, not to make good but to make bad. He was able to move outside his own class and explore the vast proletarian sub-culture of blue-collar drifters, small-time gamblers and pennyante thieves. Pushing morphine and living on his wits in New York, though yet to write a word, Burroughs became the dominant figure in a circle that included Jack Kerouac, Gregory Corso and Allen Ginsberg. Ted Morgan comments on their similarity to the Bloomsbury Group, and one can – just – see the resemblances: the same back-scratching and maverick sexuality, the same guest-appearances in each other's novels, with the astringent Burroughs as Virginia Woolf, per-haps, Kerouac as E. M. Forster and Ginsberg as Vanessa Bell . . .

One member of the circle was a bright young Barnard girl called Joan Adams, a benzedrine addict who was to become Burroughs's common-law wife and whom he tragically shot dead a few years later while playing William Tell at their house in Mexico. Ted Morgan convincingly suggests that her death, and Burroughs's grief, unlocked his literary vocation, his self-disgust coinciding with his sense of alienation from American society. Driven by his addiction, he landed in Tangier, where 'the days slid by, strung on a syringe with a long thread of blood . . .' But Tangier, Burroughs realized, might serve as the model for a novel, an 'Interzone' or limbo where anyone could act out his most extreme fantasies. Even before the book was written, Jack Kerouac had provided the title: *Naked Lunch* (the addict's fix, or the rush of pure sensation).

The sections were sent in random batches to the Paris printer, but the sequence seemed to have a logic of its own. Celebrity and controversy followed its publication, but Burroughs has for the most part spent the later years working quietly on the long series of novels that show his gift for humour and character undimmed, and constitute one of the most remarkable achievements of modern fiction, composed against the greatest conceivable odds.

Independent on Sunday
1991

Sticking to his Guns

The Letters of William Burroughs, 1945 to 1959
edited by Oliver Harris

Now living quietly in Lawrence, Kansas, at the very heart of the America he spent so many years escaping, William Burroughs has recovered from his recent heart surgery with his humour and intelligence intact, and at the age of nearly eighty is a walking advertisement for the misspent life – especially to any aspiring writer.

Burroughs has always been regarded as a maverick, roaming the wild lands of the novel beyond the walls of respectability. But this is a measure of our own conformity, and in the years to come, writers of real merit and originality may resemble Burroughs rather than the literary worthies sent jetting around the world by the British Council. Fiction today is dominated by career novelists, with the results one expects whenever careerists dominate an occupation, and the great writers of the future may need to lead lives as disordered and perverse as the one revealed in these fascinating letters. Only then are they likely to break free from the airless monoculture that threatens to entomb us.

For anyone with the courage to follow Burroughs his letters are the perfect guidebook to hell. Almost all were written to Allen Ginsberg and Jack Kerouac between 1945 and 1959. These were the darkest years of Burroughs's life, and cover the depths of his drug addiction and the death of his wife, whom he accidentally killed while trying to shoot a glass from the top of her head. His wanderings take him from the United States to South America and Europe, across a terrain of seedy hotels, sinister pharmacies and last-chance clinics where he tried to cure his addiction. From this desperate world he was able to distil his master-piece, *Naked Lunch*, one of the most original and important novels written since the Second World War.

The correspondence opens soon after his first meeting with Ginsberg, then a nineteen-year-old student at Columbia. More than ten years his senior, the Harvard-educated Burroughs at first takes a lordly line with Ginsberg, ticking him off for his misuse of language – 'Human, Allen, is an adjective and its use as a noun is in itself regrettable' – and suggesting books that might improve his mind. Their roles soon changed. Ginsberg seems to have been the great emotional and sexual passion of Burroughs's adult years, and his letters to the poet were a vital lifeline, whether he was farming in East Texas, hunting for hallucinogens in the Peruvian jungles or coping with his heroin addiction in Tangier.

The first letters show Burroughs in Texas, setting himself up as a farmer, one of the least likely people ever to worry about a carrot crop. Although preoccupied by the endless search for drugs, Burroughs writes to Jack Kerouac about his lettuces and peas, and how much he hopes to make from them. Desperate to leave the United States and its crushing suburbanism, he moves with his wife to Mexico, 'a fine, free country' where 'the cops recognise you as their superior and would never venture to stop or question an upper-class character like myself.'

But wherever Burroughs moves the cops soon get restive. His years in Mexico seem to have been his happiest, and it was there that he wrote his first novel, *Junky*. Already he is aware that the traditional novel is not for him, and in 1952 he writes to Ginsberg: 'A medium suitable for me does not yet exist, unless I invent it.' Forced to leave Mexico after his wife's death, he moves to Tangier, where he is cold-shouldered by the foreign community and snubbed by Paul Bowles and Brion Gysin, both later to become close friends. 'Maybe I will feel better when I get my shotgun and kill something,' he broods, working off his resentment by rowing in the harbour.

For all its drawbacks, Tangier played a crucial role in Burroughs's development as a writer. Interzone, the ultimate open city that is the setting for *Naked Lunch*, is a portrait of Tangier, a 'counterfeit' city, as Paul Bowles described it, with its international zone and rootless expats devoted to drugs and sex, a forerunner of the larger world emerging in the post-war years.

The letters to Ginsberg express his intense longing for the poet, whom he constantly urges to visit Tangier. It is thanks to Ginsberg that these letters have survived, and without him it is likely that *Naked Lunch* would not exist. Large sections of the novel were written in the form of extended skits – what Burroughs calls 'routines' – which were embedded in his letters to Ginsberg. These scatty monologues were Burroughs's ironic commentary on the waking nightmare through which he had moved as a heroin addict, a realm filled with corrupt doctors, deranged fellow junkies, brutal narcotics cops and the teenage boys whose fleeting embraces provided the only solace in his life. Yet the letters are never depressing. Witty, scurrilous, paranoid and philosophical, they are held together by Burroughs's comic genius and extraordinary ear for dialogue.

As Burroughs's literary skills enlarge and his visionary eye begins to shape a unique imaginative world, the mature artist emerges from the riot of cabaret turns. By the last of the letters, *Naked Lunch* has been published in Paris to huge acclaim, and Burroughs is already at the centre of the immense notoriety that has surrounded him for the past thirty years. None the less, he is never satisfied, and at the end of this correspondence he writes to Ginsberg: 'Unless I can reach a point where my writing has the danger and immediate urgency of bullfighting, it is nowhere.' How many of today's novelists would dare to agree with him?

Memories of Greeneland

Parochialism seems to me to be the besetting sin of contemporary English fiction, a fault of which Graham Greene has always been completely free. Writers, of course, can make any number of angels dance on the head of a pin and create a universe out of a nut-shell or a single room. The greatest and most influential French writers of the past fifty years – Sartre, Céline, Camus and Genet – seem, to me at least, to have taken their subject matter and inspiration from France and her territories alone, in the geographical sense, and from the most intense focus on a sometimes narrow aspect of French life, a small social class, a provincial city, a criminal milieu.

For English writers, however, a similar concentration on the life of their own country seems invariably to lead them into all the worst defects of provincialism – an obsession with obscure social nuances, with the minutiae of everyday language and behaviour, and a moralizing concern for the limited world of their own parish that would do credit to an elderly spinster peering down at her suburban side-street. The bourgeois novel flourishes in England now as nowhere else, its narrowing walls crushing its writers against their airless and over-stuffed furnishings. With few exceptions – Graham Greene pre-eminent among them – the English novel seems to me to be a branch of provincial fiction, relevant to nothing but itself.

It is no coincidence that the English novelists who triumphantly escape from this limited, entropic realm – Graham Greene, Lawrence Durrell, Anthony Burgess – are not only emigrants in the literal sense from England itself, but have taken a large part of their inspiration from the world at large. Faced with the suffocating character of English life, the writer has two stark choices – internal emigration, following the route laid down by Kafka, or a one-way ticket from the nearest airport. Now that Britain shows all too many signs of becoming an afterthought of Europe, it may be that the best British writers of the present day, like the best Irish writers of half a century ago, Joyce and Beckett, are forced by internal necessity to seek their imaginative fortunes elsewhere than in their own countries.

I first began to read Graham Greene in the mid-1950s, and will never forget the sense of liberation his novels gave me. This was the heyday of the so-called Angry Young Men – John Osborne, Kingsley Amis, John Braine, and a fraternal American colleague, J. P. Donleavy – morose recipients of a welfare state education from the wrong side of the social tracks who railed against the restrictions of English life (rich men all of them now, they sit in their grand houses, literally in some cases on top of the very hills they once sought to assault). I remember turning from *Look Back in Anger* and *Lucky Jim* to Graham Greene's *The Heart of the Matter*, and then *The Power and the Glory* and *The Quiet American*.

These remarkable novels, whether serious or 'entertainments' as Greene likes to call them, had all the tonic effect of stepping from an aircraft on to the airport tarmac of a strange country. In the novels of Graham Greene one was no longer smothered within the red-brick and lace-curtain world of English life, with its endless moral proscriptions upon everything. Instead, one could see the sights and scent the smells of the whole world. For me, a reluctant immigrant from the Far East in 1946, Greene's novels were an indefinite visa to reality. In his novels over the years one can see the shape of the post-war world as it emerged in Africa and the Far East, in Central America and the Caribbean, just as one saw the hard reality and moral ambiguities of post-war Europe in *The Third Man*.

As a writer myself, I have been enormously influenced by Greene's style, by his method of setting out the psychological ground on which his narratives rest. Within the first paragraph of a Graham Greene novel one has an unmistakable feeling for the imaginative and psychological shape of what is to come. The opening picture of a narrator/hero standing on a jetty watching the sampans drift down river and waiting with mixed feelings for his sick wife to come ashore, or of a bored police chief slapping the fly on his neck, together stamp an indelible image on the reader's mind.

And for all his most serious concern for the psychological and spiritual dilemmas of his characters, Greene never moralizes about his subject matter in that way so beloved by the English provincial writer. Their strengths and weaknesses, their dubious motives and social backgrounds are accepted without comment like the grease on the fan, the dirt under one's fingernails.

With Lawrence Durrell and Anthony Burgess, Greene keeps alive the largest and most admirable traditions of the English novel. The robustness and strength of his vision are clearly demonstrated by the fact that after half a century, and now well into his seventies, he is still producing great works of fiction.

Magazine Littéraire
1978

Visions of Hell

The Childermass, Monstre Gai, Malign Fiesta
Wyndham Lewis

Hell is out of fashion – institutional hells at any rate. The populated infernos of the twentieth century are more private affairs, the gaps between the bars are the sutures of one's own skull. Sartre's hell is other people – a lesbian, a coward and a neurotic trapped together in a hotel room and bored beyond death by their own identity. Cocteau's is the netherworld of narcissism, Orpheus snared by the images of his own mirror. Burroughs's hells are more public, their entrances are subway stations and amusement arcades, but built none the less from private phobias, like the Night-town of Leopold Bloom. A valid hell is one from which there is a possibility of redemption, even if this is never achieved, the dungeons of an architecture of grace whose spires point to some kind of heaven. The institutional hells of the present century are reached with one-way tickets, marked Nagasaki and Buchenwald, worlds of terminal horror even more final than the grave.

By comparison Wyndham Lewis's hell in *The Human Age* is a more conventional affair. Layered like a department store, the presiding bureaucracy of demons and supernal gauleiters would satisfy the most narrow-minded fundamentalist. A magisterial Bailiff, like a sinister Punchinello, presides over the émigré rabble of the dead waiting for admission to purgatory. This, called Third City, looks like Barcelona, with tree-lined avenues crammed with cafés. Now and then supernatural booms knock everyone to the ground as archangels the size of sky-scrapers move across the sky. An amiable Padishah rules this chaotic outpost of heaven like a sultanate ('social life centres on the palace'). Hell itself is a cross between Birmingham and Dieppe, governed by the Lord Sammael, a droll Lucifer who sounds like a saturnine account executive cutting a swathe through a typing pool.

Summarized like this, Lewis's Hell is hell. But on the page his annealed prose and painter's eye are able to save this vision of the judgement and resurrection of mankind from becoming a bizarre pantomime. Put on by the Third Programme ten years ago with tremendous style and panache, and with a virtuoso performance by Donald Wolfit as the Bailiff, the trilogy came over superbly as black theological cabaret. The narrative, however, asks to be taken more seriously, and the black centre at Lewis's heart casts a pall over his panorama of the afterlife.

> 'Is this Heaven?' Pullman at last blankly inquired of the air
> . . . Thousands of people overflowed the café terraces. As
> they began to pass the lines of tables nearest the road, faces
> came into view. They were the faces of nonentities; this
> humanity was alarmingly sub-normal, all pig-eye or owlish
> vacuity. Was this a population of idiots – astonishingly well-
> dressed?

Needless to say, this is not heaven. Unfortunately for the author, it is not hell or purgatory either. This malevolent vision of mankind is the fantasy of a solitary misanthrope out of touch with his times. A leader of the avant-garde before the First World War and founder of the review *Blast*, Lewis's aggressiveness and talent for polemics served him well enough in the last round of the attack on the already routed bourgeoisie. Painter, writer and propagandist, after the war he launched Vorticism, a cerebral version of cubism, and then turned his withering eye on the prominent writers of the twenties, Hemingway ('the dumb ox'), and Joyce, who comes up for special attention in *The Childermass*. Although his criticism is written with tremendous élan, a boiling irritability and impatience with fools, Lewis's reputation began to slide, particularly as his right-wing views seemed to reveal a more than sneaking sympathy for Hitler and the Nazis. *The Childermass* had been published in 1928, and a quarter of a century later he brought out the next two volumes of *The Human Age* – *Monstre Gai* and *Malign Fiesta*. When he died in 1961, blind and ignored, he was working on the notes for its projected successor, *The Divine Age*, in which the principal characters would ascend to paradise and there conclude their journey through the afterlife.

The Childermass

The inner eye of the blind painter, warped by his own bile, illuminates a landscape beyond time, space and death. Already cut off by tempera-ment from the mood of his age, he inhabits a private purgatory or, rather, sits with the other journeymen to the grave on the nominal ground outside the walls of limbo, waiting to begin his descent into hell.

> The city lies in a plain, ornamented with mountains. These appear as a fringe of crystals to the heavenly north. One minute bronze cone has a black plume of smoke. Beyond the oasis plain is the desert. Two miles across . . . the emigrant mass is collected within sight of the walls of the magnetic city. To the accompaniment of innumerable lowing horns along the banks of the river, a chorus of mournful messages, the day breaks.

Sand-devils perform on the borders of the plain, the air murmurs and thunders by the outposts of Beelzebub, in this supernatural light flares burst from the sand. There is a whiff of plague. At the ferry-station by the river a seedy-looking man in a shabby suit looks out with a speculative eye at the magnetic city, wondering how he can gain admission. The powers of this world after death seem in no hurry to set him on his way.

This sense of the constant need for choice and decision dominates Lewis's vision of hell. Unlike its obvious parallel, Dante's *Inferno*, Lewis's netherworld is a place of shifting identities and loyalties, where the characters' progress towards their ultimate trying-ground is achieved by their capacities for self-assertion, intrigue and manoeuvre. Like a party of tourists stranded outside the gates of a chaotic and perhaps hostile desert city, they have to bluff and barter their way through its guards towards whatever dubious comforts lie beyond.

The Childermass opens with the arrival of Pullman and Sattersthwaite at the refugee camp. Both have died in middle age during the First World War, but are incarnated here in their most typical guise. Pullman, a former schoolmaster, a man of sharp but pedantic intelligence, is now a young man of about thirty. Satters, his onetime fag, appears as a babyish adolescent in rugby cap and Fair Isle jumper. The indulgent relationship between this pink-lipped juvenile and the aloof intellectual, whose mind is as barbed and impatient as his author's, is carried forward through the entire trilogy, sustained by bonds that are by no means evident to the reader. How much of the high camp that mars *The Childermass* was originally satiric in intention is difficult to decide.

Taking stock of themselves, Pullman and his companion begin to explore the margins of this supernatural plain. At the refugee camp everything is uncertain. There is no formal administration, no system of processing by which the waiting émigré throng can gain entrance to the city. It is not even known whether the magnetic city, from which they are excluded by the high walls and river, is heaven or hell. Rival sects have formed themselves around the leaders of different philosophic schools, and spend their time vilifying each other and haranguing the mob. All that Pullman and Satters are sure of is that they themselves are dead, and that part of their fate, if no more, lies in the hands of the unpredictable minor demons who form the casual bureaucracy of the camp.

Principal among these is the Bailiff, to whom Pullman, with his sharp eye for self-preservation, is soon drawn. Loathed and abused by the disputing philosophical sects, the Bailiff is the presiding eminence of *The Childermass* and *Monstre Gai*, and, to give Lewis his due, one of the most droll characters in fiction. Grotesque in appearance, but with a mind of great learning and cultivation, he arrives at the camp at the head of a procession of demons and janissaries, and there holds court for the ostensible purpose of selecting entrants to the city. In fact, his authority here seems doubtful, and despite the powers of restraint and mutilation which he now and then exercises, is continually challenged by his opponents among the émigrés.

As Pullman soon realizes, behind his pose as a capricious buffoon, and the endless metaphysical and theological discourses to which he treats his audience, the bailiff's real role is to remind his listeners exactly who they are and how pathetic and vulnerable their condition, both in this life and their previous one, how meaningless and precarious their tenancy of time and space. Wheedling, raucous, vicious and cajoling by turn, a fund of low vaudeville humour and academic witticisms, the Bailiff rouses his audience to a pitch of fury. Pullman alone, realizing that this sinister but powerful figure is his one hope of escaping from the feuding and sterile self-immersion of the camp, decides to accept the Bailiff on his own terms. At the first opportunity, outside the gates of the city, he attracts the Bailiff's attention and by his ingratiating manner gains admission to the city for Satters and himself.

Monstre Gai and *Malign Fiesta*

It is here, at the opening of *Monstre Gai*, that *The Human Age* loses its way. Pullman's willingness to accept the logic of whatever situation in which he finds himself leads him to join the Bailiff's faction. Whether or not this enigmatic pasha is the Devil he can only guess, but the question is of less interest to Pullman than the need for his own advancement. In due course, an unsuccessful putsch against the palace regime is scotched when the powers of heaven send in their forces to bolster the puppet regime of the Padishah. Pullman and the Bailiff flee from Third City. In *Malign Fiesta* they arrive in hell, where Pullman deserts the Bailiff, in disfavour and exiled to the suburbs like an unsuccessful foreign revolutionary forced to return to his homeland. He now attaches himself to the entourage of the Lord Sammael. This time a more ambitious plot against heaven is abruptly forestalled, and the agents of God carry Pullman away to whatever judgement awaits in paradise – exile, one would guess, to the supernal equivalent of Elba or Mauritius.

The strange amalgam of Ruritanian intrigue, political thriller and Old Testament demonology is often entertaining, but fails to consider the most elementary questions of morality or character. Pullman's failure is not a moral one but that of a minor political opportunist who has backed the wrong horse. Pullman feels no remorse, but merely a passing regret for his errors of judgement.

However, apart from his deficiencies of character, Pullman is a wholly passive creature of circumstance. Unlike a torture chamber, a hell is made by its inmates, not its jailers. Sartre's Roquentin, in *La Nausée*, surrounded by festering furniture and cobblestones; Scobie in *The Heart of the Matter*, obsessed by his failure of compassion for his wife, God and fellow men; the legion of unknown subnormal mothers struggling with their overtoppling children – these people inhabit hells of their own devising, whose racks are despair, self-disgust and self-hate. The case histories of Freud and modern psychiatry give us a different insight into the origins of our infernos, nightmares as ghastly as the polymorphic horrors of Dali and Ernst, and very different methods for expiating our sense of sin. The hells that face us now are more abstract, the very dimensions of time and space, the phenomenology of the universe, the fact of our own consciousness.

New Worlds
1966

Memories of James Joyce

James Joyce's *Ulysses* had an immense influence on me – almost entirely for the bad. I read Joyce's masterpiece as an eighteen-year-old medical student dissecting cadavers at Cambridge, then a bastion of academic provincialism and self-congratulation. *Ulysses* opened my eyes to an infinitely richer and more challenging world. Here, I knew, was the authentic voice of heroic modernism that rang through the European and American writers I had devoured at school while trying to recover from the shock of arriving in England – Dostoevsky, Rimbaud, Kafka, Camus and Hemingway. Reading them at too early an age, long before I had the experience to understand them, was probably another mistake.

But *Ulysses* overwhelmed me. It might be set in a single day in a provincial European city, but in Joyce's eye Dublin was the whole world, and that single day lasted longer than a century. Joyce's text seemed to exhaust every conceivable possibility of narrative technique – in fact, technique became the real subject of the novel (a dead end, as the post-modernist writers demonstrate). *Ulysses* convinced me to give up medicine and become a writer, but it was the wrong example for me, an old-fashioned story-teller at heart, and it wasn't until I discovered the surrealists that I found the right model.

I read *Ulysses* again last year and was even more impressed than I was forty years ago, though clearly it's excessively interiorized, is curiously lacking in imagination and fails to engage the reader's emotions, defects that of course recommend it to academia. But if not the greatest novel of the twentieth century it is certainly the greatest work of fiction.

Guardian
1990

Kafka in the Present Day

Kafka may be *the* most important writer of the twentieth century, far more important than James Joyce. He describes the fate of the isolated man who is surrounded by a vast and impenetrable bureaucracy, and begins to accept himself on the terms the bureaucracy imposes. Human beings today are in a very similar position. We are surrounded by huge institutions we can never penetrate: the City, the banking system, political and advertising conglomerates, vast entertainment empires. They've made themselves more user-friendly, but they define the tastes to which we conform. They're rather subtle, subservient tyrannies, but no less sinister for that.

Sunday Times
1993

5 SCIENCE

Einstein, the Gene Pool,
Freud and Richard Feynman . . .

Elevators and Relativities

The Private Lives of Albert Einstein
Roger Highfield and Paul Carter

Einstein: A Life in Science
Michael White and John Gribbin

Einstein the philanderer? The notion seems as odd as Picasso the pick-pocket or Jean-Paul Sartre the arm-wrestler. Einstein is still the most famous scientist of the twentieth century, a remarkable achievement bearing in mind that few people outside the realm of theoretical physics have fully understood what relativity is about. I, for one, have never grasped the significance of those observers walking along the corridors of moving trains or firing light beams across falling elevators. And what does happen when we travel at the speed of light? It seems that we shrink and become infinitely heavy, a sensation that must be rather like meeting the tax inspector while riding the wall of death.

None the less, the theory of relativity has had immense popular appeal, especially in the uncertain years after the First World War. Everything was 'relative', in the moral sphere above all, and so anything went, which suited the temper of the times and was endorsed by Einstein's saintly appearance. With his halo of untidy hair and kindly, patient eyes, he brooded like science's conscience over the atomic revolution he had helped to create. Now all this is set to end. *The Private Lives of Albert Einstein* is a hand grenade lobbed into the sacred temple. In their scrupulously researched biography, Roger Highfield and Paul Carter reveal a very different Einstein. To their great credit these startling revelations never diminish the man but only increase our sense of wonder that a mere human being, with all the faults, frailties and pettiness shared by the rest of us, could fashion a theory that revolutionizes our view of the universe.

After Einstein's death in 1955 two of his greatest admirers, his secretary Helen Dukas and his financial adviser Dr Otto Nathan, erected a protective screen around Einstein's reputation that stood almost to this day. As controllers of his literary estate, they suppressed any damaging letters and closed the door to all but the most sympathetic researchers, virtually sealing Einstein into a monument consecrated to his own myth. It was only in 1987, when both were dead, that the real Einstein began to emerge.

During his life Einstein frequently stressed his indifference to the hurly-burly of human relationships, and many who knew him commented on his innocent and childlike nature. But in fact he was powerfully under the spell, for good and ill, of his strong-willed mother, and his behaviour in later life was that of a favourite child, who expects to be indulged, supervised and never denied. A lonely and dreamy boy, he was told after his sister's birth that he had someone new to play with. Assuming she was a toy, he said: 'Yes, but where are its wheels?' – a shrewder question than it sounds. He was an erratic pupil, and his Greek master announced that he would amount to nothing, but he excelled in physics and after leaving school entered the Polytechnical School in Zurich. There he met a fellow student, a Serb named Mileva Maric, who was to become his first wife and of whom his mother thoroughly disapproved.

Their courtship was troubled, and interrupted by Einstein's flirtations with other women. Mileva was a superb mathematician, and many have speculated that she made a significant contribution to the theory of relativity. In a letter to her, Einstein wrote: 'I'll be so happy and proud when we are together and can bring our work on relative motion to a successful conclusion!' Highfield and Carter suggest that she was no more than a sounding board for his ideas, but one less happy contribution which she did make before their marriage was their daughter Lieserl, born in 1902. Einstein was never to see her, and regarded her as a burden from which he was determined to free himself. Lieserl vanished into history and all traces of her were erased from the official records of his life, though conceivably she might still be alive.

After their marriage Mileva bore him two sons, who could never escape from the shadow of their famous father. The younger, Eduard, later suffered from mental illness and died alone in a Swiss asylum. Mileva, too, withdrew into herself. Einstein had embarked on an affair with his cousin, Elsa, later to be his second wife, and it is known that the divorce papers – still kept under seal in Jerusalem – refer to violence within the marriage. Einstein's second marriage covered the period of his fame and emigration to the United States. At first it seemed happier, Elsa having the good sense to treat the great man as a child, tolerating his tantrums and refusal to brush his teeth, and giving him pocket money. But Einstein's philandering had become a career in its own right. Rich and beautiful women flocked around him, snubbing his wife and deeply wounding her.

None of this appeared in the popular press in the 1930s, and by the Second World War he was a revered figure who had attained the status of a lay saint. After his death in 1955 his brain was removed and found to contain a larger than average number of glial cells, a sign in experimental animals of more extensive neural connections and a greater responsiveness to the environment. Needless to say, where wives fit into the wiring circuit, if anywhere, has not been discovered. An even stranger revelation was made by his former Berlin doctor, Janos Plesch, who suggested that Einstein had died of syphilis, and claimed that the abdominal aneurysm which killed him was always associated with the tertiary stage of the disease. There were rumours of a visit to a Berlin brothel, and speculation that he had sired a number of illegitimate children. Yet none of these revelations lessens one's respect. However close his appetites were to the common ground, whatever the defects of his personality, Einstein's mind was set on the universe.

Michael White and John Gribbin's *Einstein* is a superb introduction to his scientific work, the clearest and most accessible guide that I have read. After countless books explaining relativity I felt for the first time that I had begun to understand the theory – those moving observers, those mysterious trains, even that endlessly falling lift. At last I will be able to travel at the speed of light and stare the taxman in the face.

Daily Telegraph
1993

Magnetic Sleep

From Mesmer to Freud
Adam Crabtree

The history of psychiatry rewrites itself so often that it almost resembles the self-serving chronicles of a totalitarian and slightly paranoid regime. One-time pioneers are suddenly demoted and deemed to be little more than package tourists. Sigmund Freud, far from being the heroic first explorer of the unconscious mind, now seems to be one of the last to step off the gangway, as Adam Crabtree makes clear in this account of the precursors of psychoanalysis.

The unlikely figure who first raised the curtain on the era of modern psychology was Franz Anton Mesmer, a Viennese physician born in 1734, whom I have always associated with ouija boards, stage hypnotists and other assorted quackeries. In fact, he was a sceptical physical scientist deeply opposed to all paranormal phenomena. While practising as a doctor he became interested in the power that magnets seemed to exert over the workings of the human body. A Jesuit priest, with the daunting name of Father Hell, had developed a cure for stomach cramps involving the use of iron magnets. Mesmer's careful experiments convinced him that currents of force, which he dubbed 'animal gravity', moved beneficially between doctor and patient. The most important magnet, he believed, was the human body, and he enjoyed a remarkable run of success, treating everything from haemorrhoids and paralysis to epilepsy and melancholia.

Despite his immense fame, Mesmer was distrusted by the orthodox medicine of his day, but he was able to pass on his torch to the most remarkable of his French pupils, the Marquis de Puységur, a former artillery officer intrigued by the phenomenon of electricity. After being trained by Mesmer at his Society of Harmony in Paris, Puységur turned his skills upon the daughter of his estate manager, who was suffering from toothache, and began a series of experiments that Adam Crabtree claims were to alter the course of psychiatry for ever. While laying on his hands, Puységur discovered that his patients sank into what he termed 'magnetic sleep'. This was a state of sleep-walking consciousness during which the patients became extremely suggestible, developed an intense rapport with the therapist, but on awakening remembered nothing. It clearly foreshadowed both Freud's therapeutic couch and the spotlit stage of the music-hall hypnotist.

Mesmer always believed his powers of healing were physically based, but Puységur was confident that the therapeutic benefits of the magnetic trance were wholly psychological. Indeed, many physicians were already worried about the painful secrets revealed by the entranced patients and the dangers of 'unhealthy' sexual attachment. Puységur, one observer noted, placed his hands on the head of a woman patient, gently tickled her nostrils and 'pressed on her breasts in a manner that her nipples would have felt a slight rubbing'. In 'lively and sensitive women' convulsions occurred, with sudden movements of the arms and legs, the discharge of 'the sweetest emotions', followed by a state of languor and weakness. Surprisingly, the observer noted, the women felt no guilt and were ready to repeat the experience.

Well, yes, I dare say they were, and psychological medicine, as well as the arts of seduction, have never been the same since. In the nineteenth century the discovery of unconscious behaviour led to a huge popular interest in paranormal phenomena. Table-turning and wall-rapping, thought and memory transference were exploited by quacks and soberly investigated by responsible scientists. In the 1890s the French psychologist Pierre Janet elaborated the concept of the unconscious act, describing a submerged mental world that operated independently of normal consciousness and could give rise to inexplicable actions and emotions.

When Freud at last arrived on the scene, he seems from Adam Crabtree's account like the last guest at a party that had already begun to disperse. Perhaps this demotion of Freud reflects the therapeutic failure of psychoanalysis, and hints at yet another radical shift in the progress of psychology that may occur during the run-up to the next millennium. While we move the couch out of the consulting room and into the attic we would do well to reflect on what even stranger furniture might take its place.

Daily Telegraph
1994

The Evolutionary Terminus

The Language of the Genes
Steve Jones

Clasp your hands together – which thumb is on top? In half of us the right thumb is dominant and in half the left. The tendencies run in families. Again, some of us see the world through rosier spectacles than others. There are two distinct receptors for red light in the retina, and six out of ten of us have one, and the rest the other, as we discover when men with different receptors pick the jacket and trousers of a Father Christmas costume. Lastly, look around the office or your next cocktail party. One in twenty of us is not the biological child of the man we have always called our father. These differences, some trivial and some crucial to our lives, spring from our genetic codes, nature's Rosetta stone which today's biologists are rapidly deciphering. In this challenging book, drawn from his 1991 Reith Lectures, Steve Jones, of University College, London, takes the reader on an exhilarating trip around the double spiral of DNA, a rush of gravity-defying concepts and wild swerves of the scientific imagination that lurches to a breath-taking halt when he suggests that the roller-coaster ride of evolution may well be coming to an end.

He begins with an overview of genetic science today, and suggests that within ten years we may have decoded the 3,000 million letters in the DNA alphabet that shape a human being. Two-thirds of us die for reasons linked to the genes we carry, and genetics has begun to unravel the mysteries of sex, age and death, and the even greater puzzle, so dear to certain feminist hearts, of why there are men at all, or at least so many more of us than seems necessary from an evolutionary standpoint. Even our belief in our uniquely privileged place in nature is under challenge. Much of the chimpanzee's DNA is identical to our own, and we share many of our genes with mice, bananas and bacteria. As Professor Jones comments in his vivid and often poetic prose, every one of us is a living fossil, bearing a record of the past that extends far beyond the beginnings of humanity. Advances in genetics, he points out, raise the most subtle moral dilemmas. Science may soon have the power to tell many of us how and when we are likely to die. We will be able to select the sex of our children, a time-bomb packed with political dangers of every kind, and not only free them from the threat of inherited disease but even influence their physical and psychological make-up. The prospect of a world populated by Mozarts and Mike Tysons, or even by socially cooperative psychopaths with a taste for flower arranging, no longer seems one of the wilder fantasies of science fiction.

The great motor of genetic change is the mutation, and Professor Jones devotes much of his book to an exposition of the role that mutations play in the lives of species, communities and individuals. Small populations are always at danger from inbreeding, when recessive characteristics emerge unchecked, as the Pennsylvania Amish show with their tendency to produce six-fingered children. But the number of mutations, beneficial or harmful, has begun to decline. As we travel the world, and take our partners from the further shores of the gene pool, our recessive genes are paired with normal ones that mask their effects. The rate at which mutations occur accelerates with age, and most babies are now born to women who are still young. 'It may even be,' Professor Jones remarks in the last lines of this stimulating work, 'that economic advance and medical progress mean that humans are almost at the end of their evolutionary road, that we are as near to our biological Utopia as we are ever likely to get.' I always suspected that eternity would look like Milton Keynes.

Daily Telegraph
1993

Deep in the Gene Pool

The Ant and the Peacock: Altruism and
Sexual Selection from Darwin to Today
Helena Cronin

Natural selection is a ruthless taskmaster, but one with a taste for the gaudy and absurd, and capable of unexpected gentleness. The acceptance of Darwin's theory of evolution is confirmed by the way phrases such as 'nature red in tooth and claw' and 'survival of the fittest' have entered our language, truisms evident everywhere from the nearest farmyard to Prime Minister's Question Time.

None the less, there are some surprising exceptions, which have puzzled biologists since Darwin's day and are the subject of Helena Cronin's fascinating book. The preposterous size of the peacock's tail, which serves no conceivable practical purpose, runs counter to nature's sense of thrift and utility. The obsessive activities of bower birds, as they scour the countryside for bottle tops, coins and silver foil with which to decorate their mating parlours, seem to consume far more energy than propagation alone would justify. The female bower bird, after all, has nowhere else to turn. But most baffling of all, and defying the competitive drive that is the engine of evolution, are the acts of altruism found throughout the animal kingdom. The sterile worker ant has renounced all hope of reproducing itself for the good of the commune, a show of public-spiritedness that guarantees its genes go nowhere. Many animals sacrifice themselves to warn others not related to them of predators, or share food from which they themselves would benefit. Given that natural selection rewards success, why have these altruistic strains not bred themselves out of existence?

Dr Cronin plunges into her biological detective story with gusto, first tackling the conundrum of the peacock's tail. Darwin, as uneasy with the tail as he was with the almost God-inspired complexity of the human eye, attributed its size to sexual selection. The morose and dowdy peahen is sexually excited by the flamboyant tail, so males with the largest tails attract the most mates and pass on to the next generation a tendency towards larger tails. This seems confirmed by studies revealing that the more eyes in a peacock's tail, the more often he mates. However, Dr Cronin has a different explanation, drawn from modern Darwinism's belief in the collective importance of the gene pool in social animals. Whereas Darwin, who knew nothing of genes, saw evolution operating at the level of the individual and his own reproductive life, the neo-Darwinists consider the advantages which more complex strategies offer to the gene pool as a whole, and which may outweigh the sexual attractiveness of a single individual, however successful he might be.

On this reading, the conspicuous display of the peacock is precisely that – a deliberately blatant advertisement of its abundant wealth, power and confidence, the avian equivalent of the gold Rolex, the Ferrari and the Armani jacket. Mere sex, as every blonde nestling into the leopard-skin upholstery has always known, is an incidental matter, and in its wisdom the gene pool agrees, seeing to it that the sexual act takes place for more enduring and socially valuable reasons than physical attractiveness.

In her racy and provocative way, Dr Cronin tells a story that sums up the essence of neo-Darwinism. Two hunters are being chased by a bear. One stops to change into his running shoes. 'They won't help you to out-run the bear,' his companion points out. 'No,' replies the first, 'but they'll help me to out-run you.' Genes which favour such cunning will survive, and the same logic underpins acts of altruism. The cause of the gene pool as a whole may be advanced if a few genes are present which trigger socially useful acts of self-sacrifice. So the neutered worker ant toils selflessly, and heroes throw themselves on to hand-grenades to save their fellows. Their own strength and courage will not be passed on to a future generation, but this is offset by the advantages to those who survive.

Part detective story and part philosophical enquiry, *The Ant and the Peacock* offers a paradox in every paragraph, its arguments made more convincing, I happily admit, by the author's beauty – usually one would never dare to make this comment, fearing charges of sexism and flagrant irrelevance, but perhaps the gene pool in its cunning is at work again, steering her book towards a reviewer susceptible to a pretty knee and graceful wrist.

But why, I wonder? Theories of evolution are themselves subject to evolutionary pressure, from the 'survival of the fittest' Darwinism of the Victorian free-enterprise heyday, to the now discredited Lamarckism of the bogus Soviet biologist Lysenko – who claimed that strains of

Siberian wheat, in the best socialist fashion, could learn to improve themselves in their own lifetimes and pass on these acquired characteristics to the next generation – and last of all today's evolutionary theorists in our more devious and calculating times, casting a neutral eye on altruism and self-interest.

Is the new Darwinism about to bring us an unsettling message, and has the gene pool guessed that it might be most swiftly delivered by the prettiest messenger? Whatever the message is, I suspect that it is nothing to do with beauty.

Daily Telegraph
1992

Electrodynamics and Womanizing

Genius: Richard Feynman and Modern Physics
James Gleick

What is it about theoretical physics, one of the most abstract of all human activities, that attracts the eccentric and nonconformist? For all I know, geologists and bio-chemists are equally odd, but the great physicists of the twentieth century do seem to constitute a pantheon of the peculiar, as if the intense effort of wrestling with the secrets of the universe has revealed bizarre strains in their personalities.

One thinks of Einstein, with his wild hair and lack of socks, shirtless under his pullover, the epitome of the absent-minded professor. Erwin Schrödinger, the Nobel Prize-winning creator of wave mechanics, was driven by a powerful Lolita complex and must have been a menace to colleagues with pubescent daughters. Robert Oppenheimer, director of the A-bomb project at Los Alamos, was a self-torturing neurotic who flirted with the far left and claimed that a passage from the *Bhagavad-Gita* – 'Now I am become Death, the destroyer of worlds' – crossed his mind as he gazed at the first atomic explosion in New Mexico. Did it really? It seems just the sort of thing a novelist would invent.

Every bit their equal in eccentricity was Richard Feynman, the American Nobel Prizewinner whom many consider the century's greatest physicist after Einstein. Apart from his wartime years at Los Alamos, Feynman spent his entire career within the American university system. But away from the laboratory he led a life that resembled the more louche roles of Jack Nicholson – player of bongo drums, safe-cracker, lover of strip clubs and habitué of brothels, a compulsive womanizer who had devised a strategy for picking up women in bars, sadly not described by James Gleick in this entertaining biography. I would have settled for fewer pages on electrodynamics and more on the dynamics of nature's other great mystery, the female heart.

Television viewers in 1986 may remember Feynman as a member of the presidential commission on the Space Shuttle disaster. After days of testimony and stonewalling, Feynman cut straight to the source of the tragedy when he immersed a piece of flexible O-ring, a vital fuel-tank seal, in a jug of iced water and demonstrated that it became non-elastic, with the catastrophic results that occurred after a freezing night at the launch pad. This ability to tackle any problem in the most direct and simple way, ignoring the accumulated mass of conventional opinion, had inspired Feynman since his earliest days. He was born in 1918 to working-class Jewish parents in Far Rockaway, Long Island, part of the urban area surrounding New York that has produced the world's largest concentration of Nobel Prizewinners. The impoverished immigrants from Eastern Europe brought with them a deep respect for learning, and saw science as the greatest career open to a poor and determined child. After graduating from MIT, where his brilliance was instantly recognized, Feynman was summoned by Oppenheimer to Los Alamos, and soon became the enfant terrible of the bomb project. Sadly, his young wife had contracted TB, and after years of illness died in a nursing home in Albuquerque, only months before the wonder-drug streptomycin that would have saved her became available.

At Cornell University after the war Feynman continued the work which led to his Nobel Prize, remaking the theory of quantum electrodynamics and inventing the Feynman diagrams that are now part of every physicist's basic tool-kit. Like many scientists whose greatest work is over by their thirties, Feynman felt increasingly unfulfilled as he entered middle age. Fortunately, on a beach beside Lake Geneva in 1958, he saw an attractive young Englishwoman in a blue bikini, a costume that had yet to appear in the United States. Another kind of fusion reaction occurred, and Feynman invited this highly independent young woman to join him at Caltech, where she first worked as his housekeeper and later married him. By all accounts, the genius whom C. P. Snow termed a cross between Einstein and Groucho Marx had at last met his match.

Daily Telegraph
1993

The Thousand Wounds
and Flowers

The Voices of Time
edited by J. T. Frazer

If an Einstein Memorial Time Centre is ever founded, it should take its
first premises in the Museum of Modern Art. The hidden perspectives
hinted at in the paintings of Picasso and Braque, not to mention the
time-saturated images of the surrealists, say more about the subject than
anything the natural sciences can offer, for the clear reason that the
sciences are not equipped to deal with the metaphor. The thousand
wounds and flowers opened in our sides every day irrigate themselves
from a very different watershed.

Given this virtually total handicap, the collection of essays edited by
J. T. Frazer is interesting chiefly for its marginal information. The bulk
of this book is concerned, not with time, but with duration, succession,
the 'representation' of events, coexistence and the like, topics that soon
float adrift on the verbal level, if they ever had any existence at all on
any other. Enough glosses on Heraclitus, Parmenides, Newton, Shakespeare's Sonnets, Kant, Bergson and William James are provided to
pump the British Museum Library into the world's largest hot air balloon, although in other senses the book has a certain charm, like an
imaginary Borges story about a history of histories of time. Charm,
though, is probably too light a word to use – this book may not have
depth but it undoubtedly has width. Laid side by side, the tongues of
its garrulous authors would pave all the roads to Babel. Nevertheless,
they raise a number of interesting questions.

1 To take a literary example, why do so many of Shakespeare's heroes
exhibit signs of 'narrative delay'; Hamlet notably, Macbeth and Lear
(both archetypical ward bosses presumably well educated in the realpoli-
tik of when to put the knife in or back out gracefully), even Caesar and
Prospero, world-weary intellectuals not notably tolerant of fools? The
great majority of Shakespeare's heroes show all the signs of immaturity
rather than psychopathology, but it seems to me that the 'time delay'

device may well reflect some subtle dislocation of one's normal processes of recognition and action during situations of extreme danger or hazard, like the suspended time of Warhol's 'Death and Disaster' series – a deliberate holding of the camera frame for the purposes of one's own conceptual understanding. At times of crisis or bereavement one may well 'hold' events in the camera of one's mind in order to grasp the totality of the situation.

2 At London's Charing Cross Hospital, and a number of other enlightened maternity homes, the father is present at his wife's delivery, an extraordinary experience, by any standards, of the new-born child's remarkable age; lying between his mother's legs, older than pharaoh, older in fact than the great majority of his so-called biological contemporaries. From where does this sense of time come, like the sense of space one feels while looking at the Milky Way?

3 The time-values contained in the paintings of Tanguy, Delvaux and Chirico. The geometry of a landscape seems to create its own systems of time, which cinematize the events of the canvas, translating a posture or ceremony into dynamic terms. The greatest movie of the twentieth century is the 'Mona Lisa', just as the greatest novel is Gray's *Anatomy*.

4 Are there reasons to believe that our apprehension of the future is intimately associated with the origins of human speech, and that the imaginary reconstruction of events necessary for our recognition of the past is also linked with the invention of language?

In the Korsakov Syndrome, as a result of organic brain disturbance, memories fall out of place and there is no comprehension of succession and duration. Disturbance in chronology is often a first symptom of an oncoming psychotic phase. Schizophrenics may either deny the existence of time (on the basis of their infantile delusions of omnipotence), or deny that they lived at all before the onset of their psychosis. Compulsion neurotics stick to a tyrannical inner schedule out of a fear of real time. Déjà vu may be prompted by forbidden infantile wishes of which the possessor has become subliminally aware. In serious brain disturbances there can be extreme feelings of confusion which stem from the inability to 'file' daily events.

'Time does not exist for those who are absolutely without anxiety' – Kierkegaard. A melancholy prescription for immortality.

Counting rhythms are increased by rises in temperature. Psilocybin or LSD not only raise the body temperature and thus produce an overestimation of clock time, 'clock contraction', but a simultaneous expansion of space. The speed of nervous conduction is raised by three milliseconds for every degree Centigrade.

Certain patients with severe brain damage are unable to distinguish whether they are awake or dreaming.

New Worlds
1969

Spaced Out

The Next Ten Thousand Years
Adrian Berry

Science is still trying to catch up with science fiction. This 'Vision of man's future in the universe' is not a book so much as a sound-track — a hymn of joy to the wonders of space travel and the super-technologies of the future, expressed in terms that, for decades, have been the stock-in-trade of science-fiction writers. Flying city states, artificial planets, faster-than-light drives through hyperspace, the redesigning of the Solar System, and the colonization of the furthest reaches of the universe — most of these ideas, long since exhausted by s-f writers, are now being put forward seriously by reputable scientists.

Professor Freeman J. Dyson, for example, Fellow of the Royal Society and a past chairman of the Federation of American Scientists, is the architect of a project known as 'The Dyson Sphere', which involves dismantling the planet Jupiter and reassembling the pieces in a huge sphere around the Sun, in order to exploit its entire radiation. What is interesting is not the project itself, but the repeated insistence that it is entirely feasible 'even in terms of today's technological knowledge'. The perfect scheme to take Concorde's place.

In many ways, it is refreshing to see someone champion these grandiose if dotty ideas with so much enthusiasm, and the book as a whole, with its old-fashioned confidence in scientific and technological progress, has a stately period charm, like a chromium-plated replica of the *Berengaria*. The author approvingly quotes Dr Edward Teller's sly remark about the Friends of the Earth: 'Perhaps the Earth has too many friends and the energy-user too few'; and nowhere does he express any anxiety about the possible hazards of ever-increasing economic and population growth. Even a catastrophe such as a global nuclear war would, he maintains, only delay progress briefly, not prevent it. To obtain the limitless energy sources that will be needed for the exploding populations of the next few thousand years, mankind will inevitably move out into deep space, he argues, and begin the serious business of redesigning the Solar System and, ultimately, the whole Milky Way, around its own needs.

The Moon, seen primarily as a paradise for the vacuum scientist, will become a vast factory floor. Mars, lacking warmth and water, has few charms, but Venus, a hot biochemical mix, is ripe for colonization. The chapter 'Making it rain in hell' describes how its atmosphere of water vapour and carbon dioxide will be bombarded by immense numbers of rockets filled with oxygen-producing algae. After this will come whole-sale 'terra-forming' – planet-sculpting, that is, literally remodelling other worlds in the image of our own – and the construction of artificial planets, variously named New London and New New York, which will sail outwards across the galaxy, leaving behind a darkening sea of stars each dimly burning within its own Dyson Sphere . . . If I were a Martian, I'd start running now.

All this is done with vigour and panache, an impressive handling of concepts, ergs and light-years. Many of the ideas are breath-taking, to say the least, and the author is certainly a change from all the professional doomsayers and airport thinkers hawking the latest eco-crisis. Yet somehow the book is not merely unconvincing, but irrelevant. Most of the events prophesied by Adrian Berry may well take place, but within what human context? *The Next Ten Thousand Years* never seriously considers human, as opposed to scientific, evolution, and it seems obvious to me that our remote descendants will be as different from ourselves as we are from the weird algae, described by the author, which thrive on a diet of kerosene in jet-liner fuel tanks.

One value of science fiction is that its extrapolations, however far-fetched, are tested within some kind of emotional and human framework. If one regards this book as a new kind of novel, part of a recently invented category of fiction that includes books such as Herman Kahn's *The Emerging Japanese Superstate* and Desmond Morris's *The Naked Ape*, it shows up the weaknesses of this new hybrid form.

At the same time, one could just as easily speculate that none of these predictions will come true, and probably with more evidence. The brief history of the manned space programme seems to bear this out. In a sense, as far as manned flights are concerned, one can say that the Space Age, far from lasting for hundreds if not thousands of years, is already over. Why were the majority of people not only bored by the manned space flights, but indifferent to them? Partly, I think, because the science-fiction writers had reached the Moon first and formed an invisible welcoming committee, somehow reminding us of Mort Sahl's description of Cape Kennedy as Disneyland East. But most of all because, for the foreseeable future at any rate, space travel makes sense only in terms of those extravagant and overblown ideas, devoid of any human dimension, that fill Adrian Berry's book. Trying to think more realistically about space, with its utter nothingness, we become a little like laboratory volunteers floating in sensory-deprivation tanks, deranged when the only perceptible external reality becomes the interior of our own minds.

New Society
1974

Manbotching

The Body in Question
Jonathan Miller

Are books becoming another form of television? By rights, this lavishly illustrated survey of human physiology, 'linked', as the publishers say, to the new thirteen-part BBC series, should be reviewed by a television critic. Like Desmond Morris's recent *Manwatching*, another interesting example of the transformation of the book into its electronic paradigm, *The Body in Question* seems designed not to be read so much as to serve as a reminder of happier hours spent in front of the tube.

Here are the familiar huge illustrations, many of them reassuringly the size of a television screen, the TV-style graphics, the sudden zooms on to any affecting image – the constant favourite of these books is the suckling infant. The disconnected flow of images, from a full-colour reproduction of Verrocchio's 'Baptism of Christ' to a news-agency photograph of a music-hall faith-healer, makes complete sense to a viewer trained to appreciate the presentation techniques of *Civilisation* and *World in Action*, and further creates the uncanny impression that one is not really reading a book but watching a programme. Recently, while being shown round an imposingly furnished lounge in one of the smarter Thames Valley housing estates, I actually heard the hostess apologize for 'the books', a row of a dozen book-club titles occupying a lowly cell in her wall-unit. I knew what she meant. They were rather scruffy and undisciplined, totally lacking the authentic manufactured look. But she can throw them out now; *The Body in Question*, like *Manwatching*, will fit in perfectly among the stainless-steel knick-knacks, the inlaid executive bar and the 26-inch TV screen.

All this sounds like envy, and probably is – I'm only too keen for the BBC to take my own thirteen-part series on the social history of the car park. But having myself read medicine for a couple of years, which gives me about the same level of medical expertise as the average viewer with fifty *Horizons* stored away in the back of his head, I found *The Body in Question* oddly flat and unoriginal. At its best Desmond Morris's imagination can throw up a genuinely strange idea – the subliminal confusion of breasts and buttocks, for example – and *The Naked Ape* and *Manwatching* even hint at a new kind of novel. In *The Body in Question*, however, Jonathan Miller has carefully side-stepped any temptation to be speculative. He seems to have set out to explore the way in which the vital functions of the human body – respiration, the circulation, its response to illness – become a series of 'metaphors' through which we, often misleadingly, view our entire universe; but in fact this series of TV lectures soon becomes an easily digestible mix of popular medical history, A-level biology and dissecting-room anecdotes. The author was one of the last people to be described as 'brilliant' before the term went out of use in the mid-sixties, but I found not a single arresting or original idea in the entire volume. Take its opening sentence, typical of the book as a whole: 'Of all the objects in the world, the human body has a peculiar status: it is not only possessed by the person who has it, it also possesses and constitutes him.' Is that an original insight, or the smooth packaging of the banal?

A remarkable omission from this illustrated account of our vital functions is any reference to sex and reproduction. But perhaps the BBC have leased the franchise on these topics to another thirteen-parter, and at this very moment Alex Comfort is interviewing himself outside a massage parlour in Bradford. It may be that we have all had a surfeit in recent years of revelations about the functions of our bodies and that the subject needs to gather a little mystery again (or, more worryingly, is sex itself losing its charms – I keep thinking about those 500,000 women who have gone off the pill; is it in fact sex that they have given up?).

To a large extent the deficiencies of this book lie within the particular private jargon which Dr Miller displays so engagingly on TV, and which so brilliantly mimics originality without ever actually revealing it. 'Metaphor', for example, is a particularly potent term for him – 'Like blood, metaphors circulate through the intellectual community', he says in the chapter on the circulation. One of the vague fears of anyone who has ever been wheeled into an operating theatre is that the surgeon behind his mask and gown will turn out, after the operation, to have been one of those likeable impostors, usually an out-of-work actor or would-be writer, who seem so effortlessly to masquerade as senior members of the medical profession. Reading this book, and watching Dr Miller on television, I sometimes have the impression that he is reversing the process – a genuinely qualified physician who has left his hospital rounds and feels compelled to play the roles of actor, satirist, theatrical producer, TV presenter, author. But which body in question wrote *The Body in Question*?

New Statesman
1978

6 AUTOBIOGRAPHY

From Shanghai to Shepperton . . .

Unlocking the Past

One can never go home, the American novelist Thomas Wolfe has written, meaning that everything changes, the past and one's memories of it. Since coming to England in the grey, austere days after the war, I had kept alive my precious memories of Shanghai. Teeming, cruel but always exhilarating, Shanghai in my mind had become a cross between ancient Babylon and Las Vegas. But what if my memories were false? My great fear was that, far from evoking new memories, the visit might erase the old ones that had sustained me for so many years.

An hour before midnight, after flying through the darkness from Hong Kong, we approached the western rim of a vast metropolis of lights, and touched down at Shanghai International Airport, on the site of the old Hungjao aerodrome where as a boy I had played in the cockpits of rusting Japanese aircraft. A sea of superheated air covered the tarmac, carrying the forgotten scents of the Yangtse countryside. The Chinese immigration officials were amiable, asking me to declare that I suffered from neither Aids nor psychosis (except, perhaps, an excess of memory?) and that I was not importing 'salacious materials' – what did they mean? The new Julie Burchill or, conceivably, a biography of Donald Trump?

James Runcie, the director of BBC-2's *Bookmark* film, was waiting for me. I greeted him with the line I had rehearsed all the way from London, suggested by Conrad's novel about a European trader driven mad by an impenetrable Africa: 'Hello, James. Mr Kurtz returns to the Heart of Darkness.' The problem was that Mr Kurtz had arrived without his luggage, or at least the kind of luggage carried in one's hands. A few minutes earlier I had stood by the crowded carousel as suitcases were wrenched away, only to find myself alone by the eerily rotating band.

Was my tea-planter's suit, my 'costume' for the film, on its way to Caracas, Honolulu or even Darjeeling? Happily Mr Gao and Mr Zhung of Shanghai Television leapt forward and took control. Super-efficient, they exchanged telexes with Hong Kong Airport, and my suitcase was on the next flight to Shanghai. Thanking them, I remembered that, before the war, one of my parents' steamer trunks had appeared a year after the P & O boat had docked.

At midnight we arrived at the Shanghai Hilton, a forty-storey tower in the former Avenue Haig. The fuzzy street lights, perspiring trees and microwave air seemed to be those of any sub-tropical city, and I was still not sure that I had returned to the Shanghai I knew. The next morning, when I looked out from my room on the thirtieth floor, I was even less convinced. Like the London of the 1930s, Shanghai had been a low-rise city. But the Shanghai I saw from the Hilton was a panorama of immense high-rises that stretched from the northern industrial zones of Chapei and Yangtsepoo all the way to Lunghua in the south.

Dozens of huge buildings rose into the sky, roofs decked with satellite dishes. But far below I was relieved to see the old Shanghai of the 1930s was alive and well, if a little crumbling in the sunlight. There were the Provençal villas of the French Concession, and the International Settlement's handsome art deco mansions with port-hole windows and ocean-liner balconies. I gave James the slip and for an hour walked around the nearby streets through which I had cycled as a child, staring up at the faded apartment houses and office buildings that I recognized after nearly half a century's absence. I saw the old General Hospital where I had been born, the municipal park from which the Chinese had been excluded ('No dogs or Chinese'), and the modern trolley buses that still followed the routes of the giant French trams.

Shanghai, which had once been an American and European city filled with Buicks and Packards, was now entirely Chinese, packed with cyclists, its pavements lined with market stalls piled high with water melons, bootleg Hong Kong videos and mounds of writhing eels. In the Hilton lobby the *Bookmark* team was waiting for me. A thirteen-year-old Belgian boy, whose father was working for a foreign company in Shanghai, warily shook my hand. He would play my younger self in the film, and James had misguidedly told him that he resembled me.

Together we set off for our first location, my childhood home in Amherst Avenue, now the library of the Shanghai Electronic Industry Information Bureau. It had been built in the early 1930s in the classic stockbroker style of the Home Counties, though the interior was that of an American house with five bathrooms, air conditioning and a squash court-sized kitchen. The staff welcomed us in the friendliest way, but I had the weird sense that I was exploring a ghost. I walked around the dining room, now lined with shelves of electronics manuals, where my father had entertained American officers and Chinese tycoons, and the veranda where my mother had organized her bridge parties.

The affable director, Mr Chang, greeted me like a long-lost colleague and invited me into his office, crammed with computers, which had once been my mother's dressing room. We conducted an animated dialogue, neither speaking a word of the other's language, but apparently understanding everything. Later I climbed to the top floor and stood in my childhood bedroom, which still had its original pale blue paint and the bookshelves where I had methodically arranged my *Chums* annuals and American comics. Now they were stacked with scientific journals and Chinese textbooks. In the bathroom there was even the original lavatory seat on which, as a small boy, I had been ordered by the punitive White Russian nanny to sit uselessly for hours – the 1930s baby-minding equivalent of television, and probably far more educational.

That first day I moved around Shanghai in a daze. Memories jostled me like the Chinese crowds who surrounded the film crew. Watching as the Belgian lad cycled past the Cathay Hotel, where Noël Coward had written *Private Lives*, I remembered the Shanghai of gangsters and beggar-kings, prostitutes and pickpockets. I had opened a door and stepped into a perfectly preserved past, though a past equipped with a number of unattractive reflexes of my own – walking along the Nanking Road, I caught myself expecting the Chinese pedestrians to step out of my way.

Would Shanghai ever return to its former gaudy self before the Communist take-over? The beggars and cripples exhibiting their open wounds had thankfully gone for good, and there were no armies of coolies labouring under immense loads disgorged from the sampans along the Bund. The people looked confident and well fed, young couples strolling arm-in-arm past the Sun Sun and Wing On department stores, men in shirtsleeves and the women in what might have been C & A frocks. Of course, there were no bookstalls selling newspapers critical of the government, and no posters urging the merits of rival political parties. Yet everywhere, clearly, capitalism was waiting to be reborn, in thousands of small shops and back-street businesses. Like the Europeans in the years before the Opium Wars, the western visitors are again confined to their compounds – the Hilton and Sheraton Hotels

– drinking their imported Carlsberg and watching their Hollywood videos. But this time no British or American gunboat will force the Chinese to grant them concessions, which in due course will not be territorial but financial – tax havens and rent-free enterprise zones.

Already I was bored with the Bund and its great banking houses, and determined to find the last elusive piece of the past, the camp at Lunghua where the Japanese had interned some 2000 British civilians during the war. For nearly three years my father, mother, sister and I had been imprisoned there, living together in one small room.

For the next two days, as our time ran out, we embarked on a fruitless search. The unbroken expanse of paddy-fields that I remembered between Shanghai and Lunghua, eight miles to the south, had now been swallowed by greater metropolitan Shanghai – endless industrial estates and science parks, giant cement works and townships of high-rise flats. I began to despair of ever finding the camp, but at last an old policeman at a dusty wayside station confirmed that there was a high school in the Lunghua district which had once housed European prisoners, though during which war he could not remember. Ten minutes later, miraculously, I was walking through the gates of what had once been Lunghua Civilian Assembly Centre, and staring at F block, the main administrative building where the Japanese commandant, Mr Hyashi, had his headquarters – now, appropriately, his office was the headmaster's study.

Forty-five years had turned the camp into a pleasantly landscaped secondary school, filled with trees and flowers. Caretakers looked on in amazement as a sixty-year-old Englishman sprinted through the trees towards a small two-storey building – G block, where my parents, sister and I had lived in one of the forty rooms that each housed a British family. I burst into the silent entry hall, where our daily ration of rice congee and sweet potatoes had been served, and into the dark corridors where twice a day we stood to attention for roll-call. The schoolchildren were on holiday, their rooms locked, but one room was open and served as a storage cupboard, filled with cardboard boxes and assorted rubbish. This was the Ballard family room, every ceiling crack, every piece of chipped plaster, every worn window frame as familiar to me as the lines on my palm.

I was standing in the debris of my own memories when James and the film crew caught up with me. 'They've been waiting for you to come, Jim,' said our Australian cameraman. 'They even left the door unlocked for you.'

I thought about this three days later when we left for the airport. I had come to puberty in the camp and developed the rudiments of an adult brain, and I had seen my parents' generation endure years of stress and illness. I had watched a world war from the ringside, and sometimes within the ring and between the feet of the combatants. Going back to the camp had been, without my realizing it, my main reason for returning to Shanghai, and visiting Lunghua again had opened a door that I thought was sealed for forty-five years. I had made contact with a lost younger self, and confirmed that my memories of Shanghai had been clear and accurate.

As our plane took off I felt elated, my spirits as bright as the gold Rolexes on the wrists of the new China entrepreneurs who packed the Hong Kong flight. One could go home after all, and somewhere there was always one waiting door that was open and unlocked.

Daily Telegraph
1991

The Pleasures of Reading

As I grow older – I'm now in my early sixties – the books of my childhood seem more and more vivid, while most of those that I read ten or even five years ago are completely forgotten. Not only can I remember, half a century later, my first readings of *Treasure Island* and *Robinson Crusoe*, but I can sense quite clearly my feelings at the time – all the wide-eyed excitement of a seven-year-old, and that curious vulnerability, the fear that my imagination might be overwhelmed by the richness of these invented worlds. Even now, simply thinking about Long John Silver or the waves on Crusoe's island stirs me far more than reading the original text. I suspect that these childhood tales have long since left their pages and taken on a second life inside my head.

By contrast, I can scarcely recall what I read in my thirties and forties. Like many people of my age, my reading of the great works of western literature was over by the time I was twenty. In the three or four years of my late teens I devoured an entire library of classic and modern fiction, from Cervantes to Kafka, Jane Austen to Camus, often at the rate of a novel a day. Trying to find my way through the grey light of post-war, austerity Britain, it was a relief to step into the rich and larger-spirited world of the great novelists. I'm sure that the ground-plan of my imagination was drawn long before I went up to Cambridge in 1949.

In this respect I differed completely from my children, who began to read (I suspect) only after they had left their universities. Like many parents who brought up teenagers in the 1970s, it worried me that my children were more interested in going to pop concerts than in reading *Pride and Prejudice* or *The Brothers Karamazov* – how naive I must have been. But it seemed to me then that they were missing something vital to the growth of their imaginations, the radical re-ordering of the world that only the great novelists can achieve.

I now see that I was completely wrong to worry, and that their sense of priorities was right – the heady, optimistic world of pop culture, which I had never experienced, was the important one for them to explore. Jane Austen and Dostoyevsky could wait until they had gained the maturity in their twenties and thirties to appreciate and understand these writers, far more meaningfully than I could have done at sixteen or seventeen.

In fact I now regret that so much of my reading took place during my late adolescence, long before I had any adult experience of the world, long before I had fallen in love, learned to understand my parents, earned my own living and had time to reflect on the world's ways. It may be that my intense adolescent reading actually handicapped me in the process of growing up – in all senses my own children and their contemporaries strike me as more mature, more reflective and more open to the possibilities of their own talents than I was at their age. I seriously wonder what Kafka and Dostoevsky, Sartre and Camus could have meant to me. That same handicap I see borne today by those people who spend their university years reading English literature – scarcely a degree subject at all and about as rigorous a discipline as music criticism – before gaining the experience to make sense of the exquisite moral dilemmas that their tutors are so devoted to teasing out.

The early childhood reading that I remember so vividly was largely shaped by the city in which I was born and brought up. Shanghai was one of the most polyglot cities in the world, a vast metropolis governed by the British and French but otherwise an American zone of influence. I remember reading children's editions of *Alice in Wonderland*, *Robinson Crusoe* and *Gulliver's Travels* at the same time as American comics and magazines. Alice, the Red Queen and Man Friday crowded a mental landscape also occupied by Superman, Buck Rogers and Flash Gordon. My favourite American comic strip was *Terry and the Pirates*, a wonderful Oriental farrago of Chinese warlords, dragon ladies and antique pagodas that had the added excitement for me of being set in the China where I lived, an impossibly exotic realm for which I searched in vain among Shanghai's Manhattan-style department stores and nightclubs.

I can no longer remember my nursery reading, though my mother, once a schoolteacher, had taught me to read before I entered school at the age of five. There were no cheerful posters or visual aids in those days, apart from a few threatening maps in which the world was drenched red by the British Empire. The headmaster was a ferocious English clergyman whose preferred bible was Kennedy's *Latin Primer*.

From the age of six we were terrorized through two hours of Latin a day, and were only saved from his merciless regime by the Japanese attack on Pearl Harbor (though he would have been pleased to know that, sitting the School Certificate in England after the war, I and a group of boys tried to substitute a Latin oral for the French, which we all detested).

Once home from school, reading played the roles now filled by television, radio, cinema, visits to theme parks and museums (there were none in Shanghai), the local record shop and McDonald's. Left to myself for long periods, I read everything I could find – not only American comics, but *Time*, *Life*, *Saturday Evening Post* and the *New Yorker*. At the same time I read the childhood classics – *Peter Pan*, the *Pooh* books and the genuinely strange *William* series, with their Ionesco-like picture of an oddly empty middle-class England. Without being able to identify exactly what, I knew that something was missing, and in due course received a large shock when, in 1946, I discovered the invisible class who constituted three-quarters of the population but never appeared in the *Chums* and *Boys' Own Paper* annuals.

Later, when I was seven or eight, came *The Arabian Nights*, Hans Andersen and the Grimm brothers, anthologies of Victorian ghost stories and tales of terror, illustrated with threatening, Beardsley-like drawings that projected an inner world as weird as the surrealists'. Looking back on my childhood reading, I'm struck by how frightening most of it was, and I'm glad that my own children were never exposed to those gruesome tales and eerie coloured plates with their airless Pre-Raphaelite gloom, unearthly complexions and haunted infants with almost autistic stares. The overbearing moralistic tone was explicit in Charles Kingsley's *The Water Babies*, a masterpiece in its strange way, but one of the most unpleasant works of fiction I have ever read before or since. The same tone could be heard through so much of children's fiction, as if childhood itself and the child's imagination were maladies to be repressed and punished.

The greatest exception was *Treasure Island*, frightening but in an exhilarating and positive way – I hope that I have been influenced by Stevenson as much as by Conrad and Graham Greene, but I suspect that *The Water Babies* and all those sinister fairy tales played a far more important part in shaping my imagination. Even at the age of ten or eleven I recognized that something strangely morbid hovered over their pages, and that dispersing this chilling miasma might make more sense of the world I was living in than Stevenson's robust yarns.

During the three years that I was interned by the Japanese my reading followed a new set of fracture lines. The 2000 internees carried with them into the camp a substantial library that circulated from cubicle to cubicle, bunk to bunk, and was my first exposure to adult fiction – popular American bestsellers, *Reader's Digest* condensed books, Somerset Maugham and Sinclair Lewis, Steinbeck and H. G. Wells. From all of them, I like to think, I learned the importance of sheer story-telling, a quality which was about to leave the serious English novel, and even now has scarcely returned.

Arriving in England in 1946, I was faced with the incomprehensible strangeness of English life, for which my childhood reading had prepared me in more ways than I realized. Fortunately, I soon discovered that the whole of late nineteenth- and twentieth-century literature lay waiting for me, a vast compendium of human case histories that stemmed from a similar source. In the next four or five years I stopped reading only to go to the cinema. The Hollywood films that kept hope alive – *Citizen Kane*, *Sunset Boulevard*, *The Big Sleep* and *White Heat* – seemed to form a continuum with the novels of Hemingway and Nathanael West, Kafka and Camus. At about the same time I found my way to psychoanalysis and surrealism, and this hot mix together fuelled the short stories that I was already writing and strongly influenced my decision to read medicine.

There were also false starts, and doubtful acquaintances. *Ulysses* overwhelmed me when I read it in the sixth form, and from then on there seemed to be no point in writing anything that didn't follow doggedly on the heels of Joyce's masterpiece. It was certainly the wrong model for me, and may have been partly responsible for my late start as a writer – I was twenty-six when my first short story was published, and thirty-two before I wrote my first novel. But bad company is always the best, and leaves a reserve of memories on which one can draw for ever.

For reasons that I have never understood, once my own professional career was under way I almost stopped reading altogether. For the next twenty years I was still digesting the extraordinary body of fiction and non-fiction that I had read at school and at Cambridge. From the 1950s and 1960s I remember *The White Goddess* by Robert Graves, Genet's *Our Lady of the Flowers*, Durrell's *Justine* and Dali's *Secret Life*, then Heller's *Catch-22* and, above all, the novels of William Burroughs – *Naked Lunch* restored my faith in the novel at a time, the heyday of

C. P. Snow, Anthony Powell and Kingsley Amis, when it had begun to flag.

Since then I've continued on my magpie way, and in the last ten years have found that I read more and more, in particular the nineteenth- and twentieth-century classics that I speed-read in my teens. Most of them are totally different from the books I remember. I have always been a voracious reader of what I call invisible literatures – scientific journals, technical manuals, pharmaceutical company brochures, think-tank internal documents, PR company position papers – part of that universe of published material to which most literate people have scarcely any access but which provides the most potent compost for the imagination. I never read my own fiction.

In compiling my list of ten favourite books I have selected not those that I think are literature's masterpieces, but simply those that I have read most frequently in the past five years. I strongly recommend Patrick Trevor-Roper's *The World Through Blunted Sight* to anyone interested in the influence of the eye's physiology on the work of poets and painters. *The Black Box* consists of cockpit voice-recorder transcripts (not all involving fatal crashes), and is a remarkable tribute to the courage and stoicism of professional flight crews. My copy of the Los Angeles *Yellow Pages* I stole from the Beverly Hilton Hotel three years ago; it has been a fund of extraordinary material, as surrealist in its way as Dali's autobiography.

My favourite books:

The Day of the Locust, Nathanael West; *Collected Short Stories*, Ernest Hemingway; *The Rime of the Ancient Mariner*, Samuel Taylor Coleridge; *The Annotated Alice*, ed. Martin Gardner; *The World Through Blunted Sight*, Patrick Trevor-Roper; *Naked Lunch*, William Burroughs; *The Black Box*, ed. Malcolm MacPherson; Los Angeles *Yellow Pages*; *America*, Jean Baudrillard; *The Secret Life of Salvador Dali*, by Dali.

from The Pleasure of Reading, edited by Antonia Fraser
1992

Shepperton Past and Present

Shepperton, a Thames-side town fifteen miles to the west of London, has improved immensely during the thirty-five years I have lived here. When I arrived in 1960 it was a bricky enclave of pre-war houses and bungalows, a few pubs clustered around a Norman church and a manor house marking the spot where Caesar had crossed the Thames. Lines of poplars marched across the open fields towards Woking and Guildford, and the spirit of Stanley Spencer's nearby Cookham seemed to preside over the splash meadows and bosky walks.

Sheltering from all this in the comforting shadow of the film studios, the one element of modernity in the entire terrain, I felt as if I was being forced to take part in a rural pageant that had strayed from the travel-poster world of Mrs Miniver. Now everything has changed for the better. In the late 1960s the twentieth century at last arrived and began to transform the Thames Valley into a pleasing replica of Los Angeles, with all the ambiguous but heady charms of alienation and anonymity. A forest of TV aerials blotted out the poplars and church spires. Multi-storey car parks rose like the megaliths of a future Stonehenge, along with a landscape of dual carriageways and overpasses that eased and cosseted its true heir, the motor car.

Shepperton, like most Thames Valley towns, is now a suburb not of London but of London Airport, and one can see the influence of Heathrow in the office buildings that resemble control towers and the huge shopping malls whose floors remind the visitor of a terminal concourse. In the 1970s the take-over was complete with the arrival of the M3, a motion-sculpture of concrete that races past Shepperton like an immense runway.

For me, this inter-urban landscape of marinas, research labs, hypermarkets and industrial parks represents the most hopeful face of Britain at the end of the century. The countryside as we used to know it, apart from the National Trust's colour-coordinated nature trails, is now little more than an agribusiness by-product. We live in the TV suburbs, among the video shops, take-aways and police speed-check cameras, and might as well make the most of them, since there is nowhere else to go.

Sadly the architecture is relentlessly post-modern and the pitched roof rules, but this may be a passing phase. Whenever I drive to London I pass Michael Manser's superb Heathrow Hilton, part space-age hangar and part iceberg, the most exhilarating building in the British Isles today and, I hope, a model of what the Thames Valley will one day become.

Guardian
1994

First Impressions of London

My image of London was formed during my Shanghai childhood in the 1930s as I listened to my parents' generation talk nostalgically of West End shows, the bright lights of Piccadilly, Noël Coward and Gertie Lawrence, reinforced by a Peter Pan and Christopher Robin image of a London that consisted entirely of Knightsbridge and Kensington, where 1 per cent of the population was working-class and everyone else was a barrister or stockbroker. When I actually arrived in 1946 I found a London that looked like Bucharest with a hangover – heaps of rubble, an exhausted ferret-like people defeated by war and still deluded by Churchillian rhetoric, hobbling around a wasteland of poverty, ration books and grotesque social division.

To understand London now one has to grasp the fact that in this city, as nowhere else in the world, World War II is still going on. The spivs are running delis and restaurants, and an occupying army of international bankers and platinum-card tourists has taken the place of the American servicemen. The people are stoical and underpaid, with a lower standard of living and tackier services than in any comparable western capital. The weary camaraderie of the Blitz holds everything together. Bombs should fall tonight but probably won't, but one senses that people would welcome them.

How to improve London? Launch a crash programme to fill the city with pirate TV stations, nightclubs, brothels and porn parlours. London needs to become as decadent as Weimar Berlin. Instead, it is merely a decadent Bournemouth.

Time Out
1993

7 SCIENCE FICTION

Inner Space, Early Manifestos,
and the Billion Year Spree . . .

New Means Worse

The Golden Age of Science Fiction
edited by Kingsley Amis

Kingsley Amis's stormy affair with science fiction becomes more and more perplexing. In 1960, *New Maps of Hell* was the most important critical work on s-f that had yet been published, and to a large extent still remains so. Amis threw open the gates of the ghetto, and ushered in a new audience which he almost singlehandedly recruited from intelligent readers of general fiction who until then had considered science fiction on a par with horror comics and pulp westerns.

What marked *New Maps of Hell*, like Amis's reviews of the time and the considerable influence he brought to bear on publishers and literary editors alike, were his generosity and enthusiasm. Sadly, though, this was soon to change. By the mid-1960s, those of us active in science fiction began to hear the first growls of disapproval, saw ourselves glared at across the conference room, felt our kidneys punched in a jocular but unmistakably menacing way.

For the past fifteen years, in a stream of reviews, articles and interviews, Amis has vented an increasingly bilious contempt for almost everything science fiction has produced. As he writes in his introduction to this new anthology: 'Science fiction has come from Chaucer to *Finnegans Wake* in less than fifty years ... now you can take it anywhere, and it is not worth taking.' Yet Amis still returns again and again to spit into the poisoned well.

What have we done to deserve his hostility? To some extent Amis's distaste for science fiction can be put down to simple pique. Sharp observer though he was of 1940s and 1950s s-f, his prediction in *New Maps of Hell* that science fiction would become primarily a satirical and sociological medium proved totally wrong. In fact, American s-f veered away into interplanetary fantasy (Le Guin, Zelazny, Delany), while the British writers began to explore the psychological realm of inner space.

Almost the only writer to turn to sociological satire was Amis himself, in *The Alteration*, and *Russian Hide-and-Seek*. Bearing in mind the rather modest talent for s-f that Amis displayed in those works, and his restless genre-hopping, perhaps his dissatisfaction is secretly, dare I say it, with . . . ?

Whatever the root cause, Amis's contempt for post-1960 science fiction seems bound up with his growing hatred of almost everything else that has happened in the world since then. Deriding the s-f New Wave, he refers to its links with the 'Sixties scene, along with pop music, hippie clothes and hairdos, pornography, reefers.' He tells us that the writers were visited by 'restlessness and self-dissatisfaction, by the conscious quest for maturity and novelty, by the marsh-light of experimentalism.'

Worse horrors waited in the wings. 'In came shock tactics, tricks with typography, one-line chapters, strained metaphors, obscurities, obscenities, drugs, oriental religions and left-wing politics.' Good heavens, I remember now, those hairdos, that music, those oriental religions . . .

The perpetrators of all this are whipped unmercifully. Moorcock's fiction 'gives rise to little more than incurious bewilderment'. Aldiss, in *Barefoot in the Head*, 'interlards an adventure story with stylistic oddities, bits of freak talk, poems, some of them "concrete"'. As for Ballard, on whom no verdict can be harsh enough: 'Solipsistic . . . mystification and outrage . . . physical disgust . . . stories with chapters sub-divided into numbered paragraphs [not true] . . . has never been in the genre at all.'

The readers are equally despised and patronized: 'My remarks on the readership of the genre refer of course to its higher levels; the average is probably pretty low, especially today.'

To read this long-threatened postscript to *New Maps of Hell* is an unsettling experience. Apart from his sour tone, Amis is so ill-informed about the present state of science fiction, and seems to imagine that it is dominated by would-be intellectuals imitating Robbe-Grillet and Michel Butor.

In fact, science fiction today (certainly in the United States, its main centre of activity) is entering the most commercial phase it has ever known. The New Wave, along with almost all the more intelligent magazines and anthologies, has long since been inundated by a tsunami of planet fiction, sword-and-sorcery sensationalism, and *Star Wars* rip-offs, propelled by a reactionary s-f writers' guild closely interlocked with the New York publishers.

What science fiction needs now is a clear, hard and positive voice like that of the Kingsley Amis of 1960. The accurate judgments he made then are evident in his choice of 1950s s-f in *The Golden Age of Science*

Fiction, classics such as Pohl's 'The Tunnel under the World', Arthur C. Clarke's 'The Nine Billion Names of God', and H. Beam Piper's 'He Walked Around the Horses', a brilliant tale of a Napoleonic disappearance, told in the form of – what's this? – chapters subdivided into numbered paragraphs. Kingsley . . . !

Guardian
1981

Back to the Heady Future

The Encyclopedia of Science Fiction
edited by John Clute and Peter Nicholls

Does the future still have a future? As we move closer to the year 2000, which looms in front of us like a forbidding planet, we might expect all manner of millenarian fears to invade our lives. Surprisingly, we appear to have turned our backs on the future, and tend to gaze nostalgically upon a re-invented past that most of us never managed to enjoy the first time around. If anything, there appear to be fewer millenarian cults at present than there were twenty years ago in the heyday of the Moonies and the Maharishi. Perhaps our own fin-de-siècle decadence takes the form, not of libertarian excess, but of the kind of over-the-top puritanism that we see in political correctness and the assorted moral certainties of physical fitness fanatics, New Agers and animal-rights activists.

All the same, I miss the large dreams, the heady, transcendental fantasies that fill the *Encyclopedia of Science Fiction* and have been the stuff of science fiction since Mary Shelley penned *Frankenstein* nearly 200 years ago. It may be that we have already dreamed our dream of the future, and have woken with a start into a world of motorways, shopping malls and airport concourses which lie around us like the first instalment of a future that has forgotten to materialize.

Did the future arrive too soon, some time around the mid-century, the greatest era of modern science fiction? It has always struck me as remarkable that one of the twentieth century's greatest achievements, Neil Armstrong's landing on the Moon, a triumph of courage and technology, should have had virtually no influence on the world at large. The great record-breaking attempts of the 1920s and 1930s generated an endless spin-off in architecture, fashion and design. I can remember my own childhood, when even static objects like teapots were streamlined, and much of the furniture and kitchen equipment around me seemed to be forever moving past at 100 m.p.h.

Neil Armstrong may well be the only human being of our time to be remembered 50,000 years from now, but to us his achievement means almost nothing. There are no teapots shaped like an Apollo spacecraft. Chromium, the most futuristic of all materials, is disapproved of by the conservationist lobby, and everything is dominated by matt black and the Mercedes look, at once aggressive and paranoid, like German medieval armour.

One reason why the Apollo moon-landings failed to touch our imaginations is that science fiction got there first, just as it has anticipated so much of our lives, effectively taking all the fun and surprise out of existence. Fifty years ago the Hollywood film convincingly brought to life the s-f writer's visions of the future. When *Star Wars* appeared in 1977, the technology of film was so advanced that it could even show an advanced technology in decline, and cinema screens were filled with rusty spaceships like old tramp steamers and futuristic cities that resembled some forgotten World's Fair left out too long in the rain. President Mitterrand's grandiose architectural schemes, like the Défense complex in Paris, may be magnificent at first sight but are curiously unconvincing in their hold on time, since we have already anticipated their decay into the Pyramids of the future, a knack that science fiction has taught us.

Turning the pages of this remarkable encyclopedia, one has the sense that science fiction has foreseen every future that the human race can conceivably have in store for itself. Dystopias move past like sinister battleships in a menacing review. Time paradoxes pull inside out the sock of everyday reality. The furthest future is colonized, with mankind abandoning its biological past and assuming the form, first, of hyper-intelligent computers and then, finally, of electromagnetic radiation, giving birth to the stars and the planets in an act of generous play. Dreams of virtual reality dismantle our most deeply held beliefs in the difference between the real and the illusory.

All this is the stuff of popular culture, and science fiction is the folk literature of the twentieth century, with the folk tale's hot line to the unconscious. As mandarin culture gradually atrophies, and the serious novel shrinks towards the role now played by poetry, the popularity of science fiction continues to grow, exerting a huge influence on the imagery of advertising, film and television, on pop videos, paperback covers and record sleeves. One can almost make the case that science fiction, far from being a disreputable minor genre, in fact constitutes the strongest literary tradition of the twentieth century, and may well be its authentic literature. Within its pages, as in our lives, archaic myth and scientific apocalypse collide and fuse. However naively, it has tried to respond to the most significant events of our time – the threat of nuclear war, over-population, the computer revolution, the possibilities and abuses of medical science, the ecological dangers to our planet, the consumer society as benign tyranny – topics that haunt our minds but are scarcely considered by the mainstream novel. If few great names stand out in science fiction, this reflects its collaborative nature, just as no great names stand out in the design of the Boeing 747 or, for that matter, Chartres Cathedral.

In recent years more and more mainstream novelists have been attracted to science fiction – Anthony Burgess, Doris Lessing, Kingsley Amis, Angela Carter, P. D. James – drawn by its immense vitality and vocabulary of ideas. It may be that their arrival is the kiss of death that marks the end of modern science fiction, or its transformation into a new form that will carry it into the next millennium.

All these questions are covered in the thoughtful essays found in this encyclopedia. A curious aspect of science fiction is that a literature devoted to the future should now have accumulated an immense past of its own. There are countless societies and academic institutes devoted to the history of science fiction, cataloguing every obscure detail of its authors' lives. But I was pleased to read that longevity is a prominent characteristic of both science fiction and its writers. The books remain in print, and their authors, by and large, live to an advanced age. I never for a moment believed anything else.

Daily Telegraph
1993

Which Way to Inner Space?

One unfortunate by-product of the Russian-American space race is likely to be an even closer identification, in the mind of the general public, of science fiction with the rocket ships and ray guns of Buck Rogers. If science fiction ever had a chance of escaping this identification – from which most of its present ills derive – that chance will soon be gone, and the successful landing of a manned vehicle on the Moon will fix this image conclusively. Instead of greeting the appearance of the space-suited hero with a deep groan, most general readers will be disappointed if the standard paraphernalia of robot brains and hyper-drives is *not* present, just as most cinema-goers are bored stiff if a western doesn't contain at least one major gun-battle. A few westerns without guns have been attempted, but they seem to turn into dog and timberland stories, and as a reader of science fiction one of my fears is that unless the medium drastically reinvigorates itself in the near future the serious fringe material, at present its only justification, will be relegated to the same limbo occupied by other withering literary forms such as the ghost and detective stories.

There are several reasons why I believe space fiction can no longer provide the main wellspring of ideas for s-f. Firstly, the bulk of it is invariably juvenile, though this is not entirely the fault of the writers. Mort Sahl has referred to the missile-testing site at Cape Canaveral as 'Disneyland East', and like it or not this sums up the attitude of most people towards science fiction, and underlines the narrow imaginative limits imposed by the background of rocket ships and planet-hopping.

A poet such as Ray Bradbury can accept the current magazine conventions and transform even so hackneyed a subject as Mars into an enthralling private world, but science fiction can't rely for its survival on the continued emergence of writers of Bradbury's calibre. The degree of interest inherent in the rocket and planet story – with its confined

physical and psychological dimensions and its limited human relationships – is so slight as to make a self-sufficient fictional form based on
it almost impossible. If anything, however, the success of the manned
satellites will only tend to establish the limited psychological experiences
of their crews – on the whole accurately anticipated, though uninten-
tionally, by s-f writers – as the model of those to be found in science
fiction.

Visually, of course, nothing can equal space fiction for its vast perspectives and cold beauty, as any s-f film or comic-strip demonstrates, but
a literary form requires more complex ideas to sustain it. The spaceship
simply doesn't provide these. (Curiously enough, in the light of the
present roster of astronauts, the one authentic element in old-style space
opera is its wooden, one-dimensional dialogue. But if one can't
altogether blame Commander Shepard for his 'Boy, what a ride,' Major
Titov's dreamless sleep after the first night in space was the biggest
let-down since the fall of Icarus – how many s-f writers must wish they
had been writing his script!)

But my real objection to the central role now occupied by the space
story is that its appeal is too narrow. Unlike the western, science fiction
can't rely for its existence upon the casual intermittent pleasure it may
give to a wide non-specialist audience if it is to hold its ground and
continue to develop. As with most specialized media, it needs a faithful
and discriminating audience who will go to it for specific pleasures,
similar to the audience for abstract painting or serial music. The old-
guard space opera fans, although they probably form the solid backbone
of present s-f readership, won't be able to keep the medium alive on
their own. Like most purists, they prefer their diet unchanged, and
unless s-f evolves, sooner or later other media are going to step in and
take away its main distinction, the right to be the shop window of
tomorrow.

Too often recently, when I've wanted to stimulate my imagination,
I've found myself turning to music or painting rather than to science
fiction, and surely this is the chief thing wrong with it at present. To
attract a critical readership science fiction needs to alter completely its
present content and approach. Magazine s-f was born in the 1930s and
like the pseudo-streamlined architecture of the thirties, it is beginning
to look old-fashioned to the general reader. It's not simply that time
travel, psionics and teleporting (which have nothing to do with science
anyway and are so breath-taking in their implications that they require
genius to do them justice) date science fiction. The general reader is

intelligent enough to realize that the majority of the stories are based on the most minor variations on these themes, rather than on any fresh imaginative leaps.

Historically, this type of virtuosity is a sure sign of decline, and it may well be that the real role science fiction has to play is that of a minor eclectic pastime, its few magazines sustained by opportunist editorial swerves after the latest popular-science fad.

Rejecting this view, however, and believing that s-f has a continuing and expanding role as an imaginative interpreter of the future, how can one find a new wellspring of ideas? First, I think science fiction should turn its back on space, on interstellar travel, extraterrestrial life forms, galactic wars and the overlap of these ideas that spreads across the margins of nine-tenths of magazine s-f. Great writer though he was, H. G. Wells has had a disastrous influence on the subsequent course of science fiction. Not only did he provide it with a repertory of ideas that have virtually monopolized the medium for the last fifty years, but he established the conventions of its style and form, with its simple plots, journalistic narrative, and standard range of situation and character. It is these, whether they realize it or not, that s-f readers are so bored with now, and which are beginning to look increasingly outdated by comparison with the developments in other literary fields.

I've often wondered why s-f shows so little of the experimental enthusiasm which has characterized painting, music and the cinema during the last four or five decades, particularly as these have become wholeheartedly speculative, more and more concerned with the creation of new states of mind, constructing fresh symbols and languages where the old cease to be valid. Similarly, I think science fiction must jettison its present narrative forms and plots. Most of these are far too explicit to express any subtle interplay of character and theme. Devices such as time travel and telepathy, for example, save the writer the trouble of describing the interrelationships of time and space indirectly. And by a curious paradox they prevent him from using his imagination at all, giving him very little true freedom of movement within the narrow limits set by the device.

The biggest developments of the immediate future will take place, not on the Moon or Mars, but on Earth, and it is *inner* space, not outer, that needs to be explored. The only truly alien planet is Earth. In the past the scientific bias of s-f has been towards the physical sciences – rocketry, electronics, cybernetics – and the emphasis should switch to the biological sciences. Accuracy, that last refuge of the unimaginative, doesn't matter a hoot. What we need is not science fact but more science fiction, and the introduction of so-called science fact articles is merely an attempt to dress up the old Buck Rogers material in more respectable garb.

More precisely, I'd like to see s-f becoming abstract and 'cool', inventing fresh situations and contexts that illustrate its theme obliquely. For example, instead of treating time like a sort of glorified scenic railway, I'd like to see it used for what it is, one of the perspectives of the personality, and the elaboration of concepts such as the time zone, deep time and archaeopsychic time. I'd like to see more psycho-literary ideas, more meta-biological and meta-chemical concepts, private time-systems, synthetic psychologies and space-times, more of the sombre half-worlds one glimpses in the paintings of schizophrenics, all in all a complete speculative poetry and fantasy of science.

I firmly believe that only science fiction is fully equipped to become the literature of tomorrow, and that it is the only medium with an adequate vocabulary of ideas and situations. By and large, the standards it sets for itself are higher than those of any other specialist literary genre, and from now on, I think, most of the hard work will fall, not on the writer and editor, but on the readers. The onus is on them to accept a more oblique narrative style, understated themes, private symbols and vocabularies. The first true s-f story, and one I intend to write myself if no one else will, is about a man with amnesia lying on a beach and looking at a rusty bicycle wheel, trying to work out the absolute essence of the relationship between them. If this sounds off-beat and abstract, so much the better, for science fiction could use a big dose of the experimental; and if it sounds boring, well at least it will be a new kind of boredom.

As a final text, I'm reminded of the diving suit in which Salvador Dali delivered a lecture some years ago in London. The workman sent along to supervise the suit asked how deep Dali proposed to descend, and with a flourish the maestro exclaimed: 'To the Unconscious!' to which the workman replied sagely: 'I'm afraid we don't go down that deep.' Five minutes later, sure enough, Dali nearly suffocated inside the helmet.

It is that *inner* space-suit which is still needed, and it is up to science fiction to build it!

New Worlds
1962

Time, Memory and Inner Space

How far do the landscapes of one's childhood, as much as its emotional experiences, provide an inescapable background to all one's imaginative writing? Certainly my own earliest memories are of Shanghai during the annual long summer of floods, when the streets of the city were two or three feet deep in brown silt-laden water, and where the surrounding countryside, in the centre of the flood-table of the Yangtse, was an almost continuous mirror of drowned paddy fields and irrigation canals stirring sluggishly in the hot sunlight. On reflection it seems to me that the image of an immense half-submerged city overgrown by tropical vegetation, which forms the centrepiece of *The Drowned World*, is in some way a fusion of my childhood memories of Shanghai and those of my last ten years in London.

One of the subjects of the novel is the journey of return made by the principal characters from the twentieth century back into the paradisal sun-filled world of a second Triassic age, and their gradually mounting awareness of the ambivalent motives propelling them into the emerging past. They realize that the uterine sea around them, the dark womb of the ocean mother, is as much the graveyard of their own individuality as it is the source of their lives, and perhaps their fears reflect my own uneasiness in re-enacting the experiences of childhood and attempting to explore such dangerous ground.

Among the characteristic fauna of the Triassic age were the crocodiles and alligators, amphibian creatures at home in both the aquatic and terrestrial worlds, who symbolize for the hero of the novel the submerged dangers of his quest. Even now I can vividly remember the enormous ancient alligator housed in a concrete pit half-filled with cigarette packets and ice-cream cartons in the reptile house at the Shanghai zoo, who seemed to have been jerked forward reluctantly so many tens of millions of years into the twentieth century.

In many respects this fusion of past and present experiences, and of such disparate elements as the modern office buildings of central London and an alligator in a Chinese zoo, resembles the mechanisms by which dreams are constructed, and perhaps the great value of fantasy as a literary form is its ability to bring together apparently unconnected and dissimilar ideas. To a large extent all fantasy serves this purpose, but I believe that speculative fantasy, as I prefer to call the more serious fringe of science fiction, is an especially potent method of using one's imagination to construct a paradoxical universe where dream and reality become fused together, each retaining its own distinctive quality and yet in some way assuming the role of its opposite, and where by an undeniable logic black simultaneously becomes white.

Without in any way suggesting that the act of writing is a form of creative self-analysis, I feel that the writer of fantasy has a marked tendency to select images and ideas which directly reflect the internal landscapes of his mind, and the reader of fantasy must interpret them on this level, distinguishing between the manifest content, which may seen obscure, meaningless or nightmarish, and the latent content, the private vocabulary of symbols drawn by the narrative from the writer's mind. The dream worlds invented by the writer of fantasy are external equivalents of the inner world of the psyche, and because these symbols take their impetus from the most formative and confused periods of our lives they are often time-sculptures of terrifying ambiguity.

This zone I think of as 'inner space', the internal landscape of today that is a transmuted image of the past, and one of the most fruitful areas for the imaginative writer. It is particularly rich in visual symbols, and I feel that this type of speculative fantasy plays a role very similar to that of surrealism in the graphic arts. The painters Chirico, Dali and Max Ernst, among others, are in a sense the iconographers of inner space. Dali, regrettably, is now in total critical eclipse, but his paintings, with their soft watches and minatory luminous beaches, are of almost magical potency, suffused by that curious ambivalence that one can see elsewhere only on the serpentine faces in the paintings of Leonardo.

It is a curious thing that the landscapes of these painters, and of Dali in particular, are often referred to as dream-like, when in fact they bear no resemblance to the vast majority of dreams, which in general take place within confined indoor settings, a cross between Kafka and *Mrs Dale's Diary*, and where fantastic images, such as singing flowers or sonic sculpture, appear as infrequently as they do in reality. This false identification, and the awareness that the landscapes and themes are reflections of some interior reality within our minds, is a pointer to the importance of speculative fantasy in the century of Hiroshima and Cape Canaveral.

The Woman Journalist
1963

The Cosmic Cabaret

Billion Year Spree
Brian Aldiss

Brian Aldiss's exuberant title gives a fair summary of all the excitements to be found in this book – I thoroughly enjoyed it, and read it from cover to cover without a pause, a rare event for any reader these days, and a reflection of the tremendous built-in power of imaginative fiction. Even in summary (or perhaps especially in summary), these accounts of fabulous voyages, extraordinary inventions, cautionary tales and utopian satires leap off the page. *Billion Year Spree* is vividly written, witty, encyclopaedic in its scope, far ranging in its ideas, tolerant of fools (an over-abundant species in this branch of fiction), and above all affectionate towards the strange company of knaves and naives, hacks and geniuses who move through its pages like a troupe of over-excited travelling players, conning anyone they can with their unlimited blarney. The highest compliment I can pay this book is to say that hardly a single sane man appears throughout it.

Another of the great pleasures it gave me was the realization of just how little of this fiction I had read – if for no other reason, *Billion Year Spree* is guaranteed a steady sale to all those people who for some reason need to read the absolute minimum of Rider Haggard and Edgar Rice Burroughs, Asimov and Tolkien, and will now be able to breathe an enormous sigh of relief as they scan these brief – and, I'm convinced, accurate – summaries.

At the same time, a slight sense of unease came over me as I read the last chapters of this book. (These sections, where Aldiss brings the history of science fiction up to the present day, are a masterpiece of diplomacy – a sociable man, Brian clearly wants to be able to go on attending science fiction conventions here and in the United States without being clubbed over the head by some outraged author's well-aimed Hugo. On reflection, he should have commissioned me to write these last two chapters . . .) What unnerved me was the odd feeling I had of the Academy closing around me, of the plywood partitions of the Modern Literature department being erected around my mind, and around those of all the other writers exercising their talents for fantasy and invention. One of the most inaccurate jibes levelled at the so-called New Wave is that its writers suffered from delusions of literary grandeur, that they took themselves far too seriously. In fact, in my own personal experience, it is the absolute reverse which is true. The most pompous and self-important writers, both here and in the States, are those who are apparently the most 'commercial' and non-literary. It is they who are endlessly lecturing and pontificating, forming writers' societies and bogus foundations, filling the fanzines with their literary pretensions, their absurd awards and other nonsense. By comparison, most of the New Wavers I know spend their time lying around and romancing over a bottle.

Perhaps, however, the tightening embrace of Academe is merely a reflection that modern science fiction has come to an end. Anything that happened five minutes ago is already the centre of a cult, embedded in lucite and put on the display shelf. Modern science fiction (by which I mean the s-f of the thirty-year period 1926 to 1957, from Gernsback's founding of *Amazing* to the first flight of Sputnik I and the beginnings of the short-lived space age) has already become a victim of this nostalgia. Despite the protestations of its most vocal supporters, the obvious fact is that no new writers have emerged to follow on from where, for better or worse, the founders of modern science fiction – van Vogt, Heinlein, Asimov, etc. – began. And this is for the obvious reason that nothing remains to be done. The imaginary universe invented by these writers is self-defined and self-limited; the greatest weakness of this particular science fiction is that its writers have been able to define it so exactly. Unfortunately, here, unlike the western, the clock runs against it. The ever-accelerating changes brought about by science and technology have not merely transformed our lives, but made inevitable the emergence of a *new* science fiction that will more accurately and more imaginatively interpret these changes to us. There is, in fact, the curious paradox that classical science fiction (that is, pre-Gernsback) has far more relevance to us, and in a sense is far more modern than the science fiction of the 1940s and 1950s, in that it is no longer tied to a period that by its recent passing seems that much the more out-of-date. H. G. Wells's *War of the Worlds*, *Moreau* and *Time Machine* have shaken off the patina of the merely contemporary; by comparison Campbell's *Astounding* and *Analog*, with their third-rate 1950s jargonizing, their blue-collar intellectual clap-trap, are absolutely of the America of the

Reader's Digest, Betty Grable, and popular newspaper sensations such as Dianetics.

A large part of the problem faced by the protagonists of modern American science fiction is the unfortunate fact that America herself has slammed on the brakes. By this I mean that the enormous moral, psychological and imaginative reserves possessed by the United States in the 1930s, 1940s and 1950s lay in that huge system of excitements and possibilities enshrined in the notion of the 'future'. The future would be better, and America had a monopoly of the stuff. All this has now gone into reverse. The future has now been abandoned as a zone of imaginative excitement, and most of the values of modern America are under severe scrutiny. All this leaves the older generation of American science fiction writers high and dry. Most of them are now too old to change their ways – they have no place to go but forward, and the road is closed.

However, as Aldiss points out in *Billion Year Spree*, these matters are of comparatively local interest. One of the great values of this book is that we can see classical, modern and contemporary science fiction within the larger context of imaginative fiction. Arguments about whether *Gulliver's Travels* and *1984* are science fiction or whether, say, *Brave New World* should be admitted to the club (these three novels virtually designed the premises), fade away when we see the huge sweeps of cautionary and speculative fiction laid out in front of us.

Since its beginnings, roughly speaking, I would say, at the start of the Industrial Revolution (Aldiss fixes on Mary Shelley's *Frankenstein*), science fiction has been distinguished by two features: first, its imaginative response to science and technology; and second, its attempt, now more or less abandoned by the so-called mainstream novel, to place some kind of metaphysical and philosophical framework around man's place in the universe. However crudely (and most of the confusions about the position of science fiction in the literary frame of things would be avoided if it were called by a more accurate title – 'popular science fiction'), science fiction has continued to perform both these roles. As *Billion Year Spree* demonstrates, most of the major imaginative writers of the past 250 years have at some time written science fiction, and it is a tribute to the genre that they needed to do so.

Cypher
1974

Fictions of Every Kind

The Shattered Ring
Lois and Stephen Rose

Everything is becoming science fiction. From the margins of an invisible literature has sprung the intact reality of the twentieth century. What the writers of modern science fiction invent today, you and I will do tomorrow – or, more exactly, in about ten years' time, though the gap is narrowing. Science fiction is the most important fiction that has been written for the last hundred years. The compassion, lucidity and vision of H. G. Wells and his successors, and above all their grasp of the real identity of the twentieth century, dwarf the alienated and introverted fantasies of James Joyce, Eliot and the writers of the Modern Movement. Given its subject matter, its eager acceptance of naivety, optimism and possibility, the importance of science fiction can only increase. I believe that the reading of science fiction should be compulsory. Fortunately, compulsion will not be necessary, as more and more people are reading it voluntarily. Even the worse science fiction is better – using as the yardstick of merit the mere survival of its readers and their imaginations – than the best conventional fiction. The future is a better key to the present than the past.

Above all, science fiction is likely to be the only form of literature which will cross the gap between the dying narrative fiction of the present and the cassette and videotape fictions of the near future. What can Saul Bellow and John Updike do that J. Walter Thompson, the world's largest advertising agency and its greatest producer of fiction, can't do better? At present science fiction is almost the only form of fiction which is thriving, and certainly the only fiction which has any influence on the world around it. The social novel is reaching fewer and fewer readers, for the clear reason that social relationships are no longer as important as the individual's relationship with the technological landscape of the late twentieth century.

In essence, science fiction is a response to science and technology as perceived by the inhabitants of the consumer goods society, and recognizes that the role of the writer today has totally changed – he is now merely one of a huge army of people filling the environment with fictions of every kind. To survive, he must become far more analytic, approaching his subject matter like a scientist or engineer. If he is to produce fiction at all, he must out-imagine everyone else, scream louder, whisper more quietly. For the first time in the history of narrative fiction, it will require more than talent to become a writer.

It is now some fifteen years since the sculptor Eduardo Paolozzi remarked that the science fiction magazines produced in the suburbs of Los Angeles contained far more imagination and meaning than anything he could find in the literary periodicals of the day. Subsequent events have proved Paolozzi's judgement correct. Fortunately, his own imagination has been able to work primarily within the visual arts, where the main tradition for the last century has been the tradition of the new. Within fiction, unhappily, the main tradition for all too long has been the tradition of the old. Like the inmates of some declining institution, increasingly forgotten and ignored, the leading writers and critics count the worn beads of their memories, intoning the names of the dead.

Meanwhile, science fiction, as my agent remarked to me recently, is spreading across the world like a cancer – a benign and tolerant cancer, like the culture of beaches. The time-lag of its acceptance narrows – I estimate it at present to be about ten years. However, as people become more confident, so they will be prepared to accept change, the possibility of a life radically different from their own. Like green stamps given away at the supermarkets of chance and possibility, science fiction becomes the new currency of an ever-expanding future.

The one hazard facing science fiction, the Trojan horse being trundled towards its ghetto – a high-rent area if there ever was one in fiction – is literary criticism. Almost all the criticism of science fiction has been written by benevolent outsiders, who combine zeal with ignorance, like high-minded missionaries viewing the sex-rites of a fertile aboriginal tribe and finding every laudable influence at work except the outstanding length of penis. The depth of penetration of this earnest couple, Lois and Stephen Rose, is that of a pair of practising Christians who see in science fiction an attempt to place a new perspective on 'man, nature, history and ultimate meaning'. What they fail to realize is that science fiction is totally atheistic; those critics in the past who have found any mystical strains at work have been blinded by the camouflage. Science fiction is much more concerned with the significance of the gleam on an automobile instrument panel than on the deity's posterior – if Mother Nature has anything in science fiction, it is VD.

Most critics of science fiction trip into one of two pitfalls – either, like Kingsley Amis in *New Maps of Hell*, they try to ignore altogether the technological trappings and relate s-f to the 'mainstream' of social criticism, anti-utopian fantasies and the like (Amis's main prophecy for science fiction in 1957 and proved wholly wrong), or they attempt to apostrophize science fiction in terms of individual personalities, hopelessly rivalling the far better financed efforts of American and British publishers to sell their fading wares by dressing their minor talents in the great-writer mantle. Science fiction has always been very much a corporate activity, its writers sharing a common pool of ideas, and the yardsticks of individual achievement do not measure the worth of the best writers, Ray Bradbury, Asimov, Bernard Wolfe (*Limbo* 90), and Frederik Pohl. The anonymity of the majority of twentieth-century writers of science fiction is the anonymity of modern technology; no more 'great names' stand out than do in the design of consumer durables – or for that matter of Rheims Cathedral.

Who designed the 1971 Cadillac El Dorado, a complex of visual, organic and psychological clues of infinitely more subtlety and relevance, stemming from a vastly older network of crafts and traditions than, say, the writings of Norman Mailer or the latest Cape miracle? The subject matter of science fiction is the subject matter of everyday life: the gleam on refrigerator cabinets, the contours of a wife's or husband's thighs passing the newsreel images on a colour TV set, the conjunction of musculature and chromium artefact within an automobile interior, the unique postures of passengers on an airport escalator – all in all, close to the world of the Pop painters and sculptors, Paolozzi, Hamilton, Warhol, Wesselmann, Ruscha, among others. The great advantage of science fiction is that it can add one unique ingredient to this hot mix – words. Write!

Books and Bookmen
1971

Cataclysms and Dooms

Visions of world cataclysm constitute one of the most powerful and most mysterious of all the categories of science fiction, and in their classic form predate modern science fiction by thousands of years. In many ways, I believe that science fiction is itself no more than a minor offshoot of the cataclysmic tale. From the deluge in the Babylonian zodiac myth of Gilgamesh to contemporary fantasies of twentieth-century super-science, there has clearly been no limit to our need to devise new means of destroying the world we inhabit. I would guess that from man's first inkling of this planet as a single entity existing independently of himself came the determination to bring about its destruction, part of the same impulse we see in a placid infant who wakes alone in his cot and sets about wrecking his entire nursery.

Psychiatric studies of the fantasies and dream life of the insane show that ideas of world destruction are latent in the unconscious mind. The marvels of twentieth-century science and technology provide an anthology of destructive techniques unrivalled by even the most bizarre religions. As Edward Glover comments in *War, Sadism and Pacifism* (1947), 'Nagasaki destroyed by the magic of science is the nearest man has yet approached to the realisation of dreams that even during the safe immobility of sleep are accustomed to develop into nightmares of anxiety.'

As an author who has produced a substantial number of cataclysmic stories, I take for granted that the planet the writer destroys with such tireless ingenuity is in fact an image of the writer himself. But are these deluges and droughts, whirlwinds and glaciations no more than over-extended metaphors of some kind of suicidal self-hate? Though I am even more suspicious of my own motives than of other people's, I nevertheless think not. On the contrary, I believe that the catastrophe story, whoever may tell it, represents a constructive and positive act by the imagination rather than a negative one, an attempt to confront a patently meaningless universe by challenging it at its own game.

Within the realm of fiction, the writer of the catastrophe story illustrates, in the most extreme and literal way, Conrad's challenge – 'Immerse yourself in the most destructive element – and swim!' Each one of these fantasies represents an arraignment of the finite, an attempt to dismantle the formal structure of time and space which the universe wraps around us at the moment we first achieve consciousness. It is the inflexibility of this huge reductive machine we call reality that provokes infant and madman alike, and in the cataclysm story the science fiction writer joins company with them, using his imagination to describe the infinite alternatives to reality which nature itself has proved incapable of inventing. This celebration of the possibilities of life is at the heart of science fiction.

from The Visual Encyclopaedia of Science Fiction
1977

8 IN GENERAL

Coca-Cola and Walt Disney,
Mein Kampf and the Astronauts . . .

Coca-Colonization

For God, Country and Coca-Cola
Mark Pendergrast

The most famous branded product in the world, Coca-Cola enjoys the distinction of also being the most infamous, at least in the demonology of the left. Henry Ford lent his name to the soulless production lines that made his motor cars, but as far as I know no one has ever accused Hoover or Heinz of wielding the malign geopolitical influence that Marxists and anti-Americans firmly believe has been exercised by Coca-Cola.

How did a carbonated fluid, 99 per cent sweetened water with traces of caffeine and phosphoric acid, ever become one of the principal symbols of twentieth-century America and threaten, some would argue, the cultural identity of entire nations? How, too, did the company actually making the beverage, filling all those hobble-skirted bottles with caramel-coloured fizz, ever come to be taken so seriously, to the point where its functionaries abroad have often enjoyed virtually ambassadorial status, and its cheerful logo has seemed as insidious a force as the combined CIA and KGB?

Mark Pendergrast's *For God, Country and Coca-Cola* is a hilarious account of the origins of the planet's leading soft drink and its mythic place in consumer consciousness. In the headquarters city of Atlanta, Georgia, there is a museum visited by 3000 tourists a day, where the creation of Coca-Cola in 1886, in a humble three-legged kettle, is presented as a miracle equivalent to the Virgin Birth. Its inventor was John Pemberton, a 54-year-old doctor of Scottish origins and a long-suffering morphine addict. As Pendergrast shows, Coca-Cola was far from being a unique beverage. Like many other 'nerve tonics' of its time, it was a patent medicine whose distinct cocaine kick carried its chief appeal, especially to its creator. A now forgotten drink, Vin Mariani, first devised in the 1860s, already sold throughout Europe and the United States, and was a blend of Bordeaux wine and cocaine that carried lip-smacking testimonials from Edison, Zola, Queen Victoria, Buffalo Bill Cody and at least three popes.

Trying to match the success of Vin Mariani, Pemberton first marketed his French Wine Cola, adding an extract of the kola plant that contained a potent alkaloid, caffeine. But his fortified wine never caught on, and for success he turned to a new ingredient dispensed from the soda fountains of America – carbonated water. By 1900 Coca-Cola was already a commercial phenomenon, now controlled by a brilliant entrepreneur named Asa Candler. Public criticism of the drink's cocaine content led to its removal in 1901 but, surprisingly, Coke's popularity never faltered. As the company's shrewder minds realized, people were buying the image as much as the product, and Pendergrast devotes his most amusing chapters to the mind-numbing efforts which the marketing men devoted to selling the world its most refreshing burp.

Coca-Cola's heroic achievements during the Second World War were well rewarded, and its global reach matched that of American power. Few American servicemen were ever much more than an arm's length from the reassuring little bottle, and Mary Churchill, Winston's daughter, even christened a destroyer with a bottle of Coke. The drink sold almost everywhere, and its relentless advertising was a part of everyday consciousness and an emblem of American confidence.

Predictably, the first to protest against what they saw as the hidden cultural agenda were the French communists, who in 1949 talked about the 'Coca-Colonization' of Europe and tried to organize a ban. Even the usually sober *Le Monde* denounced 'the dangers that Coca-Cola represents for the health and civilization of France', and compared the company's advertising with Nazi propaganda – both 'intoxicated' the masses. Sadly for the protesters, too many people actually liked the stuff, a concept that left-wing intellectuals could never grasp. The film director Jean-Luc Godard implicitly accepted the potency of Coca-Cola and the American dream when he referred to the young of the 1960s as 'the children of Marx and Coca-Cola'.

Coke had easily defeated Marxism, but a far more sinister threat now appeared on the horizon – Pepsi. This pepsin-based drink created in 1898 by Caleb Bradham, a North Carolina pharmacist, had never matched Coke's sales, but its market share had steadily increased over the decades. Obsessed with the Pepsi challenge, Coke found itself locked in a global conflict fought to this day. Coke might have its secret formula, but Pepsi had Joan Crawford, the president's widow and a fearsome figurehead. Alone among Americans, Coke executives consider that they lost the Gulf War – to Pepsi. As Stormin' Norman Schwarz-kopf signed the ceasefire a bottle of Diet Pepsi was prominently on display beside him. At the Atlanta headquarters Pepsi was never mentioned by name but only as 'the competition', and to be caught drinking a Pepsi meant instant dismissal. Out of this bunker mentality came the biggest blunder in Coke's history – New Coke, an attempt to see off Pepsi for good, with an advanced formula which blind tastings showed the consumers preferred.

But myths die hard. A vast public clamour demanded the reinstate-ment of Classic Coke. In an appendix Pendergrast lists the ingredients of the ultra-secret '7X' formula, which has never been as secret as the advertising men have pretended. Disappointingly, the formula consists of oils of lemon, orange, nutmeg, cinnamon and coriander. I expected frankincense, gold and myrrh, at the least.

But these constitute the formula of a drink, not a dream, and the dream of Coca-Cola has now fused for ever with our notions of a certain kind of American cheerfulness, not to everyone's taste but hard to resist. Surveys, it seems, show that 'Coke' is the second most recognized word in the world. The first is 'Okay'. The genius of Coca-Cola is that it has made the two mean much the same thing.

Daily Telegraph
1993

The Mouse that Bores?

Walt Disney: Hollywood's Dark Prince
Marc Eliot

'Gee, this will *make* Beethoven!' Walt Disney exclaimed on first seeing the Pastoral Symphony sequence in *Fantasia*. However strange it now seems, this touching faith in the power of his animated films was more than justified during Disney's long reign as king of the cartoons. Apart from Coca-Cola, another modern myth, Walt Disney must be the most famous brandname of the twentieth century, stamped on to the happiest memories of countless childhoods.

All the same, is the Disney magic at last losing its grip on the imagination of the young? Euro Disney, the troubled theme-park near Paris, was described by a disgruntled French critic as a cultural Chernobyl, though perhaps a cultural Stalingrad would be closer to the truth, the battleground where the relentless advance of American popular culture was at last stopped and turned. I suspect that Mickey Mouse and Donald Duck no longer satisfy today's children, whose retinas flicker with the electronic phantoms of the arcade video games. Super Nintendo rules, and the Disney empire now merchandizes nostalgia.

Despite the lovable nature of the creatures in the Disney pantheon, their creator was a darker and more ambiguous figure, as Marc Eliot reveals in his merciless biography. Far from being the world's favourite uncle, Disney was a vicious anti-Semite and hater of communists, who for twenty-five years was a Hollywood spy for J. Edgar Hoover's FBI. Eliot describes Disney's brutal childhood, his obsessive hand-washing and heavy drinking, and his uncertainty about his own parentage. The theme of abandonment that runs through so many Disney films may have been rooted in his sense of his own lost childhood.

Eliot traces Disney's ancestry to Jean-Christophe d'Isigny, named after the village in Normandy, who remained in England after the Norman conquest and anglicized his name. His descendants emigrated to the United States in the nineteenth century, and Walt's father was an unsuccessful carpenter and farmer, a violent and alcoholic man who thrashed and terrorized his son. Fortunately the boy showed an early talent for drawing, and in due course became a successful commercial artist, making animated films of Little Red Riding-Hood and Puss in Boots. A business partner named Ub Iwerks created the famous mouse, but it was Disney's entrepreneurial genius that transformed a few sketches into a star greater than any other in Hollywood.

Paying starvation wages to animators, Disney oversaw production of the first feature-length cartoon films, *Snow White* and *Pinocchio*. By the 1930s he was world famous, meeting the Pope, Mussolini and H. G. Wells. He accepted a special medal from the League of Nations using the voice of Mickey Mouse.

Despite his enormous success, Disney was haunted by a sense of personal failure, suspecting that he was illegitimate and that his real mother was an impoverished immigrant from Mojacar in southern Spain whom his father had met in California during his search for work. Thanks to his friendship with Hoover, teams of FBI agents frequently visited Mojacar in an effort to trace Disney's parentage. But when Disney died at the height of his fame, he was still unsure of his true mother and father – the creator of the world's greatest dreams of childhood who had never really known his own.

Daily Telegraph
1994

A City of Excess

Shanghai
Harriet Sergeant

Shanghai is the lost city of the twentieth century, the Babylon or Nineveh of our age, buried for the past forty years under the dead sand of Chinese communism and only now beginning to re-emerge. The great hotels and banking houses along the Bund, unchanged since the 1930s, rise through the fading twilight of Marxist ideology, temples dedicated to Mammon and the good time, which the new China is already smartening up for business.

It is a curious feature of communist regimes, so devoted to revolutionary change in all things, that the architecture in their charge remains largely unaltered. Baroque palaces and plutocratic hotels are given a change of name but little else. Steven Spielberg, searching for somewhere to stand in for Shanghai in the film *Empire of the Sun*, almost chose the Militant republic of Liverpool – the architecture was in period and there was an endless supply of Marxists, but too few Chinese. I was glad that he decided on the real Shanghai, although a mock-Tudor mansion in Sunningdale, of all places, stood in for my childhood home in the western outskirts of Shanghai – now a near-ruin and the offices of the Shanghai Electronic Industry Information Bureau, a cover, I like to think, for a gambling den or an illicit video-games arcade.

For one of the great cities of the world, Shanghai's history has been remarkably brief. A hundred years ago it was scarcely more than a mosquito-ridden swamp near the mouth of the Yangtse, dismissively conceded by the Manchu rulers to the foreign devils – Britain and the western powers – after the Opium Wars. Eager to buy Chinese silks, porcelain and tea, but unable to trade its opium in return, the East India Company (the Medellin Cartel of its day) had fallen back on that trusty persuader, the British gunboat: in this case an armed paddle-steamer, appropriately named the *Nemesis*.

A few volleys of cannonballs brought the Chinese government to the negotiating table. In 1863 the British and Americans founded the

International Settlement, a collection of godowns and trading houses on the Whangpoo River. Fifty years later Shanghai had become a huge metropolis, a powerhouse of unrestricted venture capitalism and an international touchstone of glamour, decadence and exotic sin.

The 'whore of the Orient', home to warlords and gangsters and sing-song girls, with 400 nightclubs and the longest bar in the world (at the Shanghai Club, now a merchant seaman's hostel), was visited by endless cruise liners and European intellectuals. Noël Coward caught flu at the Cathay Hotel and sketched out *Private Lives*. George Bernard Shaw descended from the *Empress of Britain* long enough to notice that the welcoming banner misspelt his name. Aldous Huxley, writing in 1927, described Shanghai as 'life itself . . . dense, rank, richly clotted . . . nothing more intensely living can be imagined'.

Even Auden and Isherwood turned up on one of their morbid patrols, a sure sign, my parents' generation should have realized, that Shanghai's number was up. Japan, militarized and expansionist, invaded China in 1937, an action aimed as much at the European powers. The invasion led on directly to Pearl Harbor, the first sustained counter-attack by the colonized East against the imperial West.

The vicious fighting in the Chinese districts of Shanghai involved huge naval, army and air forces, and was the first full-scale rehearsal for the Second World War – a single bomb that fell in the Avenue Edward VII killed more than 1000 people, then the largest number of casualties in the history of aerial warfare. We ourselves were forced to evacuate our house when shells from rival Chinese and Japanese batteries began to pass over the roof, a pointed warning that the glory days of Shanghai were over. In 1941, on the day of their attack on Pearl Harbor, the Japanese seized the International Settlement and began to intern the Allied nationals.

For a few years after the liberation in 1945 Shanghai was its old self again, the brightest lightbulb in the Pacific and the last bastion of unchecked entrepreneur capitalism that the world has seen. But in 1949 Mao's army swept down from the north, swarming through the night-clubs, hotels and brothels, and the city passed into history.

Harriet Sergeant paints a vivid portrait of Shanghai in its prime, the capital city of a kingdom called money, the cosmopolitan meeting-ground of Europeans and Americans, of exiled White Russians and Jewish refugees, of terrorists, beggar-kings and millionaires, where Mao's future wife was a star of the Shanghai film studios and the Prince of Wales's future wife, Wallis Simpson, was photographed, so the author claims, wearing nothing but a bathing ring.

The author interviewed a large number of old Shanghai hands of all nationalities, and is particularly good on the British, who faced a special problem of having to adjust their moribund class system, designed to restrict opportunity and initiative, to the unlimited freedom that life in Shanghai offered them, both in work and play. Those Britons who shrugged off the past enjoyed rich and successful lives, while others, unable to summon either the energy or talent, retreated into petty snobbery. Lady Hayter, wife of a British diplomat, described their house as 'just like a dentist's home in Woking', but either things in Woking have changed since the 1930s or it was a paradise of gold crowns and luxurious bridgework.

Of course, Shanghai, both the city in its corrupt glory and the future city that will dwarf Hong Kong and Singapore, poses a unique challenge to the enlightened post-war sensibility. Like Auden and Isherwood, who spent just enough time away from the bathhouses to be appalled by the conditions of child factory-workers (forgetting that but for Shanghai their peasant parents would probably have killed the girls and condemned the boys to a lifetime of stoop labour), the high-minded reader of Harriet Sergeant's book will probably see nothing but the squalor and poverty, the lack of hygiene and crèche facilities and the complete absence of the social security safety net – all in all a city of dreadful night that can only inspire a refined shudder.

But for those factory youngsters, assured at least of their meals and place to sleep, there were the streets of Shanghai in its heyday, an empire of excess, possibility and ambition. I can't wait for it to return.

Daily Telegraph
1991

Alphabets of Unreason

Mein Kampf
Adolf Hitler

The psychopath never dates. Hitler's contemporaries – Baldwin, Chamberlain, Herbert Hoover – seem pathetically fusty figures, with their frock coats and wing collars, closer to the world of Edison, Carnegie and the hansom cab than to the first fully evolved modern societies over which they presided, areas of national consciousness formed by mass-produced newspapers and consumer goods, advertising and telecommunications. By comparison Hitler is completely up to date, and would be equally at home in the sixties (and probably even more so in the seventies) as in the twenties. The whole apparatus of the Nazi superstate, its nightmare uniforms and propaganda, seems weirdly turned-on, providing just that element of manifest insanity to which we all respond in the H-bomb or Vietnam – perhaps one reason why the American and Russian space programmes have failed to catch our imaginations is that this quality of explicit psychopathology is missing.

Certainly, Nazi society seems strangely prophetic of our own – the same maximizing of violence and sensation, the same alphabets of unreason and the fictionalizing of experience. Goebbels in his diaries remarks that he and the Nazi leaders had merely done in the realm of reality what Dostoevsky had done in fiction. Interestingly, both Goebbels and Mussolini had written novels, in the days before they were able to get to grips with their real subject matter – one wonders if they would have bothered now, with the fiction waiting to be manipulated all around them.

Hitler's 'novel', *Mein Kampf*, was written in 1924, nearly a decade before he came to power, but is a remarkably accurate prospectus of his intentions, not so much in terms of finite political and social aims as of the precise psychology he intended to impose on the German people and its European vassals. For this reason alone it is one of the most important books of the twentieth century, and well worth reprinting, despite the grisly pleasures its anti-Semitic ravings will give to the present generation of racists.

How far does Hitler the man come through the pages of this book? In the newsreels Hitler tends to appear in two roles – one, the demagogic orator, ranting away in a state apparently close to neurotic hysteria, and two, a benevolent and slightly eccentric *kapellmeister* sentimentally reviewing his SS bodyguard, or beaming down at a picked chorus of blond-haired German infants. Both these strands are present in *Mein Kampf* – the hectoring, rhetorical style, shaking with hate and violence, interspersed with passages of deep sentimentality as the author rhapsodizes to himself about the mystical beauty of the German landscape and its noble, simple-hearted peoples.

Apart from its autobiographical sections, the discovery by a small Austrian boy of his 'Germanism', *Mein Kampf* contains three principal elements, the foundation stones, walls and pediment of a remarkably strong paranoid structure. First, there are Hitler's views on history and race, a quasi-biological system which underpins the whole basis of his political thought and explains almost every action he ever committed. Second, there are his views on the strict practicalities of politics and the seizure of power, methods of political organization and propaganda. Third, there are his views on the political future of the united Germanies, its expansionist foreign policy and general attitude to the world around it.

The overall tone of *Mein Kampf* can be seen from Hitler's original title for the testament: *A Four and a Half Years' Struggle Against Lies, Stupidity and Cowardice: A Reckoning with the Destroyers of the Nazi Party Movement*. It was the publisher, Max Amann, who suggested the shorter and far less revealing *Mein Kampf*, and what a sigh he must have breathed when Hitler agreed. Hitler's own title would have been far too much of a giveaway, reminding the readers of the real sources of Hitler's anti-Semitic and racialist notions.

Reading Hitler's paranoid rantings against the Jews, one is constantly struck by the biological rather than political basis of his entire thought and personality. His revulsion against the Jews was physical, like his reaction against any peoples, such as the Slavs and Negroes, whose physique, posture, morphology and pigmentation alerted some screaming switchboard of insecurity within his own mind. What is interesting is the language in which he chose to describe those obsessions – primarily faecal, one assumes, from his endless preoccupation with 'cleanliness'. Rather than use economic, social or political arguments against the Jews,

Hitler concentrated almost solely on this inflated biological rhetoric. By dispensing with any need to rationalize his prejudices, he was able to tap an area of far deeper unease and uncertainty, and one moreover which his followers would never care to expose too fully to the light of day. In the unanswerable logic of psychopathology, the Jews became the scapegoats for all the terrors of toilet-training and weaning. The constant repetition of the words 'filth', 'vileness', 'abscess', 'hostile', 'shudder', endlessly reinforce these long-repressed feelings of guilt and desire.

In his preface, the translator of *Mein Kampf* describes it as written in the style of a self-educated modern South German with a talent for oratory. In this respect Hitler was one of the rightful inheritors of the twentieth century – the epitome of the half-educated man. Wandering about the streets of Vienna shortly before the First World War, his head full of vague artistic yearnings and clap-trap picked up from popular magazines, whom does he most closely resemble? Above all, Leopold Bloom, his ostensible arch-enemy, wandering around Joyce's Dublin at about the same time, his head filled with the same clap-trap and the same yearnings. Both are the children of the reference library and the self-improvement manual, of mass newspapers creating a new vocabulary of violence and sensation. Hitler was the half-educated psychopath inheriting the lavish communications systems of the twentieth century. Forty years after his first abortive seizure of power he was followed by another unhappy misfit, Lee Harvey Oswald, in whose Historic Diary we see the same attempt by the half-educated to grapple with the information overflow that threatened to drown him.

New Worlds
1969

The Future of the Future

One of the most surprising but barely noticed events of the period since the Second World War has been the life and death of the space age. Almost twenty years ago to the day, 4 October 1957, I switched on the BBC news and heard for the first time the radio call-sign of Sputnik 1 as it circled the earth above our heads. Its urgent tocsin seemed to warn us of the arrival of a new epoch. As a novice science fiction writer, I listened to this harbinger of the space age with strong misgivings – already I was certain, though without the slightest evidence, that the future of science fiction, and for that matter of popular consciousness in general, lay not in outer space but in what I had already christened 'inner space', in a world increasingly about to be remade by the mind.

None the less, I fully expected that the impact of the space age would be immediate and all-pervasive – from fashion to industrial design, from the architecture of airports and department stores to the ways in which we furnished our homes. I took for granted that the spin-off of the US and Russian space programmes would transform everything in our lives and produce an extrovert society as restlessly curious about the external world as Renaissance Europe.

In fact, nothing remotely like this occurred. Public interest in the space flights of the 1960s was rarely more than lukewarm (think, by contrast, of our powerful emotional involvement with the death of President Kennedy and the Vietnam war), and the effects on everyday life have been virtually nil. How many of us could name, apart from Armstrong himself, a single one of the men who have walked on the Moon, an extraordinary achievement that should have left a profound trace upon the collective psyche? Yet most of us could rattle off without a moment's thought the names of lone transatlantic sailors – Chichester, Chay Blyth, Tabarly, Clare Francis . . . Looking back, we can see that far from extending for ever into the future, the space age lasted for scarcely fifteen years: from Sputnik 1 and Gagarin's first flight in 1961 to the last Skylab mission in 1974 – and the first splashdown, significantly, *not* to be shown on television. After a casual glance at the sky, people turned around and went indoors. Even the test flights taking place at present of the space shuttle *Enterprise* – named, sadly, after the spaceship in *Star Trek* – seem little more than a limp by-product of a television fantasy. More and more, the space programmes have become the last great period piece of the twentieth century, as magnificent but as out of date as the tea-clipper and the steam locomotive.

During the past fifteen years the strongest currents in our lives have been flowing in the opposite direction altogether, carrying us ever deeper into the exploration not of outer but of inner space. This investigation of every conceivable byway of sensation and imagination has shown itself in a multitude of guises – in mysticism and meditation, encounter groups and fringe religions, in the use of drugs and bio-feedback devices – all of which attempt to project the interior realm of the psyche on to the humdrum world of everyday reality and externalize the limitless possibilities of the dream. So far, though, the techniques available have tended to be extremely dangerous (drugs such as LSD and heroin), physically uncomfortable (the contortions of classical yoga), or mentally exhausting (the psychological assault course of the suburban encounter group, with its staged confrontations and tantrums, its general hyperventilation of the emotions).

Meanwhile, far more sophisticated devices have begun to appear on the scene, above all, video systems and micro-computers adapted for domestic use. Together these will achieve what I take to be the apotheosis of all the fantasies of late twentieth-century man – the transformation of reality into a TV studio, in which we can simultaneously play out the roles of audience, producer and star.

In the dream house of the year 2000, Mrs Tomorrow will find herself living happily inside her own head. Walls, floors and ceilings will be huge, unbroken screens on which will be projected a continuous sound and visual display of her pulse and respiration, her brain-waves and blood pressure. The delicate quicksilver loom of her nervous system as she sits at her dressing table, the sudden flush of adrenaline as the telephone rings, the warm arterial tides of emotion as she arranges lunch with her lover, all these will surround her with a continuous light show. Every aspect of her home will literally reflect her character and personality, a visible image of her inner self to be overlaid and enhanced by those of her husband and children, relatives and friends. A marital tiff will resemble the percussive climax of *The Rite of Spring*, while a dinner party (with each of the guests wired into the circuitry) will be embellished by a series of frescoes as richly filled with character and incident as a gallery of Veroneses. By contrast, an off day will box her into a labyrinth of Francis Bacons, a premonition of spring surround her with the landscapes of Constable, an amorous daydream transform the walls of her bathroom into a seraglio worthy of Ingres.

All this, of course, will be mere electronic wallpaper, the background to the main programme in which each of us will be both star and supporting player. Every one of our actions during the day, across the entire spectrum of domestic life, will be instantly recorded on video-tape. In the evening we will sit back to scan the rushes, selected by a computer trained to pick out only our best profiles, our wittiest dialogue, our most affecting expressions filmed through the kindest filters, and then stitch these together into a heightened re-enactment of the day. Regardless of our place in the family pecking order, each of us within the privacy of our own rooms will be the star in a continually unfolding domestic saga, with parents, husbands, wives and children demoted to an appropriate supporting role.

Free now to experiment with the dramatic possibilities of our lives, we will naturally conduct our relationships and modify our behaviour towards each other with more than half an eye to their place in the evening's programme. When we visit our friends we will be immediately co-opted into a half-familiar play whose plot-lines may well elude us. Even within our own marriages we will frequently find ourselves assigned roles which we will act out with no rehearsal time and only the scantiest idea of the script – on reflection, not an unfamiliar situation. So these programmes will tirelessly unfold, a personalized *Crossroads* or *Coronation Street* perhaps recast in the style of Strindberg or Stoppard, six million scenes from a marriage.

However fanciful all this may seem, this transformation of our private lives with the aid of video-systems and domestic computers is already at hand. Micro-computers are now being installed in thousands of American homes, where they provide video-games and do simple household accounts. Soon, though, they will take over other functions, acting as major domo, keeper of finances, confidant and marriage counsellor. 'Can you afford the Bahamas this year, dear? Yes . . . *if* you divorce your husband.' The more expensive and sophisticated computers will be bought precisely to fulfil this need, each an éminence grise utterly devoted to us, aware of our strengths and weaknesses, dedicated to exploring every possibility of our private lives, suggesting this or that marital strategy, a tactical infidelity here, an emotional game-plan there, a realignment of affections, a radical change of wardrobe, lifestyle, sex itself, all costed down to the last penny and timed to the nearest second, its print-outs primed with air tickets, hotel reservations and divorce petitions.

Thus we may see ourselves at the turn of the century, each of us the star of a continuous television drama, soothed by the music of our own brain-waves, the centre of an infinite private universe. Will it occur to us, perhaps, that there is still one unnecessary intruder in this personal paradise – other people? Thanks to the video-tape library, and the imminent wonders of holistic projection, their physical presence may soon no longer be essential to our lives. Without difficulty, we can visualize a future where people will never meet at all, except on the television screen. Childhood, marriage, parenthood, even the few jobs that still need to be done, will all be conducted within the home.

Conceived by artificial insemination, brought up within the paediatric viewing cubicle, we will conduct even our courtships on television, shyly exchanging footage of ourselves, and perhaps even slipping away on a clandestine weekend (that is, watching the same travelogues together). Thanks to the split-screen technique, our marriage will be witnessed by hundreds of friends within their own homes, and pre-recorded film taken within our living rooms will show us moving down the aisle against a cathedral backdrop. Our wedding night will be a masterpiece of tastefully erotic cinema, the husband's increasingly bold zooms countered by his bride's blushing fades and wipes, climaxing in the ultimate close-up. Years of happy marriage will follow, unblemished by the hazards of physical contact, and we need never know whether our spouse is five miles away from us, or five hundred, or on the dark side of the sun. The spherical mirror forms the wall of our universe, enclosing us for ever at its heart . . .

Vogue
1977

The Diary of a Mad Space-wife

Will we ever discover alien life in outer space? The answer, almost certainly, is: 'Yes – in the year 2022. It will be thirty-five years old, female, come from Pasadena, Dusseldorf or Yokohama, be married to an astrophysicist, adore Doris Lessing and David Hockney, and live in a six-mile-long metal cylinder halfway between our own planet and the Moon.'

Faced with pollution, over-population and the microprocessor, future governments are likely to find irresistible the political and economic pressures to set off into space and place all our problems on the doorstep of the universe. Already an influential lobby in the United States, led by the Princeton physicist Professor Gerard O'Neill, is campaigning for the construction of a series of gigantic space colonies, with artificial climates variable at the flick of a switch, each housing a million people, totally self-supporting and limitlessly fuelled by a benevolent sun.

Professor O'Neill has testified before a US Congressional Committee on the economic and technical feasibility of the space colonies (though it's interesting to note that the term 'space colony' has been banned by the US State Department because of anti-colonial feelings around the world, something that might give the rest of us pause for thought), and in many ways the prospect of living in space seems beguiling. Those glass and chromium paradises, familiar from science-fiction films for the past fifty years, and the limitless technological expertise together fulfil every infantile power fantasy, and a century from now the entire population of our planet may well have moved outwards into space, abandoning its former home for ever.

We can visualize the vast satellite systems circling the Earth, with our present nation-states occupying a series of concentric orbital shells, in an order of precedence dictated by their respective GNPs. The USA and Japan will sail through the clear, star-bright ether of the outermost shells, while the still impoverished and inflation-weary UK will be down among the debris and rocket exhaust with Uganda and the Yemen. We can see the House of Commons in orbit, the MPs confronting each other across the floor of their spherical chamber, the Cup Final and Miss World celebrated in their glass and titanium pleasure-domes, and the millionth performance of *The Mousetrap* taking place in the ultimate theatre-in-the-round.

Commenting on O'Neill's projected six-mile-long satellites, the American inventor and soft-technology pioneer Steve Baer remarks shrewdly:

> Once on board, in my mind's eye I don't see the landscape of Carmel by the Sea as Gerard O'Neill suggests. Instead, I see acres of air-conditioned Greyhound Bus interior, glinting, slightly greasy railings, old rivet-heads needing paint. I don't hear the surf at Carmel and smell the ocean. I hear piped music and smell chewing-gum. I anticipate a continuous vague low-key 'airplane fear'.

A warning glimpse of what life will be like in a space colony can already be seen around us – in run-down motorway cafés, in vandalized municipal high-rises, in the once ultra-modern elevators and miles of scuffed circular corridor at the BBC Television Centre. Will we find, when we at last leave our planet, not a series of Corbusier radiant cities in the sky, but seedy housing estates and third-rate airports? More important, are we right to become nervous whenever governments begin to move into the area of fantasy? It's not only those greasy handrails that I fear. The new frontiersmen are likely to be, not Armstrong and Lovell and Borman, homespun types only a racoonskin cap away from Davy Crockett, but an army of ambitious PhDs, government planners and aerospace bureaucrats. How efficiently will these space colonies function, and what are the long-term effects likely to be on the psyches of the millions of people penned inside these orbiting Heathrows and Gatwicks? Will we see the creation of a set of unique space-age neuroses, born of that vague 'airplane fear', a half-conscious dread that will surge through the nervous system of our 35-year-old space-wife whenever the gravity system fluctuates and the soup floats out of the tureen?

Questioned about his dreams during his Skylab mission, the astronaut Russell Schweickart replied: 'I don't think anybody ever tried consciously to do any analysis of dream content. Most of the guys aren't the kind of people who even recall their dreams on Earth, let alone up there . . . I'm not even aware that I dreamt at all, but that's true here on Earth too.' Certainly NASA has not gone to great lengths to reveal the psychological effects of space travel upon the Apollo and Skylab astronauts, but the latter can't all have been as stolid as Schweickart. The subsequent, often strange careers of many of the astronauts indicate that the effects on the psyche of prolonged periods in space may be considerable. The suggestion has been made that the sensation of free-fall in zero gravity reawakens the long-forgotten but deep-laid anxieties felt by our arboreal ancestors, the ever-present fear of falling off the branch into the jaws of the predator below. Could long exposure to zero gravity generate not only neuroses but new space age cults and religions, the mythology of a second Fall of Man?

Reading through the diary kept by our space-wife during her life in one of the hundreds of satellite cities 35,000 miles from Earth, we can see the tentative evolution of a new kind of consciousness. Croydon Four, one of the older model O'Neill space colonies, is a semi-transparent cylinder 6.2 miles long and 1.25 miles in diameter, its inner surface landscaped to resemble a pleasant garden suburb, with low-rise apartment blocks, parks, schools and crèches. Through windows the size of wheatfields the tireless sun provides a limitless source of energy, and Judith, our space-wife, finds that she has little to do except lie out on her apartment balcony and let her tan deepen in the warm light of this immense solarium.

Judith's husband works a comparatively long forty-five-minute day as an astrophysicist at Croydon University – its elegant campus is a mile away, directly above Judith's head. However, he has wangled a seat on several of the voluntary committees looking into the problem of leisure in the space colony. There is a powerful Space-Wives' Union seeking a marked increase in the hours to be spent at the kitchen sink, but house-work occupies none of Judith's time. Though somewhat scuffed and dented, the metal and plastic apartment is totally dust-free and even the lightest cleaning would pollute and agitate the air. Because the artificial climate within the colony is sensitive to the slightest variations in temperature, all meals are cold and pre-packed, and the arts of cooking are now devoted entirely to the recreation of late twentieth-century airline cuisine. Even so, the excess heat produced by half a million space-wives switching on their favourite afternoon television programmes can fill the enclosed sky of the colony with a dense, dripping fog, and for some time now all television sets have been perpetually on.

For all this, Judith is happy to be here and tolerant of the minor inconveniences of this eventless, sun-filled world. Occasionally the motors which first rotated the satellite, and set its artificial gravity, malfunction and fire in reverse, with the result that everything in the apartment floats out of the windows. Judith, in fact, once spent an embarrassing twenty-four hours suspended three hundred feet in the air above her apartment when she chased her escaping handbag rather too energetically towards the bedroom window.

It is some three years after her arrival that Judith's diary reveals the first signs of a creeping malaise, that sinister combination of boredom, listlessness and self-regard which in the previous century affected Norwegian and Swedish settlers living above the Arctic Circle. Bored by the television set and the endless series of personalized video games tailored to her own needs – during one mad month she won a local beauty contest thirty times in a row (her own specifications had been defined as the ideal ones) – Judith has taken to visiting the observation deck in the basement of her apartment block. For hours she stares into space, watching the other satellites circle past, Croydon Five, Hammersmith and Tooting. Because it is always night in the observation deck, Judith soon loses her tan, and develops the first signs of space sickness. She becomes strangely drowsy, lying for ever in the artificial twilight she has chosen for her bedroom.

The day comes when she no longer recognizes her husband. Soon after, she is admitted to the nearby sanatorium. The last entries in her diary show her dreaming of her childhood in Purley. The doctors consider sending her back to Earth, but after these years in the germ-free atmosphere of the colony she would perish soon after landing. None the less, they encourage her to believe that she has never really come to the space colony, and is still living in Surrey.

So she passes her last years, with the millions of other patients in the satellite system who, like her, believe they are still living in Pasadena and Dusseldorf and Yokohama. At times she is even happy, though the zero gravity of the increasingly frequent breakdowns induces nightmares of anxiety. However, in space the canvas restraining sheets serve two roles.

Meanwhile the thousands of giant satellites continue to revolve, drawing their light from the sun and their darkness from the minds of their passengers . . .

Autopia or Autogeddon?

Automania
Julian Pettifer and Nigel Turner

The Centenary of the Car, 1885–1985
Andrew Whyte

Rolls-Royce: the Complete Works
Mike Fox and Steve Smith

Sooner or later everything turns into television. The motor car, so reviled in the 1970s as an ecological disaster, a chrome-hungry destroyer of cities, has now been restored to our affections and awarded the ultimate accolade of a thirteen-part television series. *Automania* is the book of the series being shown on ITV, and is a witty and generous tribute to this most durable of all adult toys.

Carl Benz's three-wheeler first appeared on the streets of Mannheim in 1885, and was patented the following year. As Andrew Whyte points out in his well-researched and comprehensive history of the motor car, Benz's primitive vehicle with its water-cooled four-stroke engine and electrical ignition contained the basic essentials of the modern automobile – under the bonnet, that is, for the real evolution of the motor car has taken place almost entirely at skin level. Leaving the trivial matter of transportation aside, I assume that a large part of the car's appeal lies in its combination of a comparatively primitive and static technology with a decorative shell capable of generating enthusiasms and obsessions of the most extravagant kind.

'Glorious, stirring sight!' murmured Toad of Toad Hall on falling in love with the motor car in 1908, 'O bliss! O poop poop!' His sentiments were echoed by the Italian Futurist Marinetti when he declared that 'a racing car is more beautiful than the Victory of Samothrace.'

A rich man's plaything in its early years, the car inspired owners and coachbuilders to heights of ingenuity. At the turn of the century the first European limousines featured fully equipped kitchens, silk brocade armchairs that could be converted into beds and, designed for a wealthy

American, a built-in flush toilet. From all this emerged a mammoth car-accessory industry, providing everything from tyre manicure sets and in-car fragrances to nodding doggy mascots – the greatest threat to sanity on the modern highway. Given so desirable an object, theft soon became a problem, and this in turn conjured up a host of devices, from stuffed Alsatian dogs to inflatable rubber drivers ('So life-like and terrifying that nobody a foot away can tell it isn't a real live man,' claimed an ad for Bosco's Collapsible Driver.)

But without doubt the most significant event in the history of the automobile was the decision in 1925 by Alfred P. Sloan of General Motors to introduce the annual model change. In the golden age of the Eisenhower years stylists like Harley Earl, inventor of the tail fin, and George Walker of Ford (the 'Cellini of Chrome') became kings of the industry, a reign that lasted until the failure of the over-embellished Edsel – which perhaps reflected some faltering of the American dream in the run-up to Vietnam. If the resurgence of US confidence under Reagan is as real as the commentators claim, one would expect a revival of baroque extravagance in Detroit car design.

Surprisingly, the world's first car museum, in Turin, opened as late as 1939, but today even Sotheby's and Christie's deal in motoring ephemera. The highest prices are fetched by cars with celebrity connections: Hitler's Mercedes-Benz, with its raised floor that gave the Führer an extra six inches in height; Garbo's Dusenberg with six built-in safes; Bonnie and Clyde's V8 Ford, complete with original bloodstains and 106 bullet holes. The Holy Grail, according to Pettifer and Turner, is James Dean's Porsche, which was stolen after his death-crash and has never been seen since.

In spite of the enormous freedom the car has given, the invisible destination at the end of too many route maps has been death – the authors of *Automania* estimate that 15–20 million people have been killed by the car in its first century. Between 1950 and 1980 the number of cars in the world rose from 50 million to 350 million, but the price paid in deaths and injuries seems scarcely to have dented our love affair with the car, even beyond the grave – one Texan lady infatuated with her Ferrari was buried in it. An international Gallup survey in 1983 discovered that the worst reported crime a human being can commit is not genocide, matricide or rape, but the driving away of someone else's car without permission.

Rolls-Royce: the Complete Works is an illustrated compilation of 599 stories, an ideal present for those who still believe that this is the world's best car, or are keen to recognize the number plates of Jimmy Tarbuck, Engelbert Humperdinck and Princess Margaret.

For me the heroic period of the Rolls-Royce lies well in its past, in a pre-war epoch of archdukes amd maharajahs, the latter being emperors of eccentricity – one fitted a throne, another made his steering wheel from elephant's tusks, a third crowned his Rolls with a thatched roof. Frankly, today's Silver Shadow seems a little middle class, more *Dallas* than *Debrett*, an expense-account taxi for corporation executives.

Still, I will move out of the fast lane when I next see 3 GXM bearing down on me, or hear the imperial sounds of a royal Phantom VI whose cassette holder is playing music by the band of the Brigade of Guards . . .

Guardian
1984

In the Asylum of Dreams

Theatre of Sleep
Guido Almansi and Claude Beguin

Fortunately for us all, the dream resists interpretation. Freud's royal road to the unconscious soon showed itself prone to delays and diversions, and by now is safely ensnarled in the traffic of rival theorists. For Freud the essence of dreams lay in the expression of repressed desires, while for Jung they offered reassuring glimpses of the collective unconscious and the primordial models of social behaviour. More recently, Charles Rycroft has stated that dreams are a kind of involuntary poetic activity, but Francis Crick suggests that dreams may be necessary to rid the brain of parasitic modes of behaviour.

However, as the immense richness of the dreams in this collection demonstrates, no theory ever seems likely to account for those strange safaris on which each of us sets out every night across the width of our own heads. Reason rationalizes reality for us, defusing the mysterious, but at the cost of dulling the imagination. In their preface the editors, a husband and wife team, quote Dr Charles Fisher of the Mount Sinai Medical Center: 'Dreaming permits each and every one of us to be quietly and safely insane every night of our lives.' This statement, they believe, well describes the situation of writers, who are forced by their readers to be more rational and conformist than they would like.

Literary dreams, they go on to argue, have a vital role to play in luring the reader outside his usual daily life. Frankly, I doubt this; in my experience a good many writers have notably less imagination than their readers, and cling to the props of bourgeois life like seasick passengers looking around for the furniture during a rough channel crossing.

'Comrade Lenin,' a group of Russian revolutionaries once asked the great leader, 'are we allowed to dream?' The editors maintain that his answer should have been 'no,' since dreams are an escape 'from the common world of waking people into the private fortress of the dreamer . . . in Orwell's *1984* disobedience to Big Brother starts in a dream.'

To their credit, the editors come down firmly on the side of the anarchic, mysterious and ultimately inexplicable nature of dreams. Drawing almost entirely from the western literature of the last 3000 years, from fiction and poetry, biography and philosophy, their choice ranges from Aristotle and Apollinaire to Rabelais, Richard Wagner and Nathanael West. Some of the dreams, like those of the surrealist Robert Desnos and the hapless Iranian premier Mohammad Mossadegh, are only a few lines long, though none the less poignant, while others, by Borges and Roald Dahl, are complete short stories.

Do any instant theories spring to mind? No, thankfully, though one cannot help noticing that the narrative structure of dreams, whatever the subject, seems remarkably unchanged down the centuries. The editors quote from *A Grammar of Dreams*, in which David Foulkes states: 'The typical REM dream has a linear narrative structure of a verbal narrative; first this, then this, then this, with the various "this's" having some sensible thematic connection with one another.'

Old-fashioned story-telling, in other words, with its ageless appeal and direct access to the great myths and legends that pave the floor of the individual psyche. Within the realm of the dream, Kafka is a contemporary author, and quite sufficiently up to the minute. No post-modernist meta-fictions, no room for the nouveau roman at the inn of the night. In terms of film technique, no split screens, zooms or chroma-key inlay, though one could argue that the dream cinematographers have an over-fondness for slow motion. But I have never seen a dream with a sub-title, or gone into a flashback, though the constant watching of television, apart from dimming the frontal lobes, must have some effect on the way the optical centres of the brain shape their interior world.

But perhaps, as in everything else, we already have machines to dream for us, and the collective dream of mankind is the electromagnetic sphere of the planet's television signals. Now some eighty light years in diameter, it is expanding confidently across the universe and is bringing to the natives of Proxima Centauri their first episodes of *Dallas* and the Reagan inauguration – dreams of the new Babylon that it would take a Daniel to decode.

The Lure of the Madding Crowd

The Faber Book of Madness
edited by Roy Porter

Madness has always held an immense appeal for painters, poets and novelists, fascinated by this handy and exhilarating short-cut to the secret heart of human nature. More surprisingly, the general public seems to have shared this largely misguided belief, even those with first-hand experience of mental collapse and the demoralizing ordeal of caring for those who have lost their minds. Roy Porter, in this shrewdly edited anthology, quotes Susan Sontag's remark that 'Depression is melancholy without the charm', and anyone who has visited a mental hospital will have noticed how hard it is to tell the patients from the relatives – the latter often look far more exhausted and derailed.

None the less, the mythology of madness, and the vast literature it has generated, remain as potent as ever. The insanity that closed the lives of so many philosophers, writers and composers – generally brought on, in the nineteenth century, by tertiary syphilis – seems retrospectively to illuminate their work and give it some kind of moral authority, as if by going mad Nietzsche and Schumann had deliberately burned their souls in their search for truth and beauty. Even Nijinsky's belief that he was a horse seems to have a certain simple dignity.

Our own century has romanticized madness, regarding psychiatry as a science rather than, as Thomas Szasz maintains of psychoanalysis, an ideology. The entire realm of the psychopathic has been elevated into the ultimate alternative life-style, particularly if combined with alcohol or suicide to make the headiest cocktail of them all. However, even Sylvia Plath, Hemingway and Anne Sexton never achieve the tragic pathos of Dorothy Wordsworth's uninvited self-destruction as she drifts into senile dementia in her mid-fifties, revealing those classic early symptoms, the childish resentments and irritation with relatives, of which she seems to have been aware, judging by those of her letters that Porter cites.

Porter quotes from James Boswell, who wrote a newspaper column under the pen-name 'The Hypochondriack', where he suggested that it was the done thing among the beau monde to develop depression, because its sufferings were the hallmarks of a beautiful soul, proofs of a superior sensibility. Some of the most sinister political careers of our time have openly exploited our ambiguous responses to the psychologically deviant and abnormal.

Sociopaths like Hitler and the other Nazi leaders fall outside the anthology's scope, as does the intriguing history of psychiatry during the past century, a case-study in itself. Only in the last few years has the mystique and status of psychiatrists – the dominant lay priesthood since the First World War – begun to fade, though it's hard to guess who will take their place: virtual reality programmers, New Age dieticians, eco-doomsters . . . ?

'The psychotic is a guy who knows what's really going on,' William Burroughs commented, a valid insight when applied to the paranoid inferno of *Naked Lunch*. But as this anthology convincingly illustrates, the insane have very little inkling of what is going on, either inside their own heads or in the world around them. For almost all of them, as for most neurotics fixated on some past grievance, time has stopped and they have lost the ability to learn from future experience.

To its credit, the anthology redresses the balance in favour of a far more realistic assessment of insanity. This huge compendium of texts stays close, by and large, to the asylum, where most of the insane still reside, despite recent attempts to turn them out into the streets. The accounts by patients and their physicians, especially those from the eighteenth and nineteenth centuries, show what outstations of hell these places were. Some of the more notable writings of the present day, Ken Kesey's *One Flew Over the Cuckoo's Nest* and Janet Frame's *Faces in the Water*, confirm that not all that much has changed.

The cruel and fiendish devices applied to the insane in the nineteenth century – the head restraints, cold-water immersion machines and rotating chairs – have been matched in our own day by lobotomy, electro-shock and insulin coma. The greatest breakthrough, in part because it freed nurses and doctors to practise a little therapy, came with the development of largactil and the family of tranquillizers in the 1950s, though, as Porter remarks, even these blessings are mixed, bought at the price of the lethargy and zombie-like state that make a mental hospital visit like a soirée at a house of ghosts.

For all its seriousness, madness has always been a limitless source of humour, and the anthology illustrates the weird and unconscious comedy of the seriously insane – above all James Tilly Matthews's 'Air Loom Machine', a persecuting engine which this patient believed to be pursuing him. His detailed and maniacally exact description, supported by elaborate diagrams, reads like the short story of a technologically obsessed Borges. But mental patients, and especially paranoiacs, have always shown a remarkable flair for incorporating the latest scientific marvels into their fantasies, a talent they share with science-fiction writers. Death-rays and malign super-computers are giving way at this moment, I dare say, to telepathic mobile phones and astrally guided word-processors. Today's patients imagine themselves to be, not Napoleon, but television chat-show hosts. The resilience of the wounded mind gives hope to us all.

Independent on Sunday
1991

Minstrels and the Tommy-gun

'Bonjour Blanc': a Journey through Haiti
Ian Thomson

Does travel, in its pre-package holiday sense, still exist as an independent activity, or has its place been taken by tourism? The kind of journeys on which Evelyn Waugh and Graham Greene set out in the 1930s across Africa and the Far East, protected only by their passports and the nearest British gunboat, would be unthinkable now. Away from the safety zone of the international airport, the car-rental office and the resort hotel, today's unwary traveller is soon faced with disease, civil war and the hostage dungeon. All the more credit, then, to Ian Thomson for his hair-raising but entertaining account of his journey through Haiti, which he set out to explore with little more than his toothbrush, a brazen nerve and a truffle-hound's nose for a good story.

Famous for voodoo, zombies and its late President, 'Papa Doc' Duvalier, Haiti must represent the greatest concentration of misery, cruelty and dashed hopes anywhere on our planet. From the air this one-time Caribbean paradise is a sun-scorched clinker, its forested mountains stripped bare to provide its impoverished people with fuel for their charcoal stoves. Thomson gingerly explores the capital, Port-au-Prince, scarcely more than a shanty town of garbage heaps, open sewers and tin-shack hotels, echoing to the gunfire of the latest coup and roamed by Tontons Macoute, the old Duvalierist thugs eager to hire their killing skills to any brooding general with his eye on the Presidential Palace.

But this small and desperate nation is also an endless parade of jovial, charming and garrulous characters who hail Thomson cheerfully with the 'Hey, Whitey' of his title: a euphoric taxi-driver who never uses his brakes but simply switches the ignition on and off, a voodoo priest with an IBM computer and a smooth line in psychobabble, an archly condescending teenage prostitute, and an affable, contraband-running crone who prowls the landing-beach with pocket calculator in hand. Interbred, a bewildering mix of black, white and Indian blood, they come on like actors auditioning for an insane tropical sitcom, and the whole of Haiti soon resembles a hallucinating version of the *Black and White Minstrel Show* danced to a tommy-gun beat.

As well as a personal travelogue, *Bonjour Blanc* is an intriguing history of a tragic nation, the world's oldest black republic, founded in 1804 after an uprising against the French led by the former slave, Toussaint L'Ouverture, later betrayed and done to death on the orders of Napoleon. But cruel wars between the black and mulatto factions have been endemic ever since. Ruthless dictators impose their morbid rule, the most weird and grisly being Papa Doc, who deliberately dressed in the black suit and bowler hat of Baron Samedi, chief bogeyman of voodoo, and devised his own version of the Lord's Prayer: 'Our Doc, who art in the National Palace for life, hallowed be Thy name . . .'

Bravely, Thomson allowed himself to be initiated into a sinister animist cult, which might have turned him into one of the zombies he interviews – victims buried alive after being paralysed by the puffer-fish nerve poison, tetrodotoxin, then resuscitated with damaged brains and set to work in the fields as little more than automatons. The best praise I can give to this superb and pulse-stopping book is to say that I read every page expecting it to end abruptly in mid-paragraph.

Daily Telegraph
1992

The Overlit Carousel

1963: Five Hundred Days – History as Melodrama
John Lawton

It seems scarcely credible that 1963 is almost three decades away. This was the year of the Great Train Robbery and *Dr Who*, of the Profumo affair and the fall of Harold Macmillan, of the 14th Earl of Home and the 14th Mr Wilson, of *The Avengers* and *That Was The Week That Was*, the year – according to Philip Larkin – when sex began. But, above all, it was the year when President Kennedy was assassinated and his successor, Lyndon Johnson, began to pour American troops into Vietnam, an escalation that now seems as misguided as anything in that overlit decade, and in due course destroyed his own presidency.

Although the sixties first began to swing in 1963, lurching on their gaudy way to the sound of the Beatles, some sections of the carousel now look distinctly shabby. James Bond and Dr Who reincarnated themselves a few times too many, while Profumo, Macmillan and Mandy Rice-Davies might be figures from a trouser-snatching Whitehall farce, which in a way the Profumo affair always was. But on the whole, 1963 still has a vivid period charm, an irresponsible but exciting prelude to the long, dull seventies, when the pull-up-your-socks rigours of the Thatcher years were not even a gleam in the monetarists' eye. In 1963 all the lunches were free.

For John Lawton, producer of Channel 4's *Opinions* programme, 1963 was the year in which Britain at last emerged from the grey aftermath of the Second World War and became a recognizably modern country. He stretches his 'year' to 500 days, from the arrest in September 1962 of William Vassall, the Admiralty clerk turned Russian spy, to February 1964 when the Beatles arrived in the United States and swept a continent before them. This was the year when Harold Wilson saw Britain remade in 'the white heat of the technological revolution', a dream whose time has yet to come. But the consumer culture had at last been born, and technology met more modest needs, like the Rolls washing machine which an adroit entrepreneur, John Bloom, delivered to the sculleries of a million waiting housewives. Within six months Rolls Razor went bust, which provoked an orgy of moralizing in the best British fashion, as if Bloom, for all his faults, was being punished for the naive hopes and optimism of the decade.

The Kennedy assassination alone, it seems to me, makes 1963 the most important year since the war. Kennedy's murder, the greatest mystery of the twentieth century, was the crime for which television was waiting, just as Vietnam was the war that TV needed. Together they freed the medium from the airless, studio-bound realm of stilted news announcers and staid game shows, transforming the screen into a global media landscape that soon became a direct competitor with reality itself, and may even have supplanted it. Lawton brings vividly to life this watershed year, though reading his unsparing account of follies, blunders and delusions is an unsettling experience, akin to reliving an extended hangover. The core of his book is the Profumo scandal, which doomed Harold Macmillan, to almost everyone's evident pleasure. Curiously, the Minister of Defence's affair with Christine Keeler, whom he shared with a KGB officer, echoes President Kennedy's affair with Judith Exner at a time when she was the mistress of the Mafia chieftain Sam Giancana. But Kennedy's thoughtless amours lacked the pomposities and seedy pathos of the Profumo scandal, which Lawton describes with quiet relish, setting the scene at Cliveden on that fateful July Sunday when 'a Soviet spy and the British War Minister were to be found racing each other the length of the pool, and competing for the attention of a teenage girl, watched by a member of the House of Lords and the President of Pakistan'.

But the dishevelled establishment closed ranks and waited its time. As the author points out, the Great Train Robbers always believed that their immense sentences were the establishment's revenge after being caught with its trousers down. If so, Ronnie Biggs, on the beach at Rio, is probably the last survivor of 1963, a living fossil of an often tawdry but always extraordinary year.

Daily Telegraph
1992

Rituals of a Skinny-dipper

Haunts of the Black Masseur: the Swimmer as Hero
Charles Sprawson

I have always wanted to swim across the Styx – an absurd ambition, since this is one river with a punctual ferry service. But long-distance swimming, however dangerous, does cast a potent spell, as Charles Sprawson makes clear in this fascinating book. Part social and cultural history, and part personal credo, *Haunts of the Black Masseur* is an exhilarating plunge into some of the deepest pools inside our heads.

For George Mallory, who vanished somewhere near the summit of Everest, swimming was an emotional and spiritual necessity, and on his ascents of Everest he bathed in the Kashmiri streams, stripping off his costume in some kind of self-cleansing homage to the great stone god of the mountain. Nakedness, as any skinny-dipper knows, deliciously increases the sensuality of swimming. Like shaving the legs, which Australian swimmers introduced in the 1950s, it also serves a practical purpose, knocking minutes off longer-distance times. Dawn Fraser maintained that she could have broken every record if she had been allowed to swim naked, and why not, I eagerly agree. Given that the Olympics are well on the way to becoming a contest of 'our steroids versus their steroids', it seems a pleasant bonus if the spectator's eye has something more attractive to fix itself upon than the flickering microseconds.

Besides, as Sprawson points out, nudity originated in the Greek Olympics. Water, for the Greeks, possessed magical and mysterious properties, and for the Homeric heroes ritual bathing made them resemble gods. Virginia Woolf swam naked with Rupert Brooke, and one can scarcely imagine anything more chaste or, in its eerie way, so intriguing.

Something of this search for purity, coupled with the meditative state of mind induced by solitary swimming, seems to have infused the attitudes of English swimmers in the nineteenth century, when they were widely considered to be the best in the world. The most notable of all was Captain Webb, who became a national hero after swimming the Channel in 1875 (an American had done so first, but with a rubber suit and paddle, turning himself into a one-man dinghy). Webb, exhausted by immense exhibition races, and desperately short of money for his family, died below Niagara Falls in the ferocious whirlpool that had inspired the 'Maelstrom' of Edgar Allan Poe, himself a devotee of long and mysterious river-swims.

The pre-eminent romantic swimmer was Byron, who took greater pride in having swum the Hellespont than in his poetry. Sprawson claims that almost all the great compulsive swimmers were, like Byron, strongly attached to their mothers and alienated from their fathers. But Sprawson's own motives for swimming the Hellespont, where he was nearly run down by a Russian tanker, belong more in the realm of hero-worship, and he has travelled the world searching for the swimming pools frequented by his idols. He swam in the slime-filled pool of Tennessee Williams's deserted Key West house, and in the marble baths of the New Orleans Athletic Club, after which he was painfully massaged by an attendant who might have been the sinister Black Masseur of the Williams short story.

However, he failed to swim the Tagus, another of Byron's triumphs (the river police picked him up halfway across and told him he needed a permit), and never seems to have thought of the Styx. Roaming around Greece some years ago, I tracked the Styx down to the northern Peloponnese, where it is reached by a nerve-wrenching rack-and-pinion railway. I was tempted, but my guide book warned that its waters were 'cold and treacherous'. To my everlasting regret, I decided to wait for the ferry.

Daily Telegraph
1992

Guilty Treats

A History of Food
Maguelonne Toussaint-Samat

In the long run, which casts the stronger spell, food or sex? The conventional wisdom holds that the pleasures of the table outlast those of the bed, but health, appetite and social convention are constantly changing and the truth of the matter, luckily for us, is open to endless verification. Meanwhile, the rival claims are supported by enormous literatures, often so detailed and obsessive that a curious convergence takes place, and the more specialized food guides show something of the exhausting single-mindedness of sex encyclopedias. Maguelonne Toussaint-Samat's *A History of Food* is a happy exception, a banquet of a book laid out on the broadest possible table, which examines the historical, economic, social and gastronomic factors that have shaped the foods we eat. Almost every page made my mouth water, something I can scarcely say about the *Kamasutra* or the collected works of Krafft-Ebing, but perhaps I am showing my age.

The author combines vast erudition with a charming French insistence on the health benefits, every one scientifically attested, of all our most guilty treats – wines, oysters, pâté de foie gras, caviare. Not only do the French have the world's greatest cuisine, but the menu comes with its own built-in absolution, like a VAT discount or the magical words '*service compris*'. Mlle Toussaint-Samat begins with the prehistory of food, and argues that language itself may have sprung from the lip-smacking noises our forebears emitted around the primeval cave fire. Honey was one of the earliest of all foods, a delicious and wholesome product that became a minor miracle when mixed with water and fermented, though the over-sweet and linctus-like flavour of mead has always made me wonder why it was the gods' favourite tipple.

Turning from collecting to gathering, the author gives pride of place to soya, the most widely eaten plant in the world, packed with vitamins and unsaturated fat, and a source of protein comparable to meat, fish and eggs. In the kitchens of my wartime camp I helped to grind soya beans in a stone mill, producing a 'milk' that was one of the most repellent liquids I have ever drunk, but also, I now learn, a true elixir of life.

Far more tasty is the mushroom, gathered since palaeolithic times and rich in proteins and vitamins, though I would rather not have known that it is grown commercially, at least in France, on beds of deodorized horse manure. Among other gathered foods, pride of place goes to the garlic, a miniature temple of flavour and folklore, rich in vitamin C and sulphur of allyl, and reputed, believe it or not, to be an aphrodisiac. Aioli, the sauce to end all garlic sauces, was invented by Nero. I hope the Wiener schnitzel was not invented by Hitler.

From bread, olive oil and wine, each a universe of gastronomy and myth, we move on to luxury foods, and the most expensive of all, caviare, harvested by Caesarean section from the anaesthetized female sturgeon. Lobsters meet an equally unhappy fate, but take a small posthumous revenge. After being boiled to death they resist freezing, and the Canadian lobsters we generally eat in restaurants tend to lack any flavour. The best of all come from Scotland and Norway.

Other crumbs from this feast of a book: the oyster, a true hermaphrodite, alternately male and female, can live in the wild for fifty years, but loses its flavour after five. Those repelled by pâté de foie gras may be reassured to know that the goose itself invented force-feeding, cramming food down its throat before its great migratory flights. More recently, however, French scientists have devised a method of electrically destroying the brain centres that control the bird's appetite. The bulimic and hallucinating goose gorges itself to an ecstatic death.

Lastly, a truffle-hunting sow must never be trained with second-grade truffles, or she will develop a taste for them and ignore the best. Whatever it is, it seems a moral worth pondering. As the author comments, echoing James Joyce, God made food and the Devil made seasoning.

Daily Telegraph
1993

In Search of the Last Emperor

The Empty Throne
Tony Scotland

As the communist order collapses around the world, monarchs-in-waiting have been stepping through the lobbies of their hotels in Nice and St Moritz to test the air. A tasty, nostril-twitching scent of king worship is blowing from the east, and in Romania, Bulgaria, Hungary and what was Yugoslavia, there have been calls for their return. One day, who knows, as the smoke drifts from the ruins of the last civil war, the desperate survivors may ask them to retake their thrones.

Britain, as always magnificently out of step, is showing uneasiness with its monarchy just when people elsewhere are thinking of restoring their own royal houses. By the middle of the next century, perhaps, as the exiled Windsors fret by their swimming pools in Abu Dhabi, they will be invited to make their return, and Elizabeth III or Charles IV will at last reclaim the theme-parked Buckingham Palace from its EuroDisney management. By then, ironically, no one may notice the difference between the real thing and the previous walking replicas, who dutifully waved from the balcony over the Mall, bestowed knighthoods (endorsed with a year's free membership of American Express), and strolled glassy-eyed through garden parties. There may even be complaints that the replicas were more dignified and majestic.

Curiously, the one country from which few, if any, calls for restoration have come is China, once ruled by the greatest monarchy since the pharaohs. The last emperor, P'u-Yi, the subject of Bertolucci's Oscar-winning film, died as recently as 1967, working as a seedsman in the gardens of the Imperial Palace. Tony Scotland, a veteran BBC broadcaster, had the ingenious idea of tracking down his heirs and asking if they were at all interested in taking their seats on the Dragon Throne. Aware of the BBC's unpopularity after its Tiananmen Square reporting, Scotland travelled as a tourist, but found it surprisingly easy to gain access to P'u-Yi's surviving relatives. It is only twenty-six years since the last emperor's death, but it had never occurred to the Chinese officials who spoke to Scotland that anyone might be remotely interested in reclaiming the throne.

But heirs there were aplenty. A Manchu emperor might have one empress, two secondary consorts and as many as 108 official concubines, all of whom could bear a legal heir. Despite the supreme efforts of his five wives, P'u-Yi never became a father, but it was a Manchu tradition that the emperor could assign his own successor. In his autobiography, *From Emperor to Citizen*, P'u-Yi refers to one of his nephews, Little Jiu, his constant companion during his days as a Japanese puppet ruler and in a Russian PoW camp after the war, and states that 'just before my return to China [in 1950] I nominated him as my successor in the event of my death'.

Who was this mysterious Little Jiu, never again mentioned, and was he still alive? *The Empty Throne* is a racy and entertaining account of Scotland's search for this elusive figure. He interviews a prominent Chinese historian, Professor Wang, who confirms that Little Jiu alone could rightfully claim the throne, and P'u-Yi's widow, the former Empress Li Shu-hsien, a retired nurse now living in a small flat in a Peking suburb. She vehemently insists that she is the heir, but the only royalties she is interested in are those owed to her by a French news magazine.

Scotland first sets the scene with a brilliant and disturbing account of P'u-Yi, one of the strangest figures ever to ascend a throne. The imperial court around him was a menagerie of human vices, populated by sinister officials, ambitious concubines and hundreds of eunuchs, each of whom kept his testicles in a pickling jar. The boy emperor developed an early taste for flogging, and had dozens of page-boys beaten daily, at least one of them to death. As a teenager, his favourite outfits ranged from Prince of Wales checks to Mussolini breeches, Hitler jackboots and film star glasses, and he surrounded himself with a hand-picked pleasure corps of handsome officer cadets. He liked to watch his third wife, Jade Lute, having her bath, giving her little beatings from time to time, and later read Buddhist texts to her when the courtiers assumed he was siring an heir. By comparison, one feels, Princess Diana has nothing to complain about.

Who, finally, is his successor, the unidentified Little Jiu, pretender to the Dragon Throne? Scotland discovers that he is the 75-year-old former Duke Yu-yan, a retired road-sweeper living in a mud-floored shack in Peking with his second wife, his son and the nail-clippings of the last emperor's favourite concubine. Thankfully, he is now happy with his calligraphy, and has no interest in moving to the larger and more splendid premises down the road.

Sunday Times
1993

Memories of Internment

The Way of a Boy: a Memoir of Java
Ernest Hillen

'Memory is, finally, all we own,' Ernest Hillen writes in the last line of this modest and gentle memoir. But what a memory! His recollections, fifty years on, of his wartime internment by the Japanese must be far sharper than most people's sense of their immediate present, as if the pain and horror of the events he witnessed are still so vivid that they rush in an instant across half a century and stand quivering behind him.

Hillen was seven in 1942, living on a tea plantation in Java with his Dutch father and Canadian mother. After the Japanese invasion Allied males were swiftly rounded up and interned. Hillen's strong but dour father, a stickler for 'discipline' (though thankfully the term is never spelt out), was arrested and taken away by truck – much to the reader's relief, it has to be said. The tone of this memoir lightens the moment he embraces his shy young wife for the last time and leaves its pages.

'Take care of your mother,' is his stern injunction to the seven-year-old Hillen, a remark that baffles the boy. She, after all, is supposed to take care of him. But the words are closer to the truth than he and his brother realize, and the book is a remarkable account of the way in which desperate alliances can form in the most unexpected places, even within a single family.

The Way of a Boy opens in the tea plantation after the men's departure, with Hillen's mother and the other wives trying to sustain the illusion of normality – that strange limbo which I remember well from my own childhood during a similar Japanese occupation, when the adults seemed to lose their belief in themselves, like actors in a play whose run is about to be cancelled. Hillen describes superbly how a child's watching eye soon expands to take in every detail of adult weakness and uncertainty, a disturbing lesson that lasts a lifetime.

All too soon, the scenery shifts abruptly when the Japanese decide to intern the women and children. Taking with them whatever they can carry, Hillen and his brother follow their mother to the waiting truck, bullied and berated by the ever-angry Japanese soldiers. After an over-night stop at an excrement-strewn girls' school, they are taken to their camp in Bandung, a section of the city closed off by a bamboo fence. Bloemenkamp – the Camp of Flowers – eventually held 5000 women and children, and the Hillens are crammed into a bungalow with five other families. Mrs Hillen divides their windowless room with a sheet, sleeping on one side while the sons sleep on the other, part of that subdivision of personal space that can turn an open dormitory into a Kafka-like labyrinth – the sight of sheets on a line still unsettles me.

In the heat and stench they endure boredom, starvation and incessant beatings. Hillen and his mother draw ever closer to each other, a process by no means inevitable. She risks her life by smuggling him out of the camp to a nearby hospital when he suffers an attack of blood-poisoning. But she never shares her dwindling rations with her ravenous sons, aware that a far greater danger threatens them if she dies.

The years pass as they move from camp to camp. The older brother is taken away to join the men, but they all survive and at the war's end are reunited. Hillen, interestingly, had spent three years in a women's world where the only adult males were the hostile Japanese guards, and one is curious to know what the long-term effects were upon him. Perhaps there were none. This memoir suggests that his childhood happily co-existed with a regime of hunger and brutality. He remained mischievous, dreamy and always ready to be generous, confirming that children sustained by the love of a single adult can survive anything.

Daily Telegraph
1994

Waste of Beauty

Diary of the Discovery Expedition to the Antarctic, 1901–4
Edward Wilson

Edward Wilson, doctor and zoologist, was a member of Scott's two Antarctic expeditions, on *Discovery* in 1901–4, which carried out the first inland exploration of the continent, and on *Terra Nova* in 1910–13. The tragic end of the latter partly overshadowed the *Discovery* expedition, and Wilson's diary has only now been published.

Wilson gives a brilliant picture of the southward voyage – the phosphorescent spray breaking over the huge Finner whales that sidled past the ship; the air filled with yellow-billed albatross while the expedition members flew kites and read Swinburne to each other, all in excellent humour, their dress and manner becoming more and more piratical. As they neared the Antarctic the atmosphere changed, and Wilson reported that 'jokes don't go down easily.' After the hazards of the first winter ashore he writes: 'Men don't improve when they live together . . . some of our mess have quite dropped the mask and are not so attractive in their true colouring. The Navy seems to me a most unfortunate necessity, because it spoils many otherwise excellent characters.'

Above all, the diary is remarkable for its immense detail. Wilson recorded everything: the best binoculars for observing birds (6 × Goerz rather than 6 × Zeiss, apparently), the precise process of fermentation by which the timbers of the ice-locked ship were being converted into alcohol in the bilges, weights and measurements of the expedition members, before and after (Scott put on weight). He has a sharp eye for the scene around him: the seas filled with lilac ice, the harsh jeering voices of the penguins, the snapping seals with teeth like old women, the crew jubilantly eating the first Antarctic ice taken from the sea.

Scott himself remains an aloof and isolated figure, reticent about his plans and given to the occasional calculated duplicity, but unsentimental and of iron tenacity. Wilson's character emerges more clearly: good-humoured but given to outbursts of temper, a devout Christian and obsessive taxonomist more interested in recording the unknown fauna of the Antarctic, such as the primitive insects that confirmed the continent's isolation since Cambrian times, than in the arduous sledging trips. These took him away into a blank wilderness of ice, 'a wonderful waste of beauty'.

The description of the three-month journey he made with Scott has an hallucinatory intensity: the starving dogs eating each other in their harnesses as the exhausted men dragged them along, pursued by a single skua gull that fed on the dismembered pieces, the sky full of mock suns. One's mind moves ahead a few years to when his body was found beside Scott's in the tent on the Great Ice Barrier. The letter left by the dying Scott for Oriana Wilson summed him up: 'True man, best of comrades and staunchest of friends.'

Guardian
1966

Use Your Vagina

How to Achieve Sexual Ecstasy
Stephan Gregory

Books like this one are never reviewed, although their sales – through mail order and under-the-counter outlets – are among the largest of all time, part of a huge invisible literature ignored by the critics. A factual reappraisal of these sexual handbooks, not merely as a subject for arch or clever comment, is long overdue. Most of them are profoundly earnest in tone, and deserve to be taken on their own terms in exactly the same way as the latest Ford Zephyr maintenance manual. How far any of them reflect the real world of sex is for each of us to judge. As basic primers they have the same unreality as the sort of colloquial French found in tourist guides, but this is less the fault of the publishers and authors than the impossibility of compressing the subject matter within the pages of a book.

How to Achieve Sexual Ecstasy was launched recently in a series of mail-order advertisements in magazines and underground newspapers. Elegant typography and a naked photographic model kicking up her heels suggested that this would be a fresh attempt to deal with an old subject matter. Some of the chapter titles, such as 'Beyond Sexual Infinity' and 'Threshold of the Sexual Psyche', seemed to describe a sexual version of *2001*, conjuring up a vision of a Panavision penis driving towards all the bedposts of eternity, while the Blue Danube plays from the mattress vents. The book itself is far more conservative. Although its first publication is given as 1969, it is difficult to tell when it was written. So successful have these handbooks been over the last fifty years that many of them have been revised and reprinted dozens of times. This one is American in origin, the bulk of it probably written in the late fifties, although in one section comments are made on the Masters–Johnson studies. The author's attitude is one of permissiveness governed by a strict moral code. Throughout, his text enshrines the notion that complete sexual happiness is the right of everyone in terms of that self-defeating paradox, normal sexual behaviour.

The hypothetical reader is difficult to visualize, although the sales of this book have already been enormous. Who in fact would want to read it? The preface describes it as a handbook of sex technique, though most of the amatory techniques and sexual positions described are known to any adolescent. At times one wonders whether these books are intended as fact or fiction. The lengthy description of acts of intercourse couched in detailed narrative terms are much more reminiscent of erotic fiction than they are of any handbook. However, in one sense it seems to me that these books of so-called sexual expertise provide what J. B. S. Haldane called a kinesthetic language, in this case a kinesthetic language of sex, a set of terms and descriptions by which ordinary people can describe a series of important experiences and activities for which no vocabulary previously existed.

A key to the book may come in the first chapter, in a section entitled 'Arousing the Unresponsive Wife', a suggestion that perhaps the book is designed for married couples who have begun to find a monogamous sexual relationship something of a bore. The description of an idealized sexual encounter, the set piece of the book, is presented with enormous detail, with a great deal of attention paid to the mise-en-scène: 'The place should be agreeable to both participants. If it is to be a public place such as an hotel or motel, care should be taken to ensure availability of accommodation, by reservation if possible.' Warnings are given about the hazards offered by paper-thin walls, corridor noises and highway traffic, as well as public places which cater for 'illicit sex traffic, which should be avoided for aesthetic as well as practical reasons'.

Given the appropriate situation, all is well, and the extended description of the sex act becomes a kind of seduction of the reader, presented with a notable simplicity and warmth. Careful attention is paid to the needs of elaborate foreplay and a concern for the partner's responses. Repeatedly the book stresses the traditional view of the supposed slowness of women's responses (how times have changed). However, those of us who tend to rush our fences could surely learn something from the descriptions of how to kiss our partner's elbows and savour the delights of the navel. 'Under the impetus of these attentions,' the author assures us, 'the woman will quickly reach a high level of passionate abandon. Her breath will begin to come in gasps (or sobs) and her hips will be in continuous motion. She may ask you to "put it in me" or she may say something like "Hurry, hurry". At this point you should roll her onto her back.'

An interesting comment on the psychology of the book is seen in what the author terms 'the clean-up operation immediately following the afterplay period.' He warns his readers that certain substances secreted under the duress of passion are often found offensive by both partners as passion wanes. It is wise, the author states, that clean-up begin before any feelings of revulsion may set in.

After this first extended narrative seen from the man's point of view a similar chapter follows from the standpoint of the woman. What characterizes the text is the immense concern that the author attributes to his two idealized partners. Both are so busy caring for the feelings of the other that they can have little time for any real passion, let alone the aggression and cruelty that drive in the same harness as love and tenderness.

In the second chapter, 'Specialized Coital Positions', hints are given on how to derive the maximum of pleasure from the classic sexual positions. The language throughout is simple and matter-of-fact, under headings such as 'Penetration is too shallow', 'Fit is too loose' or 'Fit is too tight'. Again, enormous attention is given to the need to satisfy the woman partner, a problem primarily solved in terms of a series of elaborate devices for bringing the clitoris into direct and continuous contact with the shaft of the penis. This continuous deference towards women reveals the archaeology of the book, that first realization of the immense sexuality of women that stunned the generation of Freud and D. H. Lawrence.

Other problems discussed are those of intercourse where the man is much taller than the woman, where the woman's buttocks are particularly large, or where, given an unusually big penis, a fuller range of sexual pastimes is possible. The author recommends what he terms 'riding high', and places great stress on the so-called 'wheelbarrow position', strongly recommending it for those women who have difficulty in achieving complete orgasm. However, he points out the hazards of using the inverted-vulva positions during pregnancy. Again and again he emphasizes the need for women to make the most of their sexual pleasure, at times even at the expense of their male partners. 'Use your vagina,' he writes, 'use it for sexual pleasure. Do not hasten towards his climax, but towards *yours*.'

Good advice, but at one point the author contrasts his idealized sexual experience with what he terms the usual and tragic pattern of sex in our society – masturbation, illicit adventures, frigidity, perversions, disenchantment, divorce, neuroses, psychoses, alcoholism and drug addiction, prostitution and sex crimes. What the book completely ignores is the fact that these activities are those which most people now seem to prefer, that sexuality is expressed more and more in terms only of its perversions and disenchantments rather than of those platonic embraces the book so humanely and affectionately describes. Too many of us would rather be involved in a sex crime than in sex. Sadly, the conceptualization of sex which has taken place along with everything else leads us away from precisely those idealized sexual encounters which these handbooks describe. To a large extent this book, like many others, is a nostalgic hymn to a kind of sexual Garden of Eden, whose doors Havelock Ellis, Marie Stopes and numerous other pioneers tried for so many years to re-open. Alas, the original tenants are no longer interested. In all probability what will put an end to the population explosion will be not birth control but buggery. Sex does not exist, only eroticism.

For all its good intentions, and its broadminded concern for our sexual happiness, *How to Achieve Sexual Ecstasy* has a strangely period quality. Above all it is a monument to marriage and the monogamous sexual relationship, and to the somewhat old-fashioned notion that someone else's pleasure is more important than our own. Far from being sent out under plain wrappers, books of this kind should be read in schools, though how far this would prepare our children for the real world seems doubtful, particularly to a generation of sub-teens brought up on Zap comics. When one thinks of successful marriages today one thinks in terms of couples who have worked out successful extra-marital relationships. A modern and much more relevant version of this manual would be concerned with the sexual perversions (some so bizarre that they have ceased to have any connection with sex), with the effects of drugs and pot on sexual behaviour, and the whole gamut of real and vicarious couplings possible when more than two people are present. It would also provide accounts of sexual intercourse with prostitutes, a specialized sub-category of sexual experience that requires its own expertise and mental attitudes. Needless to say, these ecstasies are of a very different kind.

New Worlds
1969

The Consumer Consumed

Could Ralph Nader, the consumer crusader and scourge of General Motors, become the first dictator of the United States? The question isn't entirely frivolous. Now in his sixth year as the most articulate and determined champion of the ordinary consumer, Nader already reveals an ominous degree of self-denying fanaticism that links him to the last of the old-style populist demagogues and may be making him the first of the new. Given that party and presidential politics in the USA are no longer flexible enough to admit any true outsider (the next five US presidents will probably come from a tiny pool of a hundred or so professional politicians), one would expect any real maverick with a headful of obsessions to home in on us from an unexpected quarter of the horizon.

The technological landscape of the present day has enfranchised its own electorates – the inhabitants of marketing zones in the consumer society, television audiences and news magazine readerships, who vote with money at the cash counter rather than with the ballot paper in the polling booth. These huge and passive electorates are wide open to any opportunist using the psychological weaponry of fear and anxiety, elements that are carefully blanched out of the world of domestic products and consumer software. For most of us the styling and efficiency of a soup-mix or an automobile are far more real, and far more reassuring, than the issues of traditional politics: East of Suez, balance of payments, trade union reform. Anyone who can take a housewife's trusting relationship with her Mixmaster or my own innocent rapport with my automobile and feed into them all his obsessions and unease is clearly going to be in business.

The son of immigrant Lebanese parents, Ralph Nader decided to become a defender of the common people, according to his own biography, at the age of eight. In the established tradition of populist leaders he took up his law books in their defence, but at Harvard Law School discovered that the young lawyers were being trained to defend the big corporations, not the small consumer. Nader's confrontation with the biggest of the big corporations, General Motors, contains the entire psychology of his method, and represents no mean achievement – for the first time, he made Americans feel guilty about their greatest dream image and totem object: the motor car.

At the time, Americans were so busy worrying about their cars that few of them had a chance to look at Nader's book *Unsafe at Any Speed* and the charged and emotive language he uses. This is the opening sentence: 'For over half a century the automobile has brought death, injury and the most inestimable sorrow and deprivation to millions of people.'

From this point, Nader never looked back, tapping a huge fund of insecurity about modern technology which has mushroomed into the present concern for pollution and road safety (similar efforts are now being made in Britain to make people feel uneasy over the enormous advances in sexual freedom).

What is interesting about Nader is that this champion of the consumer is himself a non-consumer. His annual income is estimated to be more than $100,000, but he lives on a minute fraction of this in a boarding-house room, without a car or a TV set. If one can divide dictators into smokers and non-smokers, Nader's potential for dictatorship is clearly of the puritanical, non-smoking kind. Described as harsh and almost unfeeling in his dedication, Nader insists over and over again that his only concern is with 'justice' – love, needless to say, has no place in his scheme of things. 'If you want to be loved, you'll be co-opted.' None of us can say we haven't been warned.

Many of Nader's targets seem ludicrously puny – did any of us, for example, ever regard breakfast cereals as anything but a good-humoured method of blocking the infant's trumpeting mouth as we recovered from our hangovers? The important point, though, is that Nader is unloading a powerful sense of anxiety and guilt on to a huge range of commonplace activities. Sooner or later, I would guess, these will crystallize around one major subject, a simple formula of antagonism, unease and wish-fulfilment that will play the same role in the technological landscape that cruder formulas played in the political landscape. Inevitably, I suppose, the consumer society must produce its own unique demagogue, but this sort of dictator may well be difficult to recognize and unseat.

As I've found to my own cost, Nader is already being taken more seriously than many politicians, precisely because the real motives at work are so hard to identify. A year ago my novel *The Atrocity Exhibition* was due to be published in the United States by Doubleday, but two weeks before publication the entire edition was withdrawn and destroyed on the orders of the firm's boss, Nelson Doubleday, an old boy of extreme right-wing views who has donated a helicopter to the California police (a nice twist – the rich man no longer bequeaths a Rubens to King's College but a riot-control weapon to keep down the student body).

What had blown Nelson Doubleday's fuses was a section of the book entitled 'Why I want to fuck Ronald Reagan'. The next firm to take the book, E. P. Dutton, were delighted with this piece, and thought seriously of using it as the book's title. That was last August. They were due to publish this month, but now they too have had cold feet. I was interested to learn that among the things that most bothered them were 'sixteen references to Ralph Nader'. In vain did I protest that anyone in public life attempting to involve us in his fantasies can hardly complain if we involve him in ours. In *The Atrocity Exhibition* a large number of public figures – Jackie Kennedy, Reagan, Elizabeth Taylor, Princess Margaret, and so on – are involved in the sexual fantasies of the hero. Although there have been threats and complaints about various sections of the book (the first publisher of the Reagan piece, Bill Butler, was tried and fined; the US Embassy put pressure on the Arts Council to stop its grant to *Ambit*, which published the Jackie sex-fantasy), these figures are generally regarded as open targets. Nader, significantly, is still considered to be on our side.

Ink
1971

The Car, the Future

Think of the twentieth century – what key image most sums it up in your mind? Neil Armstrong standing on the moon? Winston Churchill giving the V-sign? A housewife in a supermarket loading her trolley with brightly coloured food packs? A television commercial? For me, none of these. If I were asked to condense the whole of the present century into one mental picture I would pick a familiar everyday sight: a man in a motor car, driving along a concrete highway to some unknown destination. Almost every aspect of modern life is there, both for good and for ill – our sense of speed, drama and aggression, the worlds of advertising and consumer goods, engineering and mass manufacture, and the shared experience of moving together through an elaborately signalled landscape.

We spend a large part of our lives in the car, and the experience of driving involves many of the experiences of being a human being in the 1970s, a focal point for an immense range of social, economic and psychological pressures. I think that the twentieth century reaches almost its purest expression on the highway. Here we see, all too clearly, the speed and violence of our age, its strange love affair with the machine and, conceivably, with its own death and destruction.

What is the real significance in our lives of this huge metallized dream? Is the car, in more senses than one, taking us for a ride? Increasingly, the landscape of the twentieth century is being created by and for the car, a development which people all over the world are now beginning to rebel against. They look with horror at Los Angeles – nicknamed Autopia, Smogville and Motopia – a city ruthlessly ruled by the automobile, with its air clouded by exhaust gases and its man-made horizons formed by the raised embankments of gigantic freeway systems.

In Britain the first motorways are already reaching across our cities. Many of them are motion-sculptures of considerable grace and beauty, but they totally overpower the urban areas around and – all too often – below them. It may well be that these vast concrete intersections are the most important monuments of our urban civilization, the twentieth century's equivalent of the Pyramids, but do we want to be remembered in the same way as the slave-armies who constructed what, after all, were monuments to the dead?

Sadly, despite the enormous benefits which the car has created, a sense of leisure, possibility, freedom and initiative, undreamt of by the ordinary man eighty-six years ago when Karl Benz built the world's first successful petrol-driven vehicle, the car has brought with it a train of hazards and disasters, from the congestion of city and countryside to the serious injury and deaths of millions of people. The car crash is the most dramatic event in most people's lives apart from their own deaths, and for many the two will coincide. Are we merely victims in a meaning-less tragedy, or do these appalling accidents take place with some kind of unconscious collaboration on our part? Most of us, when we drive our cars, willingly accept a degree of risk for ourselves, our wives and children which we would regard as criminally negligent in any other field – the wiring of electrical appliances, say, or the design of a bridge or apartment block, the competence of a surgeon or midwife. Yet the rough equivalent of speeding on unchecked tyres along a fast dual car-riageway at the end of a tiring day at the office is lying in a hot bath with a blazing three-bar electric fire balanced on the edge below a half-open window rattling in a rising gale. If we really feared the crash, most of us would be unable to look at a car, let alone drive one.

These questions about the car – probably unanswerable for the next fifty years – I was thinking over when *Drive* invited me to join a veteran car rally across Germany to celebrate the seventieth anniversary of Mer-cedes-Benz and the launching of a new model, the 350SL grand tourer. Some eighteen cars belonging to members of the British Veteran Car Club assembled at Harwich, sailed overnight to Bremerhaven in north-ern Germany, and travelled together on a seven-day return journey to Stuttgart, the home of Mercedes.

Glad of a chance to visit the industrial landscape which was the birth-place of the car, I willingly accepted, and was duly sworn in as a passen-ger on board the AA's own veteran car, a 1904 Renault.

This was my first veteran car run, and there was no doubt by the time I reached Stuttgart that however little I knew about the modern car I knew a great deal about the old, all of it learned the hard way. Exhausting, often terrifying and always exciting, the rally to Stuttgart left me with a number of reflections on the past, present and future of the car. Whatever the appeal of veteran cars – and clearly being at the centre of a great deal of public interest is a large part of that appeal for the drivers themselves – it seems obvious to me that these antiquated and uncomfortable machines are admired chiefly because they are *machines*. Most of them are now just as efficient mechanically as they were when new, thanks to continuous rebuilding.

As machines whose basic technology is rooted in the nineteenth century – a visible and easily grasped technology of pistons, flywheels and steaming valves – these cars have the same appeal as railway locomotives and steamrollers, a far cry from the new technologies of the late twentieth century – a silent and mysterious realm of invisible circuitry, thermonuclear reactions and white-tiled control rooms. Even on the domestic level our everyday lives are now being invaded by machines whose workings we can barely guess at. How many of us could mend a faulty automatic washing machine or waste disposer, let alone a colour television set? Even if we can barely tell the difference between a sparking plug and a dipstick, the car is probably the last machine whose basic technology and function we can all understand.

At the same time, an enormous backlash of hostility now faces the automobile, part of a general anxiety about the abuses of modern science. Has the car, in the sense in which we know it, any future at all? Will legislation more and more take away the freedom that is inseparable from the private vehicle? My guess is that the car will remain much in its present form for the next thirty years. Whatever else may happen during the closing decades of the twentieth century, it is almost certain that working hours will decrease and leisure hours increase. Given more leisure, and rising incomes to spend on it, people's recreations will diversify, and only the car can provide the link. No public transit system ever devised could satisfy the vast transport needs of London, Manchester or Birmingham during the course of an ordinary weekend, and the decline of the private car is no more likely than the decline of the private house. Apart from this, driving a car clearly satisfies certain basic physical and psychological impulses, and any legislator trying to ban or significantly reduce the number of automobiles would do well to consider the alternative channels into which these impulses might flow.

None the less, it is obvious that ever more restrictive legislation will be enacted all over the world aimed at the control of the car, concerned not merely with factors such as safety and pollution but also with the overall social influences. Like most legislation, it will tend to be aimed at the mass rather than at the individual car. To a large extent, the future of the car will be the future of traffic. Within the next thirty years I see an immense network of motorway systems covering the British Isles, like the rest of the industrialized world. But simultaneously we will probably see the first traffic-free areas established in cities and large towns, blocks of several square miles where the only form of transport, other than one's own legs, will be some type of battery-powered, non-exhaust-emitting public vehicle. The roads into major cities will be controlled by toll-gates, with premium tolls charged at holiday and peak congestion periods.

It seems inevitable that we will gradually surrender our present freedom to step into our cars and drive where and when we wish across the entire area of the British Isles. Traffic movements and densities will be increasingly watched and controlled by electronic devices, automatic signals and barriers. On August Bank Holiday or Christmas Eve, for example, major holiday routes to the south coast and the West Country will be closed once a set number of vehicles has passed through the toll-gates. Electronic counters like those used by London Transport for its buses will be mounted on all roads, signalling the opening and closing of toll-gates hundreds of miles away. These controls will ensure that people stagger their holidays, and could even be used as an instrument of government policy, moving hundreds of thousands of people away from overcrowded resort areas to those that are less popular.

By the closing years of the century the first serious attempts will be made to achieve the direct electronic control of individual vehicles. Experimental schemes have already been visualized in which each car is hooked by radio to an electronic signal transmitted from a metal strip in the centre of the road, obeying its commands and matching its speed to a computer-controlled traffic flow.

Ultimately, I feel, all legislation aimed at the car is really aimed at the one feature that provides both its greatest freedom and its greatest dangers – the steering wheel. Looking beyond the next thirty years to the middle of the twenty-first century (when many children now alive will still be driving), I see its final elimination. Sooner or later, it will become illegal to drive a car with a steering wheel. The private car will remain, but one by one its brake pedal, accelerator and control systems, like the atrophying organs of our own bodies, will be removed.

What will take the place of the steering wheel? In all likelihood, a wheel of a different kind – a telephone dial. When our great-grandchildren sit down in their cars in the year 2050, they will see in front of them two objects – one that resembles a telephone, the other a telephone directory. The directory will contain a list of all possible destinations, each with a number that may be dialled. Having selected his destination, our driver will look up the number and then dial it on the telephone. His signal will be transmitted to the transport exchange, where the ever-watching computers of Central Traffic Control will hold his call, analysing it in terms of anticipated traffic flow en route, vehicle densities at the destination, metered toll charges to be recorded against the driver's account (or perhaps even instantly debited from his bank balance). If his call is accepted on the basis of available traffic information, the computer will select the best route. Electronic signals transmitted from road cables will steer the car out of its garage. Invisible eyes will guide our driver's car over every inch of his journey, adjusting speed to the traffic stream, making small detours to avoid probable delays, expertly parking it for him at his destination.

Sometimes, of course, when our driver dials his destination the number will be engaged. Central Traffic Control will have decided that there are already too many cars en route to Brighton, Blackpool or the Brontë country. A soothing recorded voice will invite the driver to try Woking, Stockton-on-Tees or Scunthorpe. Alternatively, perhaps, a harsh and threatening voice will inform him that there is insufficient money in the bank to pay the toll charges.

Clearly, the possibilities are endless. Almost anything one cares to say about the future will probably come true, and sooner than we think. I feel that most of these developments are inevitable, given rising populations, rising incomes and leisure, and that the car as we know it now is on the way out. To a large extent I deplore its passing, for as a basically old-fashioned machine it enshrines a basically old-fashioned idea – freedom. In terms of pollution, noise and human life the price of that freedom may be high, but perhaps the car, by the very muddle and congestion it causes, may be holding back the remorseless spread of the regimented, electronic society.

However, given our fascination with the machine, the car will always be with us. The veteran car rally to Stuttgart proved this for me. Our grandchildren may not be able to drive a 1904 Renault Park Phaeton, to give that bone-bruising monster its full name, but they will be able to drive a 1971 Ford Capri or Rolls-Royce.

At various points around the British Isles there will be so-called Motoring Parks, in which people will be able to drive the old cars in the old way. Baffled at first by the strange pedals and switches sprouting from the floor and instrument panel, able to vary the speed of the engine and the direction of the car with their own hands and feet, they will set off clumsily along the well-padded roads. Every so often they will come across traffic lights and road junctions, and be faced with the choice between turning left or turning right. As they become familiar with the pedals and steering wheel they will sense the exhilaration and freedom of being able to wind up these ancient engines and exceed the speed limits.

If they are really lucky they will be caught by a mock-policeman riding the strangest machine of all, something like a small metal horse, once called a motorcycle, but banned when no electronic system could be devised to control it. The real enthusiasts will even buy their own vintage cars, venerable 1971 Ford Zodiacs and 1984 Jaguars. Now and then, as part of a festival or centenary, they will hold veteran car rallies in the traffic-free pedestrian zones of major cities. And on these occasions everyone will thoroughly enjoy three rare sensations: the smell of exhaust fumes, the noise and the congestion.

Drive
1971

Grope Therapy

Travels in Inner Space
John St John

Five years ago John St John, a successful publisher in his fifties, former
Labour borough councillor, happily married and with no mental problems other than an occasional pang at the prospect of death, decided
on impulse to join a West London encounter group. With fifteen
recruits, he found himself in the ground-floor living room of a working-
class terraced house, furnished with folk-weave curtains and a circle
of cushions arranged around a chamber-pot. Here he spent the next
forty-eight hours with almost no sleep, food or exercise, stripped of his
watch and shoes by the group leader, an aggressive pug-faced blonde
from San Francisco who told him to 'get rid of that shit locked up
inside you'.

During this period, and the weekends that followed for the next six
months, he and his companions were encouraged to insult and abuse
each other, deride the most trivial personal characteristics, punch and
scream at a hapless cushion nicknamed 'Mummy', and take part in a
number of deliberately degrading games, the most enjoyable and mean-
ingful of which was apparently one called 'Mamas and Dadas': they all
lay on their backs, waved their arms and legs in the air and whimpered
pathetically. Sex played a continuing if ambiguous role, at all levels from
forced infantilism to the women dressing up as whores (they thoroughly
enjoyed this) and what seem to have been the preliminaries to bi-sexual
group copulation, when the participants took off their clothes and
crawled among each other on the floor, exploring and caressing each
other's genitalia. Of the author's nervousness with the bodies of other
nude men group-leader Maxine remarked archly: 'Of course, to be or
not to be a homosexual is an individual's personal choice.'

It says a great deal for Mr St John's sanity and good humour that he
was able to survive six months of this regime with both his confidence
and marriage undented, and even go on to explore the other forms of
'self-enlightenment' – meditation, Reichian bio-energetics, westernized

Buddhism and various fringe psychologies – that fill out the rest of his book. The notion that all the delights of psychotherapy previously reserved for the mentally ill – the hysterical outbursts and haggard confessionals, the limitless understanding and attention of others – might be more fairly shared out among the mentally sane caught on in a large way during the sixties, and on the evidence of this book the concept of 'psychotherapy for the normal' has now reached a point where one can visualize a future in which the only people suitable for psychiatric treatment will be the totally sane.

Travels in Inner Space suggests that much of popular psychology is now little more than a thinly intellectualized massage parlour. All the participants in Mr St John's encounter group were middle-class, educated, in robust health and comfortably well-off. None of them was in any way mentally ill or disturbed, and could only describe themselves as being vaguely 'angry' or 'blocked'. Many were veterans of previous encounter groups, and subsequently went off to explore other fringe psychologies. A curious aspect of these explorations of inner space is that they all took place in public, in a highly dramatized atmosphere with an appreciative audience sensitive to every nuance of exaggerated behaviour. Clearly the privacy of the consulting room and psychoanalytic couch will no longer do. Freud's view of the unconscious as a narrative stage has been taken literally, and the encounter groups now play the role formerly filled by amateur theatricals. In place of *Journey's End* or *Private Lives* at the village hall one screams at the Mummy-cushion.

Describing his first nude session, Mr St John remarks: 'I suppose you could call it an orgy, but it was a very self-conscious and structured orgy.' The encounter-group regulars were histrionic, aggressive and with a repertory of 'problems' they acted out like polished professionals. The group soon established its own taboos and hierarchies, and it was the done thing to be over-emotional. The author observed that it was frequently the same half-dozen who did the shouting and screaming and then broke down in a paroxysm of weeping as they waited for the comforting embrace of the love-in that followed.

In retrospect, what were the benefits, and did the participants do themselves any harm? A recent Stanford University survey quoted by the author indicates that 'significant pathological injury' was suffered by nearly 10 per cent of regular participants, but from the evidence of this book I would guess that Mr St John's companions were far too tough and self-centred to be hurt in any way. He himself – clearly a likeable and sensible man with an amazingly tolerant wife – is equally non-committal about the hazards and benefits. The solutions, if any, that he and his partners have found seem as undefined as the problems that sat them down round the chamber pot in the first place. All in all, my own sympathies lie with an unnamed character who, during one of the early sessions of screaming and pillow-punching, suddenly stood up, announced calmly that he had more sensible things to do with his weekends, and left. He was savagely mourned.

New Statesman
1977

Media Games

In the Psychiatrist's Chair
Anthony Clare

Interviews crowd the airwaves, a confessional babble only too open to eavesdroppers. At almost any minute of the hour, politicians and film actors, novelists and media celebrities are being relentlessly questioned about their favourite topic, themselves. Many describe their unhappy childhoods, alcoholism and failed marriages with a frankness we would find embarrassing among our closest friends, let alone complete strangers.

But how revealing are these dialogues, and what do we really learn about the subjects and their inner lives? Precious little, I suspect, though this is not the fault of the interviewers; some, like Sue Lawley or Joan Bakewell, can be remarkably shrewd. The interviewees are as professional as their questioners, and present only the image of themselves that has made them successful. The interview becomes a media game about as revealing as charades. My faults? Of course, I am too trusting, too modest, and help far too many old ladies across the road.

Another important reason is that the interviewee may not know the real truth about himself (after some 400 interviews on *Empire of the Sun* I have never yet explained why it took me forty years to write the novel). Who better, then, to tease out these hidden truths and buried traumas than a practising psychiatrist, himself a media professional, canny enough to see the tangle of neuroses behind the celebrity smile?

Enter, seated, Dr Anthony Clare, in the psychiatrist's chair. As he admits, the programme's title is misleading, since the interviews are not psychiatric, the subjects are not patients, and there is no treatment. Allowing for the entertainment format of a popular programme, to what extent do Dr Clare's professional skills add another dimension to the art and science of the interview?

Very little, as far as these twelve published interviews are concerned, and here I feel that the fault does lie with the interviewer. Dr Clare likes to begin by asking his guests why they agreed to be interviewed

272 A User's Guide to the Millennium

and gets a variety of convoluted replies, when the straight answer, as Derek Jarman is honest enough to admit, is: vanity or publicity, usually both.

Asked whether she feels comfortable, Eartha Kitt says 'Scared' and then performs her untamed-tigress act, taking the whip from Dr Clare and sitting him firmly on her stool while she stalks around the cage. None of the guests sounds in the least uncomfortable; all appear totally in control of themselves and the interview, revealing just as much about their private lives as they think will intrigue. Anthony Hopkins speaks 'frankly' about his period of alcoholism and his insecurities, but his page-long soliloquies sound like the script of one of his better roles.

During the broadcast programme, Claire Rayner, famously, broke down in tears over her unhappy childhood, and Dr Clare was criticized for distressing her. He defends himself by pointing out that she knew he would ask his questions because he had interviewed her before on his TV programme, *Motives*, and was certain that she wanted to talk about these taboo areas.

Jimmy Savile is clearly bored stiff, and sends up the whole programme, bragging about the seventeen Rolls-Royces he has owned and talking endlessly about money, which shocks Dr Clare. But what self-respecting Yorkshireman does not talk frankly about his loot? R. D. Laing, the only psychiatrist among the guests, takes the sensible precaution of being drunk. Overall, few unexpected insights emerge. Clare homes in like a truffle hound on the childhoods of his guests, rooting about in the compost of their early lives, convinced that the key to their personalities lies in their relationships with their parents.

But he ignores the one all-important fact staring him in the face: his guests are, without exception, extremely successful. The interesting things about Sir Peter Hall, Dame Janet Baker and Ken Dodd are not their weaknesses but their strengths, which psychiatry is far less equipped to cope with. None of these guests, I suspect, has ever been too trusting or too modest, for reasons that Dr Clare has probably never considered.

Daily Telegraph
1992

Kings of Infinite Space

The Right Stuff
Tom Wolfe

Now that the space age is over – or at least its heroic phase – it seems surprising that it lasted for barely fifteen years, from Yuri Gagarin's first orbital flight in 1961 to the last Skylab mission in 1974. Yet in spite of the unprecedented publicity that surrounded the American astronauts remarkably little is known about them. Compared with the gauche and determined Charles Lindbergh, Neil Armstrong remains as shadowy and mysterious a figure as Captain Scott, steering the Apollo moon-craft down to its safe landing with all the swagger of a corporation president negotiating a loan from a merchant bank.

How far was the NASA publicity machine to blame? Perhaps it deliberately created the rock-jawed, taciturn image of those heroic but somehow rather dull men, living examples, incidentally, of that wooden characterization for which science fiction writers have always been criticized. What really went on in their minds? The astronauts' subsequent careers – Aldrin's breakdown (he is now working as a Cadillac salesman in Beverly Hills), Armstrong's silence, excursions by the others into mysticism and ESP – suggest that more may have been taking place than we realized. Were they, to put once again the question which Tom Wolfe states was asked more than any others by the thousands of reporters besieging the astronauts' wives, ever *afraid*?

The answer, almost certainly is: no. Not, according to *The Right Stuff*, thanks to their superhuman courage, but for the most human of reasons. Highly trained test pilots with the 'right stuff' – that mix of skill, pride, and laconic humour under pressure – are sensitive above all else to the approval of their professional peers, and no more give way to panic than do tightrope walkers or traffic wardens.

The Right Stuff is Wolfe's sympathetic study of the first American astronauts, the seven military pilots who were recruited by NASA in the uneasy days after Sputnik 1 and carried out the earth-orbital Mercury flights that tested the runways of space before the Apollo moon-programme.

All but one of the group, Scott Carpenter, were senior test pilots, career-conscious combat veterans of Korea and World War II who had spent years on tacky desert airfields like Muroc and Edwards Air Force Bases in California, where the only local notables they mixed with socially were well-to-do automobile dealers. Wolfe amusingly describes their sudden induction into NASA, and the silly and often humiliating tests (Rorschachs and semen counts seemed to obsess the psychiatrists), which they of course passed with ease.

However, by the time they arrived at Cape Canaveral, uncomfortably wearing their cheap civilian suits and huge wrist-watches, the 'Halo Effect' had begun to transform them. Stunned by Gagarin's orbital flight, NASA and the American press presented the astronauts as models of the United States's pride and determination, always displaying 'the proper emotion, the seemly sentiment, the fitting moral tone'. The good Presbyterian John Glenn, with his interminable jogging and praying in public, took happily to his new role, prissily disapproving of the others' fighter-pilot binges.

Before any real discord could set in, *Life* magazine happily appeared on the scene with a $500,000 offer for the astronauts' exclusive stories – their annual pay at the time averaged $8000. From then on, as Wolfe says, the seven astronauts were seven slices of the same apple pie. As for the wives, looking at the group photograph on the *Life* cover with its heading 'Seven Brave Women behind the Astronauts':

> They hardly recognized each other. *Life* had retouched the faces of all of them practically down to the bone. Every suggestion of an electrolysis line, a furze of moustache, a crack in the lipstick, a rogue cilia of hair, an uneven set of the lips had disappeared in the magic of photo-retouching.

Disputes and modest rivalries simmered throughout the astronauts' training, particularly when they realized that the Mercury spacecraft was so highly automated that they themselves were passive passengers, whose most prized talent in the eyes of the NASA engineers was their ability to do nothing under stress. But the Kennedy presidency provided its own lift-off in the dark days when the Atlas rockets were failing. Making his political comeback after the Bay of Pigs disaster, JFK pledged to put an American on the moon by the end of the 1960s.

Where Eisenhower had never paid much attention to the astronauts, regarding them as service volunteers for a military experiment, Kennedy made them an integral part of his administration, including them in its social life. There were ticker-tape parades, breakfast with Johnson, adoring crowds who tore up the astronauts' lawns with their bare hands and, supreme bliss of all, water-skiing with Jackie.

In due course, by the end of *The Right Stuff*, the first flights by Shepard and Glenn put America back into the space race, and already a new group of astronauts was being groomed to carry the Stars and Stripes to the moon. Vast sums of money were spent on the most elaborate technological achievement ever seen. Yet admirable men though the astronauts were, I still miss that mad, lonely gleam in the eye of the young Lindbergh, facing the Atlantic with just his own will and a packet of sandwiches.

Guardian
1979

Project for a Glossary of the Twentieth Century

Author's note. The editors of Zone invited me to contribute to a special issue on The Body, and suggested a list of possible topics. Rather than tackle one of them at length, I provided short reflections on each of them.

X-ray   Does the body still exist at all, in any but the most mundane sense? Its role has been steadily diminished, so that it seems little more than a ghostly shadow seen on the X-ray plate of our moral disapproval. We are now entering a colonialist phase in our attitudes to the body, full of paternalistic notions that conceal a ruthless exploitation. This brutish creature must be housed, sparingly nourished, restricted to the minimum of sexual activity needed to reproduce itself and submitted to every manner of enlightened and improving patronage. Will the body at last rebel, tip all those vitamins, douches and aerobic schedules into Boston harbour and throw off the colonialist oppressor?

Typewriter   It types *us*, encoding its own linear bias across the free space of the imagination.

Zipper   This small but astute machine has found an elegant way of restraining and rediscovering all the lost enchantments of the flesh.

Jazz   Music's jettisoned short-term memory, and no less poignant for that.

Telephone   A shrine to the desperate hope that one day the world will listen to us.

Chaplin   Chaplin's great achievement was to discredit the body, and to ridicule every notion of the dignity of gesture. Ponderous men move around him like lead-booted divers trying to anchor the central nervous system to the seabed of time and space.

Trench warfare   The body as sewer, the gutter of its own abattoir, flushing away its fears and aggressions.

The pill   Nature's one step back in order to take two steps forward, presumably into the more potent evolutionary possibilities of wholly conceptualized sex.

Aerodynamism   Streamlining satisfies the dream of flight without the effort of growing wings. Aerodynamics is the modern sculpture of non-Euclidean space-time.

Pornography   The body's chaste and unerotic dream of itself.

Time and motion studies   I am both myself and the shape that the universe makes around me. Time and motion studies represent our attempt to occupy the smallest, most modest niche in the surrounding universe.

Prosthetics   The castration complex raised to the level of an art form.

Biochemical warfare   Nerve gases – the patient and long-awaited revenge of the inorganic world against the organic.

Hallucinogenic drugs   The kaleidoscope's view of the eye.

The Warren Commission Report   The novelization of the Zapruder film.

Genocide   The economics of mass production applied to self-disgust.

Phenomenology   The central nervous system's brave gamble that it exists.

Crowd theory   Claustrophobia masquerading as agoraphobia or even, conceivably, Malthusianism.

Lysenkoism   A forlorn attempt not merely to colonize the botanical kingdom, but to instil a proper sense of the puritan work ethic and the merits of self-improvement.

Robotics   The moral degradation of the machine.

Suburbs   Do suburbs represent the city's convalescent zone or a genuine step forward into a new psychological realm, at once more passive but of far greater imaginative potential, like that of a sleeper before the onset of REM sleep? Unlike its unruly city counterpart, the suburban body has been wholly domesticated, and one can say that the suburbs constitute a huge petting zoo, with the residents' bodies providing the stock of furry mammals.

Forensics   On the autopsy table science and pornography meet and fuse.

Miniaturization   Dreams of becoming very small predate Alice, but now the probability grows that all the machines in the world, like the gold in Fort Knox, might be held in one heavily guarded location, protected as much from themselves as from the rest of us. Computers will continue to miniaturize themselves, though, eventually disappearing into a microverse where their ever-vaster calculations and mathematical models will become one with the quarks and the charms.

The Vietnam War   Two wholly incompatible martial systems collided, with desperate result. Could the Vietcong, given a little more TV savvy, have triumphed sooner by launching an all-women guerrilla army against the *Playboy*-reading GIs? 'First Air Cavalry ground elements in Operation Pegasus killed 350 enemy women in scattered contacts yesterday, while Second Division Marines killed 124 women communists . . .'

Isadora Duncan   The machine had its own fling with her overdisciplined body, the rear wheel of her car dancing its lethal little jig around the end of her scarf.

Furniture and industrial design   Our furniture constitutes an external constellation of our skin areas and body postures. It's curious that the least imaginative of all forms of furniture has been the bed.

Schizophrenia   To the sane, always the most glamorous of mental diseases, since it seems to represent the insane's idea of the normal. Just as the agnostic world keeps alive its religious festivals in order to satisfy the vacation needs of its workforce, so when medical science has conquered all disease certain mental afflictions, schizophrenia chief among them, will be mimicked for social reasons. By the same token, the great appeal of alcoholism, and the reason why it will never be eliminated, is that it provides an opportunity for honourable and even heroic failure.

Body-building   Asexual masturbation, in which the entire musculature simulates a piece of erectile tissue. But orgasm seems indefinitely delayed.

Epidemiology   Catastrophe theory in slow motion.

Fashion   A recognition that nature has endowed us with one skin too few, and that a fully sentient being should wear its nervous system externally.

Automobile   All the millions of cars on this planet are stationary, and their apparent motion constitutes mankind's greatest collective dream.

Skyscraper   The eight-hour city, with a tidal population clinging to the foreshore between Earth and the yet to be navigated oceans of space.

Pasolini   Sociopath as saint.

Transistor   If the wheel is 1 on the binary scale, the transistor is 0 – but what will be 1000001?

Retroviruses   Pathogens that might have been invented by science fiction. The greater the advances of modern medicine, the more urgent our need for diseases we cannot understand.

Money   The original digital clock.

Abortion   Do-it-yourself genocide.

Science fiction   The body's dream of becoming a machine.

Answering machines   They are patiently training us to think in a language they have yet to invent.

Genetics   Nature's linguistic system.

Food   Our delight in food is rooted in our immense relish at the thought that, prospectively, we are eating ourselves.

Neurobiology   Science's Sistine Chapel.

Criminal science   The anatomizing of illicit desire, more exciting than desire itself.

Camouflage   The camouflaged battleship or bunker must never efface itself completely, but confuse our recognition systems by one moment being itself, and the next not itself. Many impersonators and politicians exploit the same principle.

Cybernetics   The totalitarian systems of the future will be docile and subservient, like super-efficient servants, and all the more threatening for that.

Disease control   A proliferation of imaginary diseases may soon be expected, satisfying our need for a corrupt version of ourselves.

Ergonomics   The Protestant work ethic disguised as a kinaesthetic language.

Personal computers   Perhaps unwisely, the brain is subcontracting many of its core functions, creating a series of branch economies that may one day amalgamate and mount a management buy-out.

War   The possibility at last exists that war may be defeated on the linguistic plane. If war is an extreme metaphor, we may defeat it by devising metaphors that are even more extreme.

International Standard Time   Is time an obsolete mental structure we have inherited from our distant forebears, who invented serial time as a means of dismantling a simultaneity they were unable to grasp as a single whole? Time should be decartelized, and everyone should set his or her own.

Satellites   Ganglions in search of an interplanetary brain.

Modernism   The Gothic of the information age.

Apollo mission   The first demonstration, arranged for our benefit by the machine, of the dispensability of man.

Zone
1992

9 AUTOBIOGRAPHY

Memories of the Rising Sun . . .

The End of My War

Had the war ended? For days, in that second week of August 1945, rumours had swept Lunghua camp. Shanghai lay eight miles to the north, beyond the abandoned villages and paddy fields, and I remember staring for hours at the apartment buildings of the French Concession along the horizon. The Swiss and Swedish neutrals who had lived there throughout the war would be tuning their short-wave radios to the latest news of the American bombing raids on Japan and the reported peace negotiations.

But in Lunghua camp we knew nothing. Their work-tasks forgotten, the British internees gathered in groups below the balcony of the Japanese commandant's offices in F block, watching the edgy guards for the smallest clue. The rest of us stood outside the huts and dormitory buildings, gazing at the strangely silent sky. Every day the Mustangs and B-29s had attacked the nearby Japanese airfield and the Shanghai dockyards, but now they had failed to appear. Our food supplies had broken down weeks ago, and we were kept alive only by the emergency rations of the Swiss Red Cross.

I waited for my father to announce that the war had ended, but he knew as little as I did. He and my mother sat in our little room in G block as Margaret, my seven-year-old sister, played outside with the other children. Two-and-a-half years of imprisonment, sharing their rice conjee and sweet potatoes with me, had desperately drained them. I sensed that they knew something they had decided to keep from me, fearing that our years of internment might end in some sudden and brutal way.

Then, on August 8, we woke to find that the Japanese guards had disappeared during the night. At last we were sure that the war had ended! People gathered silently at the open gates, peering at the dusty road to Shanghai. A few of the bolder men stepped through the barbed-wire fence, testing the empty air. I joined them, and cautiously walked to a grave-mound two hundred yards away. I looked back at the camp, at the intense, crowded world that for so long had been my home. Freedom and the war's end seemed fraught with danger, like the silent sky. I ran back to the wire, glad to be within the safety of the camp again.

Others had already decided to leave Lunghua for good. Half a dozen British men from E block stepped through the wire and set off across the fields for Shanghai, confidently waving goodbye to the camp. They returned the next day, lying unconscious in the trucks that brought another squad of Japanese soldiers to guard the camp. After carousing in the bars of downtown Shanghai the six Britons had been arrested by the Kempetai, the Japanese Gestapo, and severely beaten.

Enraged by their treatment, a crowd of English and Belgian women gathered below the commandant's balcony. Standing in their tattered cotton frocks, they screamed abuse at the impassive Japanese soldiers, necklaces of spittle shining on their breasts.

Then at last it was all over. The day after Hirohito's broadcast, we heard from the Swiss Red Cross that the war had ended. The Japanese armies had agreed to lay down their arms. We were told of the atomic bombs dropped on Hiroshima and Nagasaki, which had vapourized both cities and brought the war to a sudden halt.

'Is the war over?' I asked my father. 'Really, really over?'

'Yes, it's really over.' My father stared at me sombrely. 'Jamie, you'll miss Lunghua.'

Much as I might miss Lunghua, I was keen to see Shanghai again and visit our house in Amherst Avenue. Most of the two thousand internees remained in the camp, too tired to make their way on foot to the city, and without money or jobs to support them. Chiang Kai-shek's Chinese armies were far inland, and the nearest American forces were on the island of Okinawa. Meanwhile the countryside around Lunghua was a zone of danger, roamed by undisciplined Japanese troops, destitute peasants and gangs of leaderless soldiers of the Chinese puppet forces. It would be days before the Allied advance guard arrived and took control.

The B-29s had returned and flew slowly over the camp at little more than five hundred feet, bomb doors open. This time they were dropping food supplies, cartons of C rations filled with unimaginable treasures – tins of Spam and Klim, packs of Lucky Strikes and Chesterfields, and bars of hard, gritty chocolate that flooded my mouth with an overpowering sweetness. The parachutes sailed over the camp, landing in the nearby fields and canals, and parties of internees ran out to seize them from the Chinese peasants, forgetting that they too were Allied civilians.

Unsettled by all this, I decided to walk to Shanghai. Three days after Hirohito's broadcast, and without telling my parents, I made my way to the northern perimeter of the camp, beyond the old shower house, and climbed through the barbed wire.

In front of me was a terrain of derelict canals and deserted villages. To my right the Japanese military airfield lay between the camp and the broad arm of the Whangpoo River. Lunghua pagoda, converted by the Japanese into a flak tower, rose into the humid August air. During the American raids the pagoda had lit up like a Christmas tree, tracers streaming towards the low-flying Mustangs, but now its guns were silent and unmanned.

Avoiding the airfield, with its restless Japanese sentries, I climbed the embankment of the Hangchow–Shanghai railway line, and set off between the humming rails. Half an hour later I approached a small wayside station, where a platoon of Japanese soldiers squatted among their rifles and ammunition boxes, waiting for a train that would never come.

When I was twenty yards away I saw that they had taken a prisoner, a young Chinese in black trousers and white shirt. They had tied him to a post with telephone wire cut from the poles beside the tracks, and one of the soldiers was now slowly strangling him. The Chinese rolled his head as the wire tightened, singing to himself in a high voice.

The other soldiers had lost interest in the dying man and watched me walk up to them without comment, curiously eyeing my ragged khaki shorts and shirt. I wanted to tell them that the war was over, but I scarcely believed it myself, and I knew that the war's end carried little meaning for these Japanese soldiers. Caring nothing for their own lives, they cared nothing for the lives of others.

Leaving the station, I walked away along the railway line. The choking sing-song of the dying Chinese floated on the air as he sang himself towards his death. I have never forgotten that sound, but at the time, regrettably, I accepted this casual murder as no more than one of the minor realities of war.

Two hours later, thirsty and exhausted, I reached the western suburbs of Shanghai. At the end of Amherst Avenue I stopped at the house of my closest friends, the Kendal-Wards, who were interned in another of the camps near Shanghai. Hoping to see them, I walked up the steps to the open front door, and gazed through it at the sky above. The house was a brick shell. Everything had been stripped by the passing Chinese. Joists and floorboards, roof timbers and door-frames, pipes and electric cables had gone, leaving only the ghosts of the games we had played as children.

A few hundred yards away was the Ballard house at 31 Amherst Avenue. The roof and windows were still intact, and when I rang the bell the door was opened by a young Chinese soldier in a puppet army uniform.

'This is my house,' I told him. He tried to bar my way with his rifle, but when I pushed past him he gave up, aware that for him too the war was over. I stared at the silent rooms, which seemed strangely grand and formal after the shabby clutter of Lunghua. Everything was in place – the carpets, furniture and bookshelves, the cooker and large refrigerator in the American-style kitchen. The house had been occupied by a general in the puppet army, and the war had ended too abruptly for him to steal its entire contents.

I wandered through the airless house, trying to put a hundred memories of my childhood into their right places. But I had forgotten too much, and felt like a stranger visiting myself. I climbed to my room on the top floor and lay on the bed, looking at the empty shelves where I had kept my Chums annuals and American comics, and at the rusty hooks in the ceiling from which I had hung my model planes. Most of my mind was still in Lunghua, but a small part of it had come home.

My parents had arrived in Shanghai in 1929, aboard a P&O liner that took five weeks to make the long voyage from Southampton. I was born in the Shanghai General Hospital the following year. My father ran a textile firm, the China Printing and Finishing Company, a subsidiary of the Manchester-based Calico Printers Association. Shanghai in the 1930s was the Paris of the Pacific, one of the gaudiest cities in the world, a stronghold of unlimited venture capitalism. With a Chinese population of five million, and a hundred thousand Europeans and Americans, it was a place of bizarre contrasts, of foetid back alleys and graceful boulevards, of skyscrapers and Provençal villas, art deco apartment blocks and half-timbered Tudor mansions.

Driven to the Cathedral School by the family chauffeur, I looked out at a lurid realm of gambling dens and opium parlours, beggar kings, rickshaw coolies and mink-coated prostitutes. Each morning the trucks of the British-dominated administration toured the International Settlement and removed the bodies of the Chinese who had died during the night of disease and starvation. If Shanghai's neon lights were the world's brightest, its pavements were the hardest.

Although protected by chauffeurs and White Russian nannies, I was soon aware of a darker Shanghai, of kidnappings, gangster killings, and political bombings as the Chinese communists kept up their underground struggle against Chiang Kai-shek's Kuomintang. The first sign that the lights would really dim came in 1937, when Japanese forces invaded China and seized its coastal cities. They respected the International Settlement, the central district of Shanghai, but bitter fighting took place in the outlying suburbs. The combined land, naval and air assault was a preview of the battlegrounds of the Second World War.

Huge areas of the city were razed to the ground, and a stray bomb in the Avenue Edward VII killed more than a thousand people. Amherst Avenue lay outside the International Settlement, and when artillery shells from rival Chinese and Japanese batteries began to fly over our roof we moved to a rented house in the comparative safety of the French Concession. Neglected by its owner, the swimming pool had begun to drain. Looking down at its sinking surface, I felt that more than water was ebbing away.

When the fighting ended, Chiang's defeated armies withdrew into the vast interior of China, and we returned to Amherst Avenue. Life in the International Settlement resumed its glittery whirl. A week after the ceasefire my parents and their friends set out on a tour of the silent battlefields to the south of Shanghai. A motorcade of chauffeur-driven Packards and Buicks, filled with children, smartly dressed mothers and their straw-hatted husbands, moved past the shattered trenches and earth bunkers, like the landscapes of the Somme I had seen in the sepia photographs of the *Illustrated London News*.

Skirts in their hands, my mother and her fellow wives stepped through the hundreds of cartridge cases. The skeleton of a horse lay on the bank of a creek, and the canals were filled with dead Chinese soldiers, arms and legs stirred by the water. Belts of machine-gun bullets snaked through the grass, and live ammunition was scattered among the discarded webbing. A boy at the Cathedral School who picked up a grenade during another outing lost his hand when it exploded. Later, to his credit, he became a champion swimmer.

The Japanese controlled the Shanghai suburbs, and on the way to school I passed through their military checkpoints. By now, in 1940, I owned my first bicycle, and on the pretext of visiting the Kendal-Wards I began to take long rides around the city, pedalling through the confused traffic and avoiding the huge French trams. Sometimes I reached the Bund, and watched the Japanese cruiser *Idzumo* and the British and American gunboats, HMS *Petrel* and USS *Wake*. The amiable British tommies manning their sand-bagged emplacements often invited me to join them, getting me to clean their rifles with their pull-throughs and giving me their regimental cap badges.

As I moved through the checkpoints I was even more drawn to the Japanese soldiers. Many were ruthlessly brutal to the Chinese farmers and rickshaw coolies trying to enter the International Settlement, and in my mind I can still see an hysterical peasant woman near the Avenue Joffre tram terminal, screaming over her bayonetted husband as he died between the wheels of the passing Lincolns and Studebakers. I knew that the Japanese soldiers were brave, and I hoped the British tommies would never have to fight them. But the Japanese had a strain of melancholy that I admired, a quality not much in evidence among the party-going Europeans and Americans whom my parents knew.

By 1941 everyone was aware of the larger conflict that would soon break out. In my school classroom there were empty desks, as families left Shanghai for the safety of Hong Kong and Singapore. The steamers leaving the Bund were crowded with Europeans turning their backs on the city. Once when I cycled to a friend's home in the Avenue Foch I found his apartment abandoned to the wind, unwanted possessions scattered across the beds. Reality, I was fast learning, was little more than a stage set whose actors and scenery could vanish overnight.

Why did my parents and so many others stay on in Shanghai, risking their families' lives? They knew of the Rape of Nanking, when 20,000 Chinese civilians were butchered by deranged Japanese soldiers. They had seen for themselves how cruelly the Japanese treated the Chinese peasants in the countryside around Shanghai, the casual rapes and executions.

In part they stayed because Shanghai was now their home, where they had made successful lives for themselves away from the Depression-ridden England of the 1930s. Others were missionaries and teachers, who had committed themselves to helping the Chinese people. Together they took for granted that they would be protected by British and American power. Even though Britain was then losing the war against Germany, even after Dunkirk and the fall of France, everyone assumed that the Japanese would be no match for the British Empire and the Royal Navy.

Britain, we knew, possessed the impregnable fortress of Singapore, and a huge battle-fleet. Japanese pilots had bad eyesight and wore glasses, and their gimcrack planes would be no match for the Spitfires and Hurricanes. Over their drinks at the Country Club people boasted that the war against Japan would be over in weeks, or a month at the outside.

These arrogant assumptions were put to the test on December 7 1941, when the Japanese carrier planes attacked Pearl Harbor. In Shanghai, across the International Date Line, it was already Monday, December 8. I was lying in bed, reading my Bible in preparation for that morning's scripture exam, when I heard tanks clanking down Amherst Avenue as the Japanese began their seizure of the International Settlement.

My father and mother raced around the house in a panic, followed by the chattering and excited servants. I watched them fling clothes into suitcases. Fearful of the Reverend Matthews, the martinet who was my headmaster, I pleaded to be driven to school, but my father silenced me with the most wonderful words a child can hear: 'Jamie, there'll be no more school and no more exams, not for a very long time.'

Already I was beginning to think that the war might be a good thing.

The Japanese took control of the International Settlement, and the uneasy peace of military occupation followed. A few Britons in senior administrative posts were hunted down and imprisoned, but the thousands of British and European residents were left to themselves, their morale shattered by the sinking of the *Repulse* and the *Prince of Wales*, two huge battleships sent north from Singapore without air cover.

The little men squinting through their glasses proved to be brilliant torpedo-bomber pilots. Hong Kong soon fell, and the Singapore garrison surrendered even though it outnumbered the Japanese forces by three to one. So was nailed down the coffin of the British Empire, though the corpse was the only one not to know it was dead, and continued to kick for too many years to come.

The myth of European invincibility had died, something that an eleven-year-old brought up on G.A. Henty and tales of derring-do on the north-west frontier found hard to accept. The British Empire was based on bluff, in many ways a brilliant one, but that bluff had been called.

Throughout 1942 life in Shanghai gradually wound itself down. Cars were confiscated, and my father cycled to his office. Allied nationals wore numbered armbands. British companies still carried on their business, but the directors worked in tandem with Japanese supervisors. The time of parties was over. Having outgrown my bicycle, I rollerskated to school, which to my annoyance had reopened, as if the Reverend Matthews was unaware that the war had begun.

Meanwhile the Japanese were constructing a network of internment camps around Shanghai for the British, Dutch and Belgian civilians. In the early months of 1943 came the Ballard family's turn. Our staging post was the Columbia Country Club in the Great Western Road, and I remember it crammed with people and their suitcases, many of the women in fur coats, sitting like refugees around the swimming pool. Soon we were driven away to the coming years of captivity, and so, in many ways, began my real life.

Lunghua Camp, in the open countryside to the south of Shanghai, occupied the site of a Chinese teacher-training college. Classrooms became dormitories, wooden barrack huts housed the unmarried women, and the staff bungalows served as the quarters for the guards and commandant.

The Lunghua district, with its countless creeks and canals, was notorious as a mosquito-infested area, and soon the first cases of malaria broke out. In the humid summer heat everyone moved in a dull, sweaty daze. Our food, for the first year, consisted of grey sweet potatoes, boiled rice, a coarse brown bread and occasional dice-sized pieces of gristly meat. Rooms and corridors were a jumble of suitcases and trunks, and sheets hanging over lines of string soon converted the open dormitories into a maze of tiny cubicles. Once the 2000 internees had settled in, life in Lunghua was dominated by the overheated summers and freezing winters, by stench, noise and boredom.

I was enthralled. Like most British children in pre-war Shanghai, I had met few adult males other than my father's friends. Within a few weeks, as I roamed around the camp, chess set under my arm, I was soon on good terms with dozens of men. Architects, lawyers, engineers and plant managers, they were bored enough to play a game of chess and dispense a little cynical wisdom to an impressionable young ear.

As a family of four, the Ballards were assigned one of the forty small rooms in G block, so cramped that during the day my father propped his mattress against the wall and set up a card-table from which we could eat our meals. I had been brought up by servants and was fascinated to find myself living, eating and sleeping within an arm's reach of my parents, like the impoverished Chinese families I had seen during my cycle rides around the Shanghai slums.

But my parents must have found their talkative and hyperactive son an immense trial, and were glad to see me anywhere other than their poky room. I roved around the camp, sitting in on bridge and poker games, curious to know how people were adapting to internment. Many of the British in Shanghai had been intoxicated for years, moving through the day from office to lunch to dinner and nightclub in a haze of dry martinis. Sober for the first time, they lost weight and began to read, rekindled old interests and organized drama societies and lecture evenings.

In retrospect, I realize that internment helped people to discover unknown sides to themselves. They conserved their emotions, and kept a careful inventory of hopes and feelings. I often found that taciturn or quick-tempered people could be surprisingly generous, and that some of the missionaries who had devoted their lives to the Chinese peasantry could show a curious strain of selfishness.

A few chronic idlers refused to work, but most people buckled down to their assigned tasks. The internees ran the camp, cooking the rations and maintaining the septic tanks and water supply. A school opened for the children, a blessed relief for their parents and a valuable punitive weapon for the Japanese. After an escape attempt or any infringement of the rules they would close the school and impose a day-long curfew, forcing the parents to cope with their bored and restless offspring.

Still intrigued by the Japanese, I soon met some of the guards. Hanging around their bungalows, I realized that they were also imprisoned in Lunghua. The younger soldiers invited me into their bare and unfurnished rooms. They strapped me into their kendo armour and taught me to fence, a whirl of wooden swords that usually sent me back to G block dazed, head ringing from a dozen blows.

They were friendly to me while the war went well for Japan, but when the tide turned after the Battle of Midway conditions in the camp began to worsen. Winters in the unheated cement buildings seemed arctic. A few Red Cross supplies arrived, overalls and shoes with soles cut from motor-car tyres. Our rations fell. The rice and cracked wheat, an animal feedstuff I found especially tasty, were little more than warehouse sweepings, filled with nails and dead insects. We pushed hundreds of weevils to the edges of our plates, until my father decreed that we needed the protein and would henceforth eat the weevils.

He and I tended a small garden plot, hoisting buckets of excrement from the G block septic tank to fertilize the beds. All over the camp cucumber frames rose from the carefully tilled soil. Tomatoes and melons supplemented our diet, but by 1944 I had long forgotten the taste of meat, milk, butter and sugar.

By the last year of the war I was aware of a certain estrangement between my parents and myself. We had seen too much of each other, and they had none of the levers that parents can pull, no presents to give, no treats to withhold. Lunghua camp was a huge slum, and as in all slums the teenage boys ran wild. I sympathize now with the parents in English sink-estates who are criticized for failing to control their children.

Our rations continued to fall, and the American bombing raids on the Japanese airfield next to the camp provoked the guards into senseless acts of brutality. Mr Hyashi, a former diplomat who was the camp commandant, was no longer able to control the soldiers. But he was a decent man, and after the war my father flew down to Hong Kong and testified in his defence at the war crimes trials. Justly, Hyashi was acquitted.

VJ Day, everywhere else in the world, lasted for twenty-four hours, but in the countryside around Lunghua it seemed to go on for days. The war-clocks had stopped. At last the first American warships moored opposite the Bund, and their forces took control of Shanghai. The city swiftly became its old self, its bars and brothels eager for business. Gangs of whores roamed the streets in the backs of pedicabs, chasing the American servicemen in their jeeps.

The Ballard family left Lunghua a week after the ceasefire, but I often returned to the camp, hitching rides from passing American trucks. I still felt that Lunghua was my real home. I had come to puberty there, and developed the beginnings of an adult mind. I had seen adults under stress, a valuable education I would never have received in peacetime Shanghai.

I now knew, as my parents revealed when we returned to Amherst Avenue, of the extreme danger we had faced. They had heard from Hyashi that in the autumn of 1945 the Japanese military intended to close Lunghua and march us up-country. There, far from the European neutrals in Shanghai, they would have killed us before preparing to face the expected American landings at the mouth of the Yangtse.

American power had saved our lives, above all the atomic bombs dropped on Hiroshima and Nagasaki. Not only our lives had been spared, but those of millions of Asian civilians and, just as likely, millions of Japanese in the home islands. I find wholly baffling the widespread belief today that the dropping of the Hiroshima and Nagasaki bombs was an immoral act, even possibly a war crime to rank with Nazi genocide.

During their long advance across the Pacific, the American armies liberated only one large capital city, Manila. A month of ferocious fighting left 6000 Americans dead, 20,000 Japanese and over 100,000 Filipinos, many of them senselessly slaughtered, a total greater than those who died at Hiroshima.

How many more would have died if the Americans and British had been forced to fight for Singapore, Saigon, Hong Kong and Shanghai? Huge Japanese armies were falling back to the mouth of the Yangtse and would have turned Shanghai into a vast death-ground. The human costs of invading Japan became clear during the fierce struggle for Okinawa, an island close to Japan, when nearly 200,000 Japanese were killed, most of them civilians.

Some historians claim that the war was virtually over, and that the Japanese leaders, seeing their wasted cities and the total collapse of the country's infrastructure, would have surrendered without the atombomb attacks. But this ignores one all-important factor – the Japanese soldier. Countless times he had shown that as long as he had a rifle or a grenade he would fight to the end. The only infrastructure the Japanese infantryman needed was his own courage, and there is no reason to believe that he would have fought less tenaciously for his homeland than for a coral atoll thousands of miles away.

The claims that Hiroshima and Nagasaki constitute an American war crime have had an unfortunate effect on the Japanese, confirming their belief that they were the victims of the war rather than the aggressors. As a nation the Japanese have never faced up to the atrocities they committed, and are unlikely to do so as long as we bend our heads in shame before the memories of Hiroshima and Nagasaki.

The argument that atomic weapons, by virtue of the genetic damage they cause to the future generations, belong to a special category of evil, seems to me to be equally misguided. The genetic consequences of a rifle bullet through the heart are even more catastrophic, for the victim's genes go nowhere except the grave and his descendants are not even born.

In 1992, nearly fifty years after entering Lunghua camp, I returned for the first time. To my surprise, everything was as I remembered it, though the barrack huts had gone, and the former camp was now a Chinese high school. The children were on holiday, and I was able to visit my old room. Standing between the bunks, I knew that this was where I had been happiest and most at home, despite being a prisoner living under the threat of an early death.

But to survive war, especially as a civilian, one needs to accept the rules it imposes and even, as I did, learn to welcome it.

Sunday Times
1995

Index